A guide to studying, diagnosing, and fixing information flow in organizations

Clay Spinuzzi

Urso Press
Austin

Urso Press, Austin, Texas 78757
© 2018 by Clay Spinuzzi
All rights reserved. Published 2018.

clayspinuzzi.com

Acknowledgements for the Second Edition

In 2013, I published the first edition of *Topsight* with hopes that its friendly prose and integrated research approach would find an audience. And it has. That edition has been assigned in undergraduate and graduate classes, handed to Ph.D students, and used by new professors seeking to strengthen their research agendas. It's been used in industry as well. I've even seen it cited in research papers, which I certainly didn't expect.

Beyond those readers at other institutions, *Topsight*'s readers have included my own students at the University of Texas: undergraduates in my RHE 330c, Designing Text Ecologies; MA students in HDO 390, Qualitative Research; and Ph.D students who used *Topsight* independently as an introduction to their own research. In using *Topsight* to teach these classes, I have seen places where it could be improved. More importantly, the students have willingly elaborated on what they would like to see from a second edition. Based on semesters of feedback from these classes, and on feedback from workshops and readers, I've improved some chapters and expanded the book to include a design approach. Thanks to these readers for giving me the guidance to improve.

Finally, thanks to Fredrik Matheson (Bekk Consulting), who generously took time out of a very busy schedule to comment on this second edition. I've spent a long time writing for academics, and I've picked up a tendency to use complicated words and concepts when plain ones will do. Fredrik has gently but firmly pointed out this tendency, helping me to make the text more accessible to broad audiences. If you find this version easier to read than the last one, he's the one to thank.

Table of Contents

List of Figures

List of Tables

Foreword

In David Gelernter's 1993 book, *Mirror Worlds*, he argues that we often have trouble getting to the big picture—understanding the entire system. Instead, he says, we get mired in the details, something that he calls *ant-vision*. "Ant-vision is humanity's usual fate; but seeing the whole is every thinking person's aspiration. If you accomplish it, you have acquired something I call *topsight*."

Topsight—the overall understanding of the big picture—is something that we must "pursue avidly and continuously, and achieve gradually." Gelernter proposed accomplishing this through software models. But much of what we do in our own systems—organizations, workplaces, teams, and communities—is not amenable to software modeling because it is unrecorded, unspoken, and unstandardized. Team members tend to develop their own workarounds, their own tips and tricks for getting things done. They tend to push a lot of information around their organizations. Since they don't have the big picture, they aren't always aware of when and where the information gets stuck or distorted. In these cases, getting past the ant-vision and achieving topsight into the social system can be very difficult.

But it doesn't have to be.

I've been achieving topsight into various organizations for over 20 years. Along the way, I've developed an approach in which I gather clues, confirm details, model social interactions, and systematically achieve topsight. I've taught this approach in classes, workshops, and seminars. And now, I've put the approach into a book—this book.

This book describes how information flows, and why it sometimes doesn't flow, in complex organizations. It distills all the tips, tricks, and insights that I have developed over 20 years of field research in organizations. It is accessible and easy for the general public to read. It is suitable for undergraduate students, graduate students who are looking for a gentle introduction to research methods, academics, consultants, and people who need to solve complex problems in their own organizations.

This book is above all *friendly*. I've tried to write it in a casual voice that presents field research in a simple, nonthreatening way. But if you want to delve deeper, see Appendix A, where I provide references to the sources I consulted, and the books and articles that I wrote, as I developed this approach.

In this book, you'll learn how to

- design a field study at your organization;

- convince your organization and individuals to take part in the field study;

- conduct the field study, collecting solid data;

- characterize the data you collect;

- analyze the data using several different models that can provide insights into systemic issues that haven't yet been understood within the organization;

- write a solid recommendation report that presents your findings and recommends ways to solve those systemic issues; and

- use participatory design techniques to implement your recommendations with feedback loops.

Along the way, I provide a lot of advice, but I also provide examples, models, and exercises that will help you make your field study happen. Since I can't cover everything about field research in one book, I provide further resources so that you can learn more on your own.

This book isn't comprehensive; it covers just one out of many approaches to field studies. But the approach has served me well, and is fine-tuned for developing multileveled recommendations. I hope you'll find it useful for thinking out how to effectively solve problems within organizations.

Finally, I'm interested in your comments and questions. To leave these, or just to get in contact with me, see the book's website:

http://clayspinuzzi.com/book/topsight/

Good luck!

CHAPTER 1

Achieving Topsight

Organizations come in all shapes and sizes. But they all tend to develop complex, multileveled issues over time—wicked problems that are hard to solve because they are hard to identify, diagnose, and define. Those issues start to drag at the organization, making it harder to circulate information, coordinate work, and get things done.

Let's start with an example based on an actual research study that I conducted a few years ago. I've changed some details here to make the example more illustrative; you can see the original study referenced at the end of this chapter.

The SEO Case: Dealing with Rapid Change at an Internet Marketing Firm. Imagine that you're a consultant who has been called in to examine how workers handle rapid change at an Internet marketing firm, SEObrate. These workers focus on search engine optimization (SEO), which involves finding ways to make clients' websites rank high in keyword searches. Since there's no college degree in SEO, workers come from very different backgrounds (e.g., information studies, history, marketing, etc.). The problem is that the Internet is changing incredibly rapidly, so the things that work today might not work tomorrow. Not only do workers have to constantly learn new SEO techniques on the job, they also have to teach those techniques to their coworkers. *In a rapidly changing field, how do people circulate the up-to-date information they need?*

Notice some of the factors that make this problem so complex and multileveled:

Unforseen circumstances (contingencies). Internet marketing, particularly SEO, is changing constantly.

Circulating information. The workers not only have to constantly learn new techniques to deal with these contingencies, they also have to teach those techniques to each other and share other sorts of information.

Coordination. Although workers often work alone, they also must coordinate frequently to produce monthly reports.

Varied backgrounds. The workers don't share the same background, so they don't necessarily know the same things, see problems in the same way, or share the same expectations or tools for dealing with problems.

Varied clients. The company serves clients from very different fields and disciplines, and to serve clients well, the workers must learn a little bit about their clients' work and the customers that their clients serve.

In fact, a big part of what makes this problem so difficult to address is that we have a hard time getting the big picture. We can easily see when people encounter specific problems in the organization, such as forgetting to share information with someone on their team, missing an important change in SEO techniques, or misunderstanding which customers a client is targeting. But we often can't put our finger on how all these things are related. We can't get *topsight*: an understanding of the big picture.

In a complex organization—really, any organization that draws together people from different fields so that they can combine their different sets of expertise—it might seem almost impossible to achieve topsight. Complex organizations develop complex problems, problems that might involve values, interpretations, culture clashes, roles, rules, confusing tools, and even unspoken habits. These problems are often undefined or underdefined. Although everyone seems to have an opinion about how to fix them, no one seems to be able to get the big picture.

But by the end of this book, you will. You'll be able to confidently visualize and explain aspects of the organization, such as

- the organization's overall **activity** (the work it repeatedly achieves)

- how that activity relates to a **network** of other activities;

- the **resources** that people use to get things done (such as tools and materials);

- the **chains** of communication that people use in the organization;

- how people **combine and substitute resources** to address their tasks (such as using two tools together or replacing one tool with another); and

- the unspoken **habits** people use as they do their work.

You'll be able to use these visualizations to detect *systemic issues* in your organization—the issues that underlie problems that your organization regularly encounters. By the end of the book, you'll be able to confidently analyze these underlying problems, resulting in concise statements that get to the heart of the issue, like these:

- "Since search engines keep changing their search algorithms, SEObrate has limited control over search rankings, but internal and external communication patterns haven't addressed this problem consistently."

- "No standardized project tracking exists, resulting in confusion when specialists have to communicate project status to each other or account managers."

You'll also be able to use your analysis as a basis for improvement, making specific, actional recommendations like these:

- "Develop a note in SEObrateMax to indicate search algorithm changes."

- "Develop a routine to automatically detect algorithm changes."

- "Establish standardized project tracking."

Finally, you'll be able to develop and test your hypotheses through specific implementations of those recommendations, allowing you to find out how well they work and to fine-tune them before you actually deploy them in the organization.

So that's what we're after: topsight. Here's how to gain it.

Gaining Topsight

How can we gain topsight so that we can solve this wicked problem? How can we establish patterns and commonalities in this kind of work, identify common disruptions, and move toward best practices? The task may seem very hard, just like solving wicked problems in your own organization, one that you've decided to study, or one for which you are consulting. And it *is* hard. But it's not that hard. I'll show you how to do it.

As you go through this book, you'll learn practical techniques for gaining topsight in your organization. I'll walk you through the steps:

I. **Designing** a field study at your organization and convince the organization and individuals to take part in it.

II. **Conducting** the field study, collecting solid data like professional researchers do.

III. **Characterizing** the data you collect, allowing you to see connections you haven't seen before.

IV. **Analyzing** the data using several different models that can collectively provide insights into systemic issues that haven't yet been understood within the organization—systemic issues that cause the everyday symptoms of dysfunction in the organization.

V. **Writing** a solid recommendation report that presents your findings and recommends ways to solve those systemic issues.

VI. **Redesigning** implementations and testing them to make sure they actually solve the issues.

By the end of my investigation into the Internet marketing firm, I was able to gain and express topsight. That allowed me to pinpoint two systemic issues and to make three solid recommendations for addressing them. We'll revisit this case throughout the book, showing how you can apply these techniques to your own organization. If you follow along and apply these lessons to your own organization, by the end of the book, you too will develop topsight, identify systemic issues, and provide solid recommendations and implementations.

Before we get started on these major steps, though, let's establish how we'll think of these organizations. Getting to topsight means understanding organizations systematically. And that means that we have to look past what we usually call *problems* to the underlying systemic issues that cause them. Often, the problems that you can see are not really the problems you want to address. They're more like symptoms or clues. And until you start thinking of them as symptoms or clues, you won't be able to develop topsight.

Thinking About Organizations as Systems

To get to topsight, you must think about organizations as systems, just as doctors think about illnesses or detectives think about cases.

Thinking Like a Doctor

Imagine that you're not feeling well, so you go to see the doctor. "What symptoms do you have?" the doctor asks. You list the symptoms: a bad headache, a high fever, a sore throat, and weakness. As the doctor listens, she makes notes.

As the patient, you've been trying to treat the symptoms. For instance, you've taken aspirin for the headache, you've been drinking coffee to raise your energy levels, and you've been popping cough drops for your sore throat. But treating the symptoms isn't useful because you haven't addressed the underlying illness.

What's the illness? Your doctor should be able to figure it out just from listening to you and examining you. That is, she sees the relationship among the symptoms and determines the underlying illness—in this case, the flu. With that information, she can recommend a course of action that actually attacks the illness, not just the symptoms.

As you look at the problems you see in the organization, you may be tempted to treat the symptoms. Instead, think like a doctor: look at all the symptoms you can find then figure out what they tell you about the underlying illness.

Thinking Like a Detective

Or imagine you're enjoying your favorite detective show: *CSI* or, maybe, *Scooby Doo*. As you watch, you examine the clues that the TV detective finds: the blood stains on the carpet, the laundry stub in the victim's pocket, or the suction cups hidden in the fruit bowl.

You're not collecting the clues just to have them; you're trying to fit them together in a way that allows you to solve the mystery. Even if all signs point to the same suspect—especially if that happens—you look at other possibilities. Eventually, the culprit will shake his fist and complain that he could have gotten away with it, if it hadn't been for those pesky kids and their dog.

As you look at the obvious, visible problems in the organization, don't think of them as the mystery. They're just clues. Think like a detective: gather all the clues you can, then figure out how they fit together to help you solve the real mystery.

Thinking About the Organization as a System

If you're thinking like a doctor or a detective, you're thinking about the organization as a system. And that's critical if you're going to truly address the underlying issues in the organization. Unfortunately, people often don't approach the issues this way. They mistake the symptoms for the disease and the clues for the mystery. Consequently, they try piecemeal solutions that don't quite address the entire issue.

So how do you approach the organization as a system? You need an approach that will let you honestly gather different perspectives on the organization, cross-check them against each other, catalogue the symptoms, and inductively develop a more comprehensive understanding of the underlying issues at play within the organization. Once you understand the illness, you can prescribe the cure.

How do you accomplish this? You conduct a field study.

Field Studies

In this book, I use *field study* to mean a study in which you enter an organization, collect data on how people operate within that organization, and analyze the data to gain topsight into how the organization works.

 If that sounds very broad, it should. Often, we enter an organization with only a vague idea of what we're looking for, and sometimes we might even have an incorrect idea of how the organization works. Field studies involve a lot of watching, listening, and examining as we figure out what data to collect, what's important, what's problematic, and what's working well in the organization. The process is inductive: we have to make sense of it as we go along (as opposed to a deductive process, in which the investigator starts with a general, known law and infers particular instances).

The Process

Fortunately, this book lays out a specific process for field research in organizations, based on my many field studies and fine-tuned for finding systemic issues in such organizations. As you follow this book, you will learn the phases in Table 1.1.

Table 1.1. Phases, their key questions, and the materials you will produce to answer them.

Phase	Key Questions	Materials
I. Design	What do you want to study? How do you prepare to study it?	Research questions; research design matrix; research proposal; consent form; protocol; study description; elevator pitch; site letter
II. Conduct	How do you follow through on the study you've planned? How do you push past obstacles and get your data?	Field notes; interview transcript; interim report
III. Characterize	How do you characterize the data you've collected? How do you start fitting the data together and seeing relationships?	Coding scheme
IV. Analyze	How do you make sense of the data? How do you work inductively to discover and understand the systemic issues in the work?	Models for discovering systemic issues, both blank and filled out

V. Report	How do you communicate your analysis? How do you develop a solid set of recommendations?	Recommendation report
VI. Redesign	How do you redesign parts of the work to address the organization's systemic issues? How do you communicate your changes?	Mockups and proto-types, organizational games, future work-shops

This is a complex process! But don't worry; I've included plenty of documents, models, and examples to help you get through this process.

The Ground Rules

The process comes with some ground rules. Just like a doctor will want to hear about the patient's symptoms, but will *also* examine the patient herself—and just like a detective will want to get eyewitness testimony, but will *also* look for clues—you will need to be careful about what you collect and what you believe. Your field study will have to follow the following ground rules:

Be systematic. If your doctor is seeing five people who might all have the same disease, she examines them all the same way, using the same tests. She doesn't just check the first patient's temperature, the second patient's blood pressure, and so on. Similarly, you have to be systematic, collecting roughly the same data from each *participant* (person who agrees to be in your study). In Chapter 3, we'll discuss how to systematically design a field study.

Collect verifiable data. When your doctor asks you about your symptoms, she also tries to independently verify them. For instance, if you complain that you have a fever, she also takes your temperature. She trusts, but verifies. After all, if you're wrong, she doesn't want to misdiagnose you and prescribe the wrong cure. In Chapter 3, we'll talk about how to design your study to collect verifiable data, and in Chapter 11, we'll talk about how to *triangulate* or systematically compare the data to verify it.

Field studies involve a lot of uncertainties. Fortunately, we know some things about how organizations generally work. These things will be our starting point, and will underlie the entire process that we'll follow throughout the book. We'll focus on activities and information resources.

Activities

Complex organizations form around some sort of objective that people have to accomplish over and over. Without that core objective that they have to accomplish on a given cycle, organizations don't persist, and thus they don't have the time to develop the complex mechanisms that make an organization work well.

For instance, take a graphic design firm that specializes in designing company identities. The firm regularly meets with a client, discusses the client's vision and market, and then develops a set of texts (e.g., logo, letterhead, website, etc.) that cohesively communicate the client's identity. The firm may work for different clients from engagement to engagement, but it will follow the same processes and produce the same sorts of texts. Or consider a nonprofit organization that regularly applies for grants. As the grant writers approach different foundations, they must read and produce different texts: calls for proposals, inquiry letters, emails, internal communications among the team, the job histories or resumes of different team members, a budget spreadsheet, and finally the grant proposals themselves. Again, every situation might be different, but the nonprofit organization has developed a regular set of procedures and tools for addressing this sort of situation.

This cyclical nature of work helps to anchor organizations. Over time, these organizations develop at three levels:

The macro level. The level of culture and history: think of it as the *organization level* in terms of the organization's mission and vision—accomplished on the scale of years or decades. This is the "Why" level—why does the organization do what it does?a

The meso (or middle) level. The level of goal-directed actions: think of it as the *human level* in terms of what the individual is consciously trying to accomplish on the scale of minutes or hours. This is the "What" level—what is the individual trying to do?

The micro level. The level of habits and reactions: think of it as the *habit level* in terms of what the individual does unconsciously on the scale of seconds. This is the "How" level—how does the individual reach her meso-level goals?

To understand how an organization works and develops, we must look at all three of these levels (see Chapter 3). As we do, we'll discover various *disruptions* at each level—points at which the organization does not function well. These disruptions tend to become exacerbated over time. At first, people tend to try to deal with them via workarounds; as they grow more severe, people will try to address them via bigger changes. We'll examine such disruptions in Phase IV.

Finally, as people in the organization do the same thing over and over, they develop routines, tools, and roles to *mediate* their work—to help them achieve their work.

They usually get these mediators from other places. For instance, if Person A is setting up a new student organization at your university, he might set up officers such as a president, vice president, secretary, and treasurer; not because these are naturally the best officer positions to use, but because it's how most student organizations are set up. If Person B is opening a new business, she might read books and websites to discover how to set up billing procedures and handle taxes. If Person C is just starting a new job, he might handle an issue by using the same familiar kinds of information resources that he used at his old job.

We'll learn much more about activities in Chapters 3 and 20. But for now, let's focus on information resources.

Information Resources

People use various information resources in their work. *Information resources* is a broad term that I'm using to cover the regular and semi-regular types of information that workers circulate in an organization (e.g., types of documents, instant messages, hallway conversations, meetings, and even sticky notes). (Elsewhere, I have termed these information resources *genres*. For more details, see the resources in Appendix A.)

For instance, in the SEO case, workers recorded and circulated many types of information. They wrote monthly reports, gave presentations, had phone meetings with clients, and entered notes into a database. They communicated with each other in hallway conversations, instant messages, and meetings. They coordinated their own work through lists, spreadsheets, and handwritten notes. They shared expertise through mentoring meetings and internal blogs. In fact, they used a lot of information resources—but that's surprisingly common in organizations. As you look closely at organizations, you may be amazed at how many types of information resources they use.

Information resources are regular and recurrent. We can recognize them, share them, and use them in predictable ways. They're a way to mediate our own cyclical work and the cyclical work of others. In fact, information resources tend to represent crystallized problem-solving.

For instance, at some point in the company's history, someone put together the format for the monthly report. They made several choices about what to include (e.g., aims, keyword performance, and next actions) and what not to include (e.g., general news about search engines, the bios of each worker, and workers' favorite colors). That person put a lot of work into fine-tuning the report's format so that it answered most client questions.

That problem-solving work is now baked into the report format. When a new SEO specialist begins work, she doesn't have to make up a new format for her monthly reports. Instead, she learns the standard report format that everyone else uses. In the process, she learns what sorts of things clients expect her to report.

As you can imagine, we can learn a lot about how people do and understand their work when we examine information resources and how they're used. We can especially learn about the cycles that people face in their work, how the information resource grows out of solving problems in those cycles, and how the information resource fits into the overall logic of that work.

But things are often more complicated than that. As I noted earlier, we tend to import solutions, including information resources, from other places. Those solutions might not fit the new activity well.

For instance, suppose the worker wants a change, so she quits her job at the Internet marketing firm and joins a small graphic design firm. As she begins to work with her own clients, she might decide that she wants to keep these clients updated on their projects. Naturally, she turns to the same solution that worked so well at the Internet marketing firm; she begins writing monthly reports in the same format.

But in this case, the information resource doesn't work as well. It was originally developed to solve the problem of providing detailed monthly updates for clients in long-term contracts. In her graphic design work, clients don't need the same level of detail. In fact, most of them have short-term contracts with her.

In other words, the monthly report addresses a different problem with different constraints; it's not a good fit, because it doesn't fit the logic of the new organization.

Of course, the above scenario is an extreme case. More often, we pull in information resources that work reasonably well, but not perfectly. In fact, you'll often find that in a given organization, workers pull in information resources from very different places, representing very different logics, but somehow these information resources hold together. As workers encounter new problems, they tend to add new information resources from various other activities to solve them. Eventually, these resources tend to develop considerable tensions among themselves that impact the work (see Chapter 16).

Getting Started

Now that we've covered field studies and some of the concepts that we'll use throughout the book, it's time to get started. First stop: designing a field study.

The Case Study: SEObrate

Throughout this book, we'll use a fictional case study. This study is loosely based on one I conducted a few years ago and published here:

> Spinuzzi, C. (2010). Secret sauce and snake oil: Writing monthly reports in a highly contingent environment. *Written Communication*, 27(4), 363–409.

However, it's not the same study. I've added details, problems, characters, and events to make it more suitable for explaining the concepts within this book.

As you read each chapter, you'll see examples based on this case. So if you start to feel a little lost, it might help to bookmark this page so that you can return here and review the case details.

The Organization

The Internet marketing firm, SEObrate, has been in business for just a few years. Although the firm started as a fairly small shop of about 10 people, SEObrate now employs about 50. These people have many jobs, including search engine optimization, paid search, account management, and various other jobs.

In this study, we'll focus on search engine optimization (SEO).

Search Engine Optimization

SEObrate employs about 15 analysts, whose job is to figure out how people search for clients' products, such as which keywords they type into Google or Yahoo. Then the analysts use various techniques to make sure that when people search those keywords, they'll see clients' websites in the first few pages of search results. These techniques might include cleaning up and developing the client's website as well as building links pointing to the client's website.

For instance, suppose a person is looking for information, perhaps, without knowing exactly what she is looking for. She might enter a few keywords into a search engine (e.g., "cleaning wine spill" or "hotels near disneyland") and skim through the list of results. Typically, individuals start at the top, looking at each result to see if it offers the right information, products, or services. The most highly ranked sites—the ones in the first few pages of results—are more likely to secure business.

So clients, such as vendors who sell cleaning supplies or who own hotels near Disneyland, will pay to rise higher in the rankings. And SEObrate is one of the companies they pay.

But SEO is a complex space. SEObrate and other Internet marketing firms face several challenges as they operate.

Challenge 1: "Snake Oil"

The first challenge is that many clients don't trust SEO, sometimes for good reason. Some Internet marketing firms use unscrupulous tricks (a.k.a., "snake oil") to make their clients' websites rise in the search rankings, such as embedding invisible keywords in the site or embedding irrelevant keywords that don't really characterize the site's content (e.g., "Britney Spears"). Others guarantee top ranking, but only for a specific, long phrase for which people are unlikely to search (e.g., "red and white hotels near Disneyland with covered parking and shuttle service").

SEObrate doesn't use these unscrupulous tricks. To keep clients' trust, SEObrate generates detailed monthly reports, showing the clients' ranking on given keywords and proposing adjustments that will help the clients better meet their goals.

Challenge 2: Education

The second challenge is finding people with the appropriate background for SEO. After all, no universities offer a major in SEO (i.e., not at the time of writing). So SEObrate tends to hire analysts from various backgrounds (e.g., information, American studies, history, and computer science). These analysts must be highly motivated, organized, and self-reliant—beyond that, they have very different backgrounds.

Challenge 3: Keeping Up

Once they're hired, these analysts discover that the SEO space changes very rapidly. For instance, new sites and services pop up every day, all of which are potential sources for links. Search engines tweak their algorithms constantly, so a site that ranks highly on Monday may drop 20 spaces by Friday. News items can crowd the search results. For instance, if a scandal erupts that involves a Hollywood celebrity cleaning a wine spill, a client who has bought the keyword "cleaning wine spill" might find that its website drops from the first screen of search results to the 14th.

To keep up, the analysts must maintain awareness of these factors, communicate them to each other when necessary, and adjust their techniques appropriately.

SEObrateMax

SEObrate has developed an in-house system to handle the firm's SEO efforts: SEObrateMax. SEObrateMAX helps them track keyword performance, log their efforts, note problems and changes, and generate first drafts of monthly reports. Although other vendors sell SEO software, SEObrateMax lets the company add customized functionality.

SEObrate's Workers

For this case study, we'll look at the work of four people:

Dani, a senior analyst, has worked at SEObrate for just over a year. This is her second job after graduating with a degree in information.

Elizair, a senior analyst, has worked at SEObrate for two years, initially as an intern while he finished his bachelor's degree in advertising. He has just been promoted to senior analyst.

Craig, a junior analyst, has worked at SEObrate for just six months. During that time, he worked with Elizair to learn the ropes. This is Craig's first job out of school; he graduated with a history degree from a local college.

Sonia, an account manager, has worked at SEObrate for eight months. She has a bachelor's degree in public relations and has worked in other jobs as an account manager, but never in the tech industry, until now.

CHAPTER 2

About Organizations and Activities

In the remainder of the book, we will be talking a lot about *activities*. Organizations form to carry on activities, so we will need to understand what activities are and what characteristics they have. We will discuss activities in much more detail in Chapter 19, but for now, here are some of the basics.

What are Activities?

Activities are ongoing, collective attempts to cyclically transform a shared objective.

For instance, in the SEObrate case, the SEO specialists take on clients whose websites rank low in search rankings. Every month, the specialists work with others at SEObrate and with the client; in this work, they make changes that are intended to improve each client's website rank for a specific set of search terms.

Here, their work is:

- **Ongoing**. They continue this work over time. It's not just "one and done."

- **Collective**. Each specialist works with others in the organization as well as clients. Although each has her or his own duties, and sometimes works individually, they all contribute to the overall effort.

- **Cyclical**. They report monthly, and as a result, they complete a monthly cycle that includes fine-tuning the client's site, building links, examining statistics, and developing a monthly report.

- **Transformative**. They are attempting to make the site rank more highly each month. That is, they are trying to transform the website rank, not just keep it at a steady state.

- **Oriented toward a shared objective**. Even though the specialists, account managers, and clients have different roles and expertise, they all ultimately want the same thing: To continue improving the site's rank. This shared objective is what guides their efforts individually and collectively.

When I talk about "activities," I'm referring to these characteristics.

What are Organizations?

When I refer to *organizations* in this book, I don't just mean groups of people who draw their paycheck from the same employer. Yes, they might—but sometimes we see organizations of people who work across employers. So in this book, I'll use a broader definition: durable collections of people who share both an objective and a historically developed authority relationship.

For instance, SEObrate is an Internet marketing firm. A big part of its business involves the shared objective of improving site rankings. To make that happen effectively, it *hires* people, promising them regular pay. Those people accept the authority of the company: they understand that as long as they work in the company, they must fulfill assigned duties (within legal bounds). Within the company, people take on different duties, and they may even be given the discretion to execute those duties in the ways they see fit. But ultimately they must work within the authority framework of the company if they are to remain engaged in the organization's activity.

(Notice that an organization does not have to establish its authority through hiring. For instance, if you have served in a volunteer organization, you have had the experience of accepting someone's authority over your work even though you were not paid to do so.)

Importantly, although specialists at SEObrate may work *with* individuals working for the client, they aren't part of the same organization. Their collaboration is not characterized by mutual authority relations. That is, even though Elizair might work closely with a client, he is still working *for* SEObrate. Although we often hear that "the customer is always right," ultimately Elizair accepts direction from his organization and uses its rules, tools, methods, procedures, and organizational perspective to solve the client's problems.

How Do Activities Impact Organizations?

We have already seen some basic characteristics of activities. But let's look more carefully at three more characteristics of activities that impact organizations. (For more on these characteristics, see Spinuzzi 2015.)

Activities are Stable, Structured, and Pulsing

Activities are relatively *stable* because they try to solve the same basic problem over and over. In fact, that's how they improve over time. That is, they are oriented to cyclically transforming an objective.

Let's take manufacturing. If you want to manufacture a one-off item, such as a unique piece of furniture, you will likely have to do it by hand. It will be a creative act, and since no one has produced anything quite like this before, you will be inventing the way to create it as you go. Your process will probably be quite inefficient. But that's okay, because you will only be making this one unique piece of furniture.

But if you want to manufacture thousands or millions of copies of that furniture, you will likely change the way that you manufacture the furniture. You'll hire industrial designers to establish strict specifications, identify material sources, set up the appropriate machinery in a factory, and do the other things manufacturers do in order to begin cranking out furniture. And over time, the people you hire will get better at their jobs (because they do them over and over). Your managers will (ideally) get better at managing, your floor workers will (ideally) become more familiar with your procedures and equipment, and your human resources department will get better at hiring the right people for the factory.

Notice that the activity will also become more *structured*. People will take on different roles and specialize in them. You'll add new tools (such as equipment). You'll add new rules—and some rules will be imposed on you from regulatory agencies. And you may take on investors, which means that you'll have to think about how those stakeholders see things.

One more thing. This activity is set up to turn raw materials into furniture over and over again— that is, to regularly transform the objective:. So the activity *pulses* quickly, manufacturing hundreds or thousands of pieces of furniture per day. But it may *also* have other pulses, such as the annual pulse in which you report to shareholders and reevaluate your company strategy.

Activities are Kinetic

In fact, organizations have to reevaluate their activities on a regular basis. That's partly because activities are *kinetic*: Each activity interacts or comes into contact with other activities. They impact each others' conditions. For instance, SEObrate's activity is in contact with those of its different clients as well as the search engines whose behavior SEObrate tries to predict. When a client decides to start a new product line, or SEObrate takes on a new kind of client, or a search engine changes its ranking algorithm, SEObrate has to adapt. The activities are analytically separate, but they affect each other.

Activities are Dynamic

And this leads to the point that activities are *dynamic*. When they interact, they change each others' conditions.

Let's go back to SEObrate. As you recall, SEObrate's activity involves cyclically improving search rankings for its clients' websites: every month they enter a new round of changes to iteratively change these rankings. But that activity comes into contact with many other activities, such as their different clients and search engines themselves. If SEObrate finds that it can't help certain kinds of clients, it might decide to specialize in just certain types of clients. If a search engine radically changes its ranking formula, SEObrate may have to respond by hiring different specialists or changing its services. In both examples, an activity changes because of other activities impacting it.

How Do Activities Face Disruptions?

The dynamic nature of activities means that organizations usually encounter *disruptions*—disruptions that can vary from momentary confusion to wholesale change across the organization. They must periodically (or constantly) adjust to these disruptions, no matter how smoothly they function. These disruptions can be related to an organization's *lifecycle*, *scale*, *complexity*, and *interactions with other organizations*.

Let's use one more example: a university student organization dedicated to photography.

In the beginning, the organization is started by an enthusiast with a few others who, though also enthusiastic, are perhaps a little less enthusiastic. Following the rules of the university, they take on official roles (President, Vice President, Secretary, Treasurer) and write up some required documents. Everyone is unfamiliar with the tasks of running an organization—they've never done this before—so they encounter many small disruptions as they figure out these tasks. In fact, they are almost shut down that first year because the president forgot to file a piece of paperwork.

Over time, they get the hang of it. They adopt tools and rules that make their lives easier (such as a schedule for meetings and a structure for running meetings). They divide up the labor in regular ways so the President doesn't end up doing everything. And they get a clearer idea of what they want the organization to do. Disruptions still happen, but they aren't as regular, nor are they as big a deal. The organization flourishes.

But after a while, the organization flourishes so much that it outgrows the systems that keep it running. The tools and rules that worked for a ten-person organization don't do so well at running a more complicated, 100-person organization. The four officers can't keep up with all of their duties. And as the organization puts on larger events, it has to coordinate more with other organizations to make them happen. The number and severity of disruptions rise. Eventually, the student organization has to change a lot of things—new bylaws and procedures, new officers, new informal rules—to address them. As these take effect, disruptions begin to drop again.

But that happy ending doesn't always take place. Organizations sometimes reach intractable crisis points that lead to their split or collapse. In this organization, after a decade, two constituencies emerge: people who enjoy taking casual snapshots with their phones and people who want to learn more about high-end photography. Although they share the same general interest in photography, their specific objectives are too different to be well served by one organization. Eventually, after several tries to reconcile these two objectives, the organization either splits in two or disintegrates (Figure 2.1).

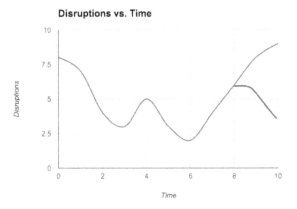

Figure 2.1. Disruptions vs. time. At the end, the organization either splits in two, eliminating the contradiction (the downward line) or disintegrates (the upward line).

No matter how smoothly they function, organizations typically face disruptions. Since they are *pulsing*, *dynamic*, and *kinetic*, these complex organizations are in a constant push-pull, both internally and with the activities in which they come into contact. Yet these disruptions sometimes develop so gradually that they aren't perceived or addressed systematically; people live with them or put together workarounds until they become so severe that they *must* be addressed. And when people do finally address these disruptions, they often have trouble seeing underlying systematic issues that cause them.

How can we systematically investigate an organization so that we can understand the underlying systemic issues it faces? The first step is to plan a solid study of the organization—a study that will allow us to understand and address these systemic issues before they become so severe that they threaten the organization.

Planning a Study

Starting a study can be nerve-wracking at first. In this section, we'll answer two questions:

- What do you want to study?

- How do you prepare to study it?

CHAPTER 3

Developing a Research Design

To gain topsight, you have to establish your game plan for investigating the organization. What are you trying to discover? How will you discover it?

In this chapter, we'll go through the process of developing a research design, including developing a research question or concern, then developing a research design based on the question or concern.

As you read this chapter, you'll get a jump start on developing your research design. You may find that it's useful to read Chapters 2-4 all together before getting started, since your research design will depend in part on what your potential site and participants will let you do. Read Chapters 7-10 to learn more about each research method that you might include.

Developing a Research Question or Concern

Traditionally, in academic research, you select a *research question*—a one-sentence expression of the issue that you want to study. With open-ended field research, you might also start with a *research concern*—something that you can't put into a precise question, but that still concerns you or others:

An academic studying an office might ask, "What documents do people need to use in order to develop and produce monthly reports?" (Spinuzzi 2010).

A consultant might ask, "How does a unit in the client's organization move information around, and where does that information get blocked?"

Someone in an organization might say, "I want to know more about the advantages and disadvantages of the way we're currently handling records in this office."

Notice that these questions and concerns are not very precise. In fact, we may not be quite sure *what* we're looking for, which is to say that we are following an exploratory process. So you may refine your research question/concern quite a bit. In fact, you will probably have to as you begin to

- develop your research design (this chapter);

- express your research design for others (Chapter 4); and

- persuade people in the organization to allow you to do research (Chapter 5).

But you do need a starting point, because your research question or concern drives your research design. In other words, you need a general idea of what you want to know before you can begin to look for it. So let's generate a research question/concern now.

Types of Research Questions or Concerns

You can generate a research question or concern from at least three places.

What *you* want to know. If you're a student working on a senior thesis, master's thesis, or dissertation, you may already have a good idea of the phenomenon you want to study. You'll draw from previous studies or theory to generate an idea, and you'll work with your advisor to develop your question.

What the *client* wants to know. If you're a consultant or contractor, on the other hand, your research question or concern will be driven by client needs. You can generally get those needs from a request for proposals (RFP), a formal meeting, or an informal meeting with stakeholders (see Chapter 5). At the same time, you are the expert, which means that, although you'll fold their concerns into your research question/concern, you will need to formulate the research question/concern yourself.

What *your organization* needs. Maybe you're looking at your organization or unit and thinking, there has to be a better way to run this process. In this case, like a consultant, you'll need to talk with stakeholders (see Chapter 5). But you'll also need to consider your own understanding of the organization's or unit's needs. Ultimately, like the consultant, you'll need to formulate the research question/concern yourself.

Formulating Research Questions

A research question expresses what you're trying to find out. But it's not that simple. Your research question will be constrained by the available data too. In other words, you need to ask a research question that you can plausibly answer, given the methods available to you and the access the site is willing to give you.

For instance, in the SEO study, I would *not* be able to answer these research questions through a three-month field study of five people at SEObrate:

Poor RQ: *How is the SEO industry going to change over the next three years?*

This question is predictive—it looks into the future—but field studies are geared to understanding what's happening right now. The question also has too large a scope: You are looking at one company, not an entire industry, and you're gathering data over three months, not three years.

Poor RQ: *How do people's specific college degrees prepare them to do SEO?*

This question can't be answered with the small number of people in this study: if we see differences in how participants do their work, we don't have enough comparison points to be confident that these differences come from their college experience as opposed to their personalities or other life experiences.

Poor RQ: *What do clients think of the reports?*

Since the study is restricted to people working at SEObrate, not clients, we can't really answer this question either. We might find out what our participants assume, or we might look at the feedback that clients have given to the participants, but we can't be confident that we really know what the clients think without some direct way to address that question.

Poor RQ: *How many reports are produced each month?*

This research question could certainly be answered with a three-month field study. But you don't really need to conduct a field study to get the answer—you could just ask one well-placed person. More than that, the question isn't that interesting. Does anyone really care?

A good research question needs to be suitable for what you can investigate:

- **Opportunity**. It should be answerable given the data that you can reasonably expect to collect.

- **Scope**. It should be small enough in scope—in terms of timeframe, organization, and people—that you can investigate it and provide a solid, meaningful answer.

- **"So what."** It should answer a question that you and the site actually want to be answered.

Notice that these three elements interact. For instance, if you can come up with a really compelling "so what," it might convince the site to give you more access (changing your opportunity and scope). For that reason, you might have to revise the research question a few times to fine-tune it for your study. Eventually, you can develop a research question that is well tuned to the opportunity, scope, and "so what," like these:

RQ1: *How do people in this organization manage projects? What tools and texts do they use?*

RQ2: *How, and to what extent, do they collaborate in management?*

RQ3: *How, and to what extent, do they share information?*

RQ4: *What training have they received?*

RQ5: *How has project management changed in their organization?*

These research questions are tuned to the *opportunity* being sought: a three-month field study. They delineate a reasonable *scope*: they can be answered within the time and participant limitations. And they have a compelling "*so what*," since SEObrate's managers were interested in the answers.

Research Questions vs. Interview Questions

Research questions aren't the same as *interview questions*. A research question is a question that you and the site want to answer; an interview question is a question that you ask each participant in order to eventually answer the research question.

To understand the difference, imagine that you're a police detective trying to solve a murder mystery. Your big question—the research question, so to speak—is: *Who committed the murder?* But when you interview suspects, you won't just ask them this research question. Imagine what that would be like:

DETECTIVE: Who committed the murder?

SUSPECT: (Shrugs) I don't know.

DETECTIVE: Okay, you're free to go.

Asking the suspect the research question won't do much good. If the suspect knew the answer, he would have either volunteered the information already or he has decided to hide it!

Instead, you have to ask other questions that will help you to answer that main research question. These might include:

Where were you on the night in question? Can anyone else corroborate your whereabouts?

Did the victim have any enemies?

Did the victim have any money trouble?

Did you know of any arguments the victim had had recently?

These questions can help the detective build a larger picture of the events, motivations, and opportunities that surrounded the murder.

You won't be using the Topsight approach to investigate any murders (I assume), but like the detective, you'll be talking to people who won't be able to answer your research question. Your interview questions, which we will discuss in Chapter 8, will help you to answer that research question.

Vocabulary for Research Questions/Concerns

The methodology in this book is focused on how information flows through an organization or unit, how it moves through information resources and routines, and how roles and objectives affect it. So when you're developing your research question/concern, think in these terms:

- Information

- Documents

- Roles

- Tools

- Rules

- Flow

- Processes

- Routines

- Disruptions

Once you have a basic research question/concern, it's time to develop a research design.

Developing a Research Design

The research question/concern gives you a general idea of what you want to know. You have established that you want to get from Point A (no knowledge) to Point B (some knowledge). But how do you get from Point A to Point B? You need to make sure you use the right methods to gather the right data to allow you to make this journey.

What are Methods?

Data collection methods are ways that you can gather facts about the organization. You can think of these as ways to hunt for clues or evidence. For instance, if you're visiting an office to understand how it works, you might

- observe people as they work;

- interview them about their work;

- get copies of the information resources they use;

- take photos of their work environment;

- install keylogging software on their computer—with their permission, of course—so that you can see what keys they hit; or

- ask them to draw how they feel about a particular task.

Below are several different data collection methods you might consider using. But you might end up inventing your own data collection methods, which is fine as long as you can use them to systematically gather data.

- **Observations** (see Chapter 7). Visit the workers, watch them as they work, and take notes. This method lets you see their actual work, not just what they say about it.

- **Interviews** (see Chapter 8). Talk with workers about their work. Typically, you'll audio record these interviews. You'll usually ask a list of questions you've developed ahead of time, but you'll also follow up on issues you saw during the observations. Through this method, workers can explain why they do things and how these things fit into their other work.

- **Artifacts** (see Chapter 9). Pick up artifacts or copies of artifacts (e.g., information resources and tools) that the workers use or generate during their work. These can help you better understand the genres people use to accomplish their work. In aggregate, they can help you understand how the organization has changed over time.

- **System monitoring** (see Chapter 10). The worker lets you install software on her computer so that you can see what they do during the day. This approach can collect precise data about what they do on the computer—if they're comfortable with it.

- **Diaries** (see Chapter 10). The worker fills out forms describing what she is doing at certain parts of the day, like a detailed diary or a timesheet. Diaries capture the worker's impressions when you can't be there.

- **Pictures** (see Chapter 10). Ask workers to draw pictures that describe their experiences or feelings. These pictures can help people to talk about their experiences and feelings in ways that might not come out during interviews.

- **Participatory design techniques** (see Chapter 10 & Phase VI). Collaborate with workers to develop new solutions, using techniques such as prototyping. Participatory design puts workers in an active problem-solving role.

The data collection methods that you use will depend on what you're trying to find out. Some sound unusual ("pictures?"), but they allow you to systematically get at something you need to know, they allow you to collect *data*.

What are Data?

Data are facts about the organization that you systematically gather so that you can infer a general statement. Once you develop that general statement, you can use these data as *evidence* to support that statement (see Phase IV).

In the example above, you are gathering data:

- Observation notes

- Interviews

- Copies of texts

- Photos

- Keylogs

- Pictures

You use these data to build up a picture of how people are working in the environment. They're your clues for solving the mystery. Since they're such important clues, you need to make sure that you collect them systematically.

For instance, suppose that you hear an offhand remark from one participant, talking about someone else in the organization, "Fred is such a foul-up." There's a piece of data. You might start thinking: is Fred *really* a foul-up? Maybe. But you can't conclude that from this offhand remark. The participant might have been exaggerating, kidding, lying, or mistaken. In any event, this judgment might be an opinion that no one else shares.

If you're going to use this piece of data to say something significant, you need to collect similar data systematically. For instance, you can

- **observe** Fred and others doing the same job (Does Fred make more mistakes?);

- **interview** the participant (Does she really believe Fred is a foul-up? Why?); and

- **interview** other participants (What do they think of Fred's performance? Why?).

I've been talking about collecting data in terms of solving a mystery. And just as you wouldn't want a detective to build a case based on one neighbor's hearsay, you shouldn't try to build an analysis based on just one piece of data. By collecting data systematically, you can build a better, more comprehensive picture of what's going on.

But how do you know what clues to gather, and how to gather them systematically? You need a *research design*.

Developing the Research Design Matrix

Let's switch metaphors. Suppose that you're investing money. You *could* put all of your money into one stock. Very few people do that, because it's very risky. If the stock goes up, maybe you win big. But if it goes down, you lose money—maybe lots of it. Just ask the people who bought Facebook stock on opening day.

Instead, most people who invest tend to mitigate their risk by *diversifying* their investments. They invest in a mix of stocks (which provide higher yields, but are more volatile) and bonds (which provide lower yields, but are much less volatile). People who don't avidly follow the stock market—like me—might also invest in index funds, which bundles together an index of different investments across different sectors in an attempt to approximate the movement of the entire financial market. Since financial markets have historically tended to go up over time, index funds are generally a good way to mitigate risk, while making sure you get something out of your investment.

Think of the research design matrix (table 3.1) as an index fund for research methods. Here, the "risk" is the risk of not gathering the data you'll need.

Table 3.1. The research design matrix.

	Methods that yield...	Methods that yield...
	Your etic perspective (What you can see about their work)	*Their emic perspective (What they can tell you about their work)*
Macro (organiza-tion) level: *Culture and history; objectives and outcomes; usually unconscious*		
Meso (human) level: *Actions and goals; conscious*		
Micro (habit) level: *Habits and reactions; unconscious*		

This table helps you to diversify the risk of not getting the right data. Using it, you can gather data at the three levels of activity discussed in Chapter 1 with two perspectives.

Three Levels of Activity

As discussed in Chapter 1, we can think of human activity as occurring at three *levels*:

- **The macro level.** The level of culture and history: think of it as the *organization level* in terms of the organization's mission and vision—what it accomplishes on the scale of years or decades. This is the "Why" level—why does the organization do what it does?

- **The meso level.** The level of goal-directed actions: think of it as the *human level* in terms of what the individual is consciously trying to accomplish on the scale of minutes or hours. This is the "What" level—what is the individual trying to do?

- **The micro level.** The level of habits and reactions: think of it as the *habit level* in terms of what the individual does unconsciously on the scale of seconds. This is the "How" level—how does the individual reach her meso-level goals?

To get a full understanding of what's going on in the study, you need to be able to collect data at all three levels. That is, you'll need to answer the "Why", the "What", and the "How". To see how this works, let's look at a particular scenario:

You're investigating how people write monthly reports at the Internet marketing firm. To get a fuller understanding of this work, you investigate at the three levels.

At the macro level, you gather information about why the organization does what it does. You pick up several annual reports describing the company's work; you look at its mission or vision statement; you examine a list of clients; and you interview the office's director to better understand how she sees the organization's mission.

At the meso level, you want to see what the work actually involves. You observe different people in the office as they work on reports at different times of the month. You interview them about how they write the reports and where they get their information. You collect copies of the reports and look at how they're marked up.

At the micro level, you want to see how people work. So as you observe them, you especially note their habits, mistakes, and recoveries. For instance, you notice that in a certain dialog box, people often click "Cancel" when they mean to click "OK."

By collecting data at these three levels, you can gain a fuller picture of what's going on. In Phase III, we'll see how to analyze data at the three levels then integrate them into a fuller picture.

Two Perspectives

In addition, you need to be able to coordinate two *perspectives*: yours (sometimes called the *etic* perspective, the perspective from outside the social group) and your research participants' (sometimes called the *emic* perspective, the perspective from within the social group). Let's look at a particular scenario:

You're visiting a participant in his office. As you observe him working, you see him open a file folder and take out its contents: a heavily annotated report and a sticky note. He puts the sticky note on his computer monitor and places the report to the right of his computer. Then he opens a word processing file, which looks like the report, and starts typing. Twice in the next hour, he instant messages someone—you're not sure who—with questions about the report.

What is happening? It looks like he's editing the report, but you're not sure why or where he's getting the information for the edits. From your (etic) perspective, you can see some aspects of what he's doing, but you can't get to his interpretation of it and you're missing important bits of context.

After the hour is up, you interview him about what you saw. He says:

"Yeah, that printout was last month's report. I'm working on this month's report, so what I do is make a of copy last month's file [in the word processor], change the name and date, then edit it to show what happened this month. I wrote all over the printout, as you saw. The sticky note is from my supervisor."

Now you're getting his (emic) interpretation, including the context. But notice what's missing; he hasn't discussed his Instant Messaging (IM) use. In fact, he might not bring it up, unless you prompt him. Using IM might be such a habitual part of his workflow that he doesn't even think about it, any more than he thinks about breathing.

By gathering data that represent both perspectives, you can get a fuller understanding of the work. Importantly, you'll be able to triangulate them (see Chapter 12).

Filling Out the Research Design Matrix

Now that you have a good idea of what the research design matrix does, you can begin thinking about the data collection methods that you can use.

What you can collect will depend on the nature of the work as well as what the organization and participants will let you collect.

For instance, you might *want* to interview people as they do their work, but if they're doing something that involves talking with a customer (e.g., phone sales) or something that involves a lot of concentration (e.g., brain surgery), you won't be able to collect data that way. You also may want to install keylogging software on a participant's computer to capture all of their work. But the participant might refuse—let's face it, keylogging is very intrusive—or the participant might not remember to turn on the keylogging software at the right time.

Nevertheless, you should be able to collect some sort of data at all three levels and both perspectives, even if you have to hit multiple levels with the same technique. For instance, you might use a post-observation interview to get the participant's perspective on the organization's objective (macro level), what the participant did during this observation (meso level), and the participant's explanation of micro-level mistakes he made during the observation (micro level).

Table 3.2 shows a research design matrix for the SEO case described above. The research design in table 3.2 represents a nicely diversified set of data collection methods, which together should provide systematically collected data that you can triangulate.

Table 3.2. The research design matrix for the SEO case.

	Methods that yield...	Methods that yield...
	Your etic perspective (What you can see about their work)	Their emic perspective (What they can tell you about their work)
Macro (organization) level: Culture and history; objectives and outcomes; usually unconscious	Copies of mission or vision statement; copies of annual reports; list of clients who read monthly reports	Interview with office manager; interviews with writers
Meso (human) level: Actions and goals; conscious	Observations; copies of reports and annotations; photos of office	Post-observation interviews
Micro (habit) level: Habits and reactions; unconscious	Observations; copies of annotations; keylogging	Post-observation interviews

So now you have a research question/concern and a research design that allows you to investigate it. But you still don't have a lot of specifics. How many participants do you need? Who should they be? How will you approach them? How will you protect their confidentiality? And how will you persuade them to take part in your study? In the next few chapters, we'll answer these questions.

Exercises

- Develop a research question or concern.

- Based on the research question or concern, develop a research design matrix for your case. Make sure to "diversify"—to fill in all the cells.

Examples

The next page has a set of research questions from the SEO case and a blank research design matrix for you to fill out.

Research Questions

- How do people in high-tech knowledge work organizations manage projects? What tools and texts do they use?

- How, and to what extent, do they collaborate in management?

- How, and to what extent, do they share information?

- What training have they received?

- How has project management changed in their organization?

Research Design Matrix

	Methods that yield...	Methods that yield...
	Your etic perspective (What you can see about their work)	*Their emic perspective (What they can tell you about their work)*
Macro (organization) level: *Culture and history; objectives and outcomes; usually unconscious*		
Meso (human) level: *Actions and goals; conscious*		
Micro (habit) level: *Habits and reactions; unconscious*		

CHAPTER 4

Building in Protections

Studying how people work can be nerve-wracking. Think about it from *their* perspective:

Workers are trying to get things done. They don't have a lot of time to talk. More than that, they aren't really sure what you're after, but they know you're looking for problems. Will you tell their boss about every mistake they make? Will your observations go into their job review? Worse, will you tell the boss that their job is redundant?

Managers are interested in improving things, but they don't want their unit to take a productivity hit because you're asking questions. Will you pull employees off of the job for lengthy interviews? Will you interfere in their work? Worse, will you turn up problems with management style and put the managers themselves on the spot? Will you make them and their organization look bad?

You can see how your humble little research study can seem like a high-stakes risk for both groups. These risks are real. In fact, *you* face risks yourself:

You want to get a better understanding of the work so that you can recommend positive changes, but you face the problem of gaining the workers' and managers' trust, because without that, you won't be able to perform the study well or draw accurate conclusions. In fact, if these people don't trust you, they can do various sorts of damage to your own reputation as a researcher, consultant, or member.

How do you manage these three sets of risks?

Managing Workers' Risks: Human Subjects Research Guidelines

These problems aren't new. In fact, in United States universities, *human subjects research*—research that involves studying human participants—must be approved by an institutional review board (IRB) before it can proceed. The reasons are varied and go back to historical violations of participants' well-being (see the resources in Appendix A, especially the *Belmont Report*). The bottom line is that for academics to conduct research, they must meet certain guidelines to minimize the risk to participants.

Field researchers in industry, such as consultants, don't have an IRB to which they must report; however, I strongly suggest that they follow these guidelines as well. Not only will the guidelines help researchers to conduct ethical research, they also help researchers to build trust with the participants, which is critical, as we'll see later in the chapter.

Here are some human subjects research guidelines:

Privacy. If they choose, participants should have the right to be anonymous in research reports. For instance, if you're studying a work environment, participants may worry that you'll report an incident that will negatively affect their job reviews or employment. Typically you should handle this by making sure each participant is anonymous in reports; for instance, it's common to give each participant a pseudonym so she or he can't be identified. You should also remove any *identifying information* from reports. For instance, if there's only one male in the group you're studying, you're not protecting that participant by simply giving him a male pseudonym!

Confidentiality. Participants are trusting you with information that could put them at risk. So you must protect them, not just in the final reports, but also in how you keep your data. Typically you should handle this by keeping any data (i.e., observational notes, interviews, etc.) in a locked area to which only you have access, such as a locked filing cabinet or an encrypted hard drive.

Control over participation. Participants should have the right to say no to the study at any time; they should never feel coerced to be in the study. This means managers cannot tell people to participate in the study; it should be their own decision. Participants should be able to drop out of the study at any time, for any reason; if they do, you should destroy their data (e.g., delete their files, shred any papers they gave you).

Control over time. Participants should not face an undue burden when participating. For instance, if they do you the favor of participating in your study, they should know what they're getting into. That means that you should provide clear expectations about how many visits there will be, for how long, and what you'll ask them to do during each visit.

Additionally, participants should be free to decide when you'll interview them, when you'll observe them, and what other data you can collect.

At the end of this chapter is a sample research proposal, based on the template provided by my institution, the University of Texas at Austin. If you're in an academic institution, it probably has its own templates.

In addition, you'll want to present each participant with a consent form (see end of chapter). Notice that the consent form describes the same study as the research proposal, but is written to the individual participant in plain language. You'll have each participant sign two copies: then you'll keep one and let the participant keep the other.

Managing Managers' Risks: Human Subjects Research Guidelines

As we've seen, managers can also perceive risks, both to themselves and their organizations. That's especially true in big, complex organizations, in which the right hand often doesn't know what the left hand is doing. They face risks letting someone into their organization:

- Giving away a competitive advantage

- Revealing damaging information, such as poorly executed parts of a work process

- Revealing regulatory violations before the organization itself is aware of them

Managers consider letting you into their organization because they want your help in improving the organization, but they also often worry that you'll cause more damage than benefit.

Managers are human too, and that means that they fall under the human subjects guidelines too.

Privacy. Like participants, organizations should have the right to be anonymous in research reports, if they choose. You can accomplish that by making sure each organization is anonymous in reports and by expunging any *identifying information* from reports. For instance, describe the organization in terms that are general enough that they could refer to a number of similar organizations.

Confidentiality. Also like participants, organizations are trusting you with information that could pose risks to them. So you must protect them, not just in the final reports, but also in how you keep your data. Typically, you should handle this by keeping any data (observational notes, interviews, etc.) in a locked area to which only you have access, such as a locked filing cabinet or an encrypted hard drive.

Control over participation. Like participants, organizations should have the right to say no to the study at any time. After all, they are your hosts. If they choose to discontinue the study, you must destroy the data.

Control over time. Organizations have to get things done, which means that they have to make sure your research won't interfere unduly with their operations. That means that you should provide clear expectations for how many visits there will be, for how long, and what you'll ask them to do during each visit.

Additionally, organizations should be able to determine (or veto your suggestions for) when you'll interview participants, when you'll observe participants, and what other data you can collect.

Some organizations may also work up a non-disclosure agreement (NDA) for you to sign. Generally, these NDAs are meant to reduce the organization's risk, rather than to interfere with your study. Don't be shy about negotiating the NDA or even walking away, if the terms won't allow you to do your job.

If you're submitting your research proposal to an IRB, you will also ask for a *site letter*. This document is a short letter from a person in authority at your organization, spelling out their understanding of what you will be doing at the organization. Typically, I write the site letter based on the research proposal, then negotiate the specifics with the site before having them sign it (see the example at the end of the chapter).

Managing Your Own Risks: Trust Building and Reciprocity

Traditionally, academic research guidelines have assumed that the researcher poses risks to the participants. After all, she or he may plan to publish the research, while the participants do not have a publishing outlet.

But, realistically, participants and organizations always pose risks to the researcher as well. Organizations in particular have many ways to communicate with the public, ways that can be used to threaten the researcher's reputation. And in the age of social media, even individual participants can often reach a greater audience than the researcher can.

Unfortunately, IRBs are not set up to address those risks. So you, the researcher, will have to take measures to protect yourself from such risks—by building trust with your participants, by making sure that your participants know that they have a say in how you represent them.

Trust Building through Documents

I recommend building trust through the following measures:

Establish terms in writing and stick to them. You have three documents that serve this purpose (examples at the end of the chapter):

- The research proposal

- The consent form

- The site letter

Establish a set of documents to keep managers in the loop.
In this book, I'll walk you through these documents: the interim
report and the recommendation report.

Establish member checks to confirm participants' data. As
you collect, analyze, and interpret the results of your study, you
might consider using *member checks* to make sure that you and the
participants are on the same page. Member checks might involve
showing participants the following things and asking for their
comments:

- The researcher's observational notes pertaining to a participant (see Chapter 7)

- The participant's interview transcripts (see Chapter 8)

- Drafts of interim reports (see Chapter 13)

- Models based on the participant's work (see Chapters 15-23)

- Drafts of the recommendation report (see Chapter 26)

You can conduct member checks at any of these stages. See Chapter 11 for more on member checks.

**Establish the right for management and participants to
review publications.** If you plan to publish your results, strongly
consider circulating drafts to management and participants to
gather their feedback. Yes, doing this can lead you to pull your
punches, but it can also lead you to better understand the situation from different perspectives.

Trust Building through Actions

In addition to these formal document-based processes, you can
build trust simply by *establishing expectations, and meeting them*.

Think about it this way: suppose an acquaintance, Alan, wants to meet you to talk about a job opening in your organization.

"Okay," you tell him, "just let me know when you can meet and we'll grab a cup of coffee."

He does. And that's when the trouble starts. He cancels the first meeting at the last minute, explaining that he had a conflict. He doesn't show up to the second meeting, then apologizes later and says he forgot. At the third meeting—yes, you meet him a third time—he has some vague questions, and it's clear he doesn't really know what he needs from you. How much are you inclined to help him at this point?

Now let's suppose that another acquaintance, Bertha, wants to meet you about the same job opening. She suggests a meeting time and sends you a link to her LinkedIn page. When you get to the meeting, she's already there with a cup of coffee for you. Over the course of the meeting, it becomes clear that she's done her homework. She asks a series of well-focused questions that are obviously based on research that she's done. How much are you inclined to help her at this point?

The critical difference is that Bertha respects your time and has done everything possible to make it easy for you to help her. More than that, she has demonstrated what kind of coworker she would be: a coworker that carries her own load, thinks ahead, and makes your job easier. You can see yourself working with Bertha, but not Alan.

As a researcher, obviously, you want to be more like Bertha. Your participants are giving up part of their busy day for you. Make them glad to do this:

- Set clear appointments with specific agendas.

- Follow through on those appointments on time and respect time limitations.

- Be flexible enough to work around any emergencies they face.

- Come well prepared with appropriate questions.

How do you do this? Put together a research protocol (see example at end of chapter).

Think of your research protocol as a detailed plan for your visit with a participant. It's a to-do list that should help you to implement the research measures from the consent form in a timely fashion. In this example, follow this research protocol:

- Introduce yourself and explain the consent form.

- Have them sign the consent form.

- Conduct the observation.

- Conduct the interview (including questions).

As you can see, the research protocol is a detailed checklist that you set up based on the consent form. The protocol includes the interview questions you will ask; in Chapter 8, we will discuss how to formulate these interview questions.

Exercises

- Based on the **research proposal example**, **your research question**, and your **research design matrix**, write a **research proposal**.

- Based on the **consent form example** and the **research proposal draft**, write the **consent form**.

- Based on the **site letter example** and the **research proposal draft**, write a **site letter**.

- Based on the **data collection protocol example** and the **consent form**, write the **data collection protocol**.

- Review the documents to make sure they line up—whether they are still describing the same study.

- In groups, discuss **member checks**. What member checks will you use?

Examples

On the next few pages are examples of the research proposal, consent form, and data collection protocol for the SEO case, as well as a site letter.

Research Proposal

TITLE

Project Management in a High-Tech Organization: A Field Study

PRINCIPAL INVESTIGATOR

Clay Spinuzzi, University of Texas at Austin

PURPOSE

I seek to answer the following research questions:

- How do people in a high-tech knowledge work organization manage projects? What tools and texts do they use?

- How, and to what extent, do they collaborate in management?

- How, and to what extent, do they share information?

- What training have they received?

- How has project management changed in their organization?

PROCEDURES

Data collection involves these methods for exploring participants' training and practices:

- **Site interviews**: Researcher will conduct one short (average 30 minute) semi-structured interview with a manager before contacting participants. Interviews will be audio recorded.

- **Pre-observational interviews**: Researcher will conduct one short (average 15 minute) semi-structured interview with each participant immediately before the first observation to collect information about their professional biography and history with project management, collaboration, and related tools and practices. Interviews will be audio recorded.

- **Naturalistic observations**: Researcher will visit participants at work and conduct up to three two-hour observations of each participant's work. During the observations, researcher will record events relating to project management, collaboration, information sharing, and training. Recordings will be in the form of detailed field notes.

- **Post-observational interviews**: Researcher will conduct one semi-structured interview with each participant immediately after each observation (average .5 hours). Interviews will be audio recorded.

- **Artifact collection**: Researcher will collect artifacts from the participant's workplace that are related to project management, collaboration, information sharing, and training. Artifacts might include copies or photos of project lists, to-do lists, training documentation, generic contracts, screen shots, and email. To ensure privacy of others, participants will redact artifacts before turning the artifacts over to researcher.

Researcher will analyze the observational, interview, and artifact data using ethnographic methods:

- **Coding** (i.e., starts with but not limited to the extant categories: communication, time and project management, understanding, relationships, strategy, and training)

- **Models** (i.e., activity systems, activity networks, resource maps, handoff chains, triangulation tables, breakdown tables, and topsight tables)

- **Member checks** (i.e., researcher circulates drafts to participants for comments)

LOCATION

Research will be conducted at the organization, _____.

RESOURCES

This research requires no resources.

STUDY TIMELINE

Data collection: April 1-July 1, 2016

Data analysis: July 1-July 30, 2016

Write-up: August 1-September 1, 2016

MEASURES

Interview questions are in the research protocol.

PARTICIPANTS

TARGET POPULATION

Researcher will recruit up to five participants in a single organization. Participants will be company employees working in various web-related and software-related areas, such as search engine optimization, social media, and web development.

INCLUSION/EXCLUSION

None

BENEFITS

This study will have implications for understanding project management and collaboration in this organization. In addition, the project should serve as a way for participants to articulate, reflect upon, and justify or improve their project management practices respective to their work.

RISKS

The research may uncover weaknesses as well as strengths in the participants' work. Reports will remind readers that this should happen and that the role of this research is to better understand the organizations' project management as a whole, not to evaluate individual work styles. In addition, the participants' identities and organizational affiliations will be kept secret. Participants will be assigned pseudonyms in any publications resulting from this research.

RECRUITMENT

Researcher will contact participants through personal connections with management in this organization.

OBTAINING INFORMED CONSENT

Participants will be presented with consent forms.

PRIVACY AND CONFIDENTIALITY

Participants can choose to discontinue participation at any time; if they choose to do so, their data will be destroyed. Participants can determine acceptable times for interviews and observations. The participant's identity will not be disclosed in reports. Researcher will refer to participant with a pseudonym and redact any identifying characteristics in reports. Data will be kept confidential and secure. No publications resulting from this research will include identifiers of participants or their organizations. Finally, the researcher will explain to management that it is entirely up to team members whether they wish to participate in the study; the organization will not require team members to participate, and team members can drop out of the study at any time, for any reason. The organization's site letter will assert this fact, and the researcher will explain this fact to team members before having them sign consent forms.

CONFIDENTIALITY OF THE DATA OR SAMPLES

Research data will be kept in a locked cabinet at researcher's office and on an encrypted laptop hard drive

For interviews, (a) the interviews will be audio recorded; (b) the digital files will be coded so that no personally identifying information is visible on them; (c) they will be digitally secured with a password; (d) they will be heard or viewed only for research purposes by researcher; and (e) they will be destroyed after they are transcribed (by July 30, 2016).

COMPENSATION

Participants will not be compensated.

Example

Consent Forms

PROJECT MANAGEMENT IN A HIGH-TECH ORGANIZATION: A FIELD STUDY

INTRODUCTION

The purpose of this form is to provide you information that may affect your decision as to whether or not to participate in this research study. The person performing the research will answer any of your questions. Read the information below and ask any questions you might have before deciding whether or not to take part. If you decide to be involved in this study, this form will be used to record your consent.

PURPOSE OF THE STUDY

You have been asked to participate in a research study about your organization. The purpose of this study is to better understand how people in organizations like yours manage projects, collaborate, and share information.

WHAT WILL YOU BE ASKED TO DO?

If you agree to participate in this study, you will be asked to

- Be interviewed for about 15 minutes about your professional biography and history with project management, collaboration, and related tools and practices.

- Be observed up to 3 times, for two hours each, as you conduct your normal work.

- Be interviewed for up to 30 minutes immediately after each observation.

- Provide copies or allow the researcher to take photos of documents and other artifacts. You may refuse to allow copies or photos. You may also redact (cut or black out) information on these before handing them to the researcher.

This study will take a total of 7 hours 45 minutes of your time. It will include approximately five study participants.

Your participation will be audio recorded.

WHAT ARE THE RISKS INVOLVED IN THIS STUDY?

There are no foreseeable risks to participating in this study.

WHAT ARE THE POSSIBLE BENEFITS OF THIS STUDY?

You will receive no direct benefit from participating in this study; however, this study will have implications for understanding project management and collaboration in this organization. In addition, the project should serve as a way for you to articulate, reflect upon, and justify or improve your project management practices respective to their work.

DO YOU HAVE TO PARTICIPATE?

No, your participation is voluntary. You may decide not to participate at all or, if you start the study, you may withdraw at any time. Withdrawal or refusing to participate will not affect your relationship with The University of Texas at Austin (University) in any way.

If you would like to participate, please sign this form and return it to the researcher. You will receive a copy of this form.

WILL THERE BE ANY COMPENSATION?

You will not receive any type of payment participating in this study.

HOW WILL YOUR PRIVACY AND CONFIDENTIALITY BE PROTECTED IF YOU PARTICIPATE IN THIS RESEARCH STUDY?

Your privacy and the confidentiality of your data will be protected by the following measures:

- Your identity will not be disclosed in reports. Researcher will refer to you with a pseudonym and redact any identifying characteristics in reports.

- Data will be kept confidential and secure.

- No publications resulting from this research will include identifiers of participants or their organization.

- Research data will be kept in a locked cabinet at researcher's office and on an encrypted laptop hard drive

- For interviews, (a) the interviews will be audio recorded; (b) the digital files will be coded so that no personally identifying information is visible on them; (c) they will be digitally secured with a password; (d) they will be heard or viewed only for research purposes by researcher; and (e) they will be destroyed after they are transcribed (by July 30, 2016).

Example

If it becomes necessary for the Institutional Review Board to review the study records, information that can be linked to you will be protected to the extent permitted by law. Your research records will not be released without your consent unless required by law or a court order. The data resulting from your participation may be made available to other researchers in the future for research purposes not detailed within this consent form. In these cases, the data will contain no identifying information that could associate it with you, or with your participation in any study.

If you choose to participate in this study, you will be audio recorded. Any audio recordings will be stored securely and only the research team will have access to the recordings. Recordings will be kept until July 30, 2016 and then erased.

WHOM TO CONTACT WITH QUESTIONS ABOUT THE STUDY?

Prior, during or after your participation you can contact the researcher [NAME] at [PHONE NUMBER] or send an email to [EMAIL ADDRESS] for any questions or if you feel that you have been harmed.

WHOM TO CONTACT WITH QUESTIONS CONCERNING YOUR RIGHTS AS A RESEARCH PARTICIPANT?

For questions about your rights or any dissatisfaction with any part of this study, you can contact, anonymously if you wish, the Institutional Review Board by phone at [PHONE NUMBER] or email at [EMAIL ADDRESS].

PARTICIPATION

If you agree to participate, please sign the form and return to the researcher.

SIGNATURE

You have been informed about this study's purpose, procedures, possible benefits and risks, and you have received a copy of this form. You have been given the opportunity to ask questions before you sign, and you have been told that you can ask other questions at any time. You voluntarily agree to participate in this study. By signing this form, you are not waiving any of your legal rights.

_____
Printed Name

_____
Signature   Date

As a representative of this study, I have explained the purpose, procedures, benefits, and the risks involved in this research study.

_____

Printed Name of Person Obtaining
Consent

_____

Signature of Person Obtaining   Date
Consent

Example

Protocol checklist

OBTAIN CONSENT

☐ Introduce self to participant.

☐ Describe project and goals.

☐ Describe the eventual product: a report discussing how people manage projects in their organization.

☐ Describe eventual benefits: An improved understanding of project management in rapidly changing organizations.

☐ Explain consent form and ask them to sign.

☐ Conduct pre-observation interview. (See questions below.)

☐ Conduct observation.

☐ Conduct post-observation interview. (See questions below.)

PRE–OBSERVATION INTERVIEW QUESTIONS

• What is your job history? Could you tell us about the sorts of jobs you have held beyond this one?

• What is your academic background? Could you tell us a bit about your educational experience?

• How would you describe your current job? What are your most important duties or activities?

• What team or teams do you work in? Can you describe your current project?

• How does this team manage this project (e.g., objectives, milestones, and delegation)? What tools and texts do they use?

• How does your team share information? To what extent?

• What training have you received in teamwork and project management?

• How has project management changed in your organization?

Post-Observation Interview Questions

- I noticed that some of your activities included **(list from observation).** How did you learn how to deal with these project-related duties and activities?

- Would you say that this was a typical day? Tell me about where you are in this project.

- I noticed that you **(observation about how they communicate within their temporary networks)**. Could you tell us a bit about the ways that you communicate with clients, vendors, subcontractors, and others?

- These projects tend to be pretty complex, with a lot of things to coordinate. I noticed that you **(observation about time and project management)**. Could you talk a bit about how you manage your time and projects?

- I also noticed that you **(observation about working with others)**. To make these projects successful, do you need to know much about the work of clients, vendors, subcontractors, and others? If so, how do you learn about their work?

- Do you tend to work frequently with the same vendors or subcontractors? How do you maintain those relationships?

- Where do you see your business or unit five years from now? What are your goals? Do you see projects like this one contributing to those long-term goals?

Example

Site Letter

[date]

To whom it may concern:

SEObrate is interested in [researcher]'s efforts to study project management in high-tech organizations. We will allow [researcher] to conduct the following research with a designated team at our organization:

Site interviews. Researcher will conduct one short (average 30 minute) semi-structured interview with a manager before contacting participants. Interviews will be audio recorded.

Pre-observational interviews. Researcher will conduct one short (average 15 minute) semi-structured interview with each participant immediately before the first observation to collect information about their professional biography and history with project management, collaboration, and related tools and practices. Interviews will be audio recorded.

Naturalistic observations. Researcher will visit participants at work and conduct up to three two-hour observations of each participant's work. During the observations, researcher will record events relating to project management, collaboration, information sharing, and training. Recordings will be in the form of detailed field notes.

Post-observational interviews. Researcher will conduct one semi-structured interview with each participant immediately after each observation (average 30 minutes). Interviews will be audio recorded.

Artifact collection. Researcher will collect artifacts from the designer's workplace that are related to project management, collaboration, information sharing, and training. Artifacts might include copies of project lists, to-do lists, training documentation, generic contracts, screen shots, and email. To ensure privacy of others, participants will redact artifacts before turning the artifacts over to the researchers.

We understand that [researcher] will keep team members anonymous; when he discusses data, findings, and recommendations, the discussion will be in general terms that identify systemic issues rather than specific personnel issues. We also understand that it is entirely up to team members whether they wish to participate in the study; we will not require team members to participate, and team members can drop out of the study at any time, for any reason. If [researcher] publishes his research, he will use pseudonyms for team members as well as for our organization. We also understand that [researcher] will compare our anonymous results with those of other organizations participating in the study. [researcher] will present us with a recommendation report at a later date, outlining issues and suggesting improvements.

Sincerely,

[site manager]

[site title]

Example

68

Topsight 2.0

CHAPTER 5

Permissions and Preparations

Planning your study is one thing; following through is another. In this chapter, we'll discuss two things that are often glossed over in field methods guides: how to get people to agree to your study in the first place and how to get ready for your first visit so that it goes off without a hitch.

Gaining Permission

Several years ago, I contacted an acquaintance to see if I could gain permission to study his organization. He was a fairly new hire at this small company, but assured me that I could conduct the study—he had discussed it with the CEO. I sent him a site letter, which he himself signed. Hmm, I thought, that's odd.

When I arrived at the company, the acquaintance introduced me to the CEO. We chatted a bit, and then I began approaching people for observations and interviews. They hadn't been expecting me. I left after a couple of disappointing interviews.

Within a few hours, an executive vice president emailed me to ask what on earth was going on. No one else seemed to know about the study! It turns out that even though my acquaintance had cleared the study with the CEO, neither one had let anyone else in the organization know about it. Although I smoothed things over in a later meeting, no other participants volunteered and I ended up abandoning the study.

It's one thing to design the study, another to get permission to study it. So, now that you've developed the documents for the study, you'll need to make sure you gain that permission. To do that, you'll need to answer four key questions:

- Who can advocate for you within the organization?

- Who gives permission formally?

- Who needs to give permission informally?

- What arguments can persuade each of these stakeholders?

Who Can Advocate for You within the Organization?

If you're approaching an organization—as opposed to them approaching you—your best bet is to have someone within that organization who can advocate for you. In the example above, I had an acquaintance who served as an advocate—although not successfully. I've similarly found advocates in many of the other studies that I've conducted.

I typically advise my students to identify organizations by starting with their network of contacts: their roommates, coworkers, fellow students, and members of their student organizations. That's because their primary job is to find a site to study.

But even if you are approaching an organization as a consultant or other nonacademic researcher, you should attempt to find and develop an advocate. That's because the advocate does the following key things for you:

- Tells you who can give you formal permission

- Tells you who can give you informal permission

- Tells you what arguments might persuade other stakeholders

For instance, the advocate can

- show you an organization chart that shows the key stakeholders;

- provide information on which stakeholder will have the most say over the decision to greenlight the study;

- tell you how much discretion other "off the radar" stakeholders might have over the decision (e.g., administrative assistants often have considerable discretion over what goes on in their units); and

- tell you a bit about how each stakeholder makes decisions and what their key concerns might be.

Who Gives Permission Formally?

Who is the key stakeholder you'll need to persuade?

In some cases, you might go to the top of the organization. For instance, with a small organization such as the one in the example above, it was possible to drop in and chat with the CEO. In fact, when my students study cases, they typically select small organizations with this profile (e.g., small businesses, franchises, student organizations, etc.).

But even in that situation, as we've seen, you may have to identify other key stakeholders; one obvious example is the head of the unit you want to study. Even if you can get the highest-ranking stakeholder on board, the study might face insurmountable difficulties unless the unit head is also on board.

How do you identify key stakeholders? Presumably, you have already asked an advocate in the organization for their advice. You might also look at the organization's publicly available documentation, such as an organization chart, list of officers, or website description. Finally, you might examine the social media presence for each potential stakeholder.

How do they give permission? I typically ask for a site letter, which I write and send to the representative to modify and sign. The site letter is based on the research proposal and clearly describes the methods I'll be using, the length of the engagement, and the benefits they will receive (see the end of Chapter 4 for a copy of a site letter).

Who Needs to Give Permission Informally?

As noted above, beyond the key stakeholders, others might need to give permission for the study to be a success.

Most obviously, you will need to convince the individual participants. Remember, as we saw in Chapter 4, participants can drop out of the study at any time. So you'll need to persuade them that it's in their best interests to stay.

In addition, as discussed above, other stakeholders such as administrative assistants may also need to give permission.

What Arguments Can Persuade Each of These Stakeholders?

As we discussed in Chapter 4, stakeholders perceive risks in allowing you to investigate their organization. So why should they let you do it?

There are several possible reasons. Below are a few of the most common. Notice that I've used the vague term "problem" below, because, most of the time, stakeholders will be interested in how you can help them identify and solve problems that keep their organization from achieving their objectives.

They want to know *whether* they have a problem or an opportunity. Perhaps some stakeholders are interested in your research because, even though they don't know of any problems in their operation, they would like to have early warning of problems—problems that might include issues with specific tools, organizational frictions, operations, or unwritten rules. If you can give them insight into these problems as well as a solid recommendation, they can head them off at the pass before they become critical issues.

They know—or think they know—that they have a problem, but they don't know exactly what it is. Other stakeholders might believe that the organization has a problem, but they are not sure what it is or where it is occurring. For instance, they might hear rumors that the reimbursement system is hard to use or that two units are not communicating well, but they don't know the root or the scope of these problems. If you can investigate a possible problem, confirm it, and describe it more exactly; they can have assurance that they are dealing with the issue.

They know (or think they know) that they have a problem and exactly what it is. Still other stakeholders might believe that they know about a problem, but they want you to confirm it, so that they can gain permission to fix it or the insight to fix it more precisely. These stakeholders may be highly motivated to host your study, but they also might try to drive your process. Be careful not to simply confirm what they believe; make sure to design your study broadly enough to investigate other possibilities.

They are sure—or say they're sure—that no problem exists. This is the most difficult scenario to address, but also the least likely one to face. The fact is, in a complex organization, problems always exist. The key challenge is to detect and address them without disrupting other parts of the work. How do you find out which arguments will gain the most traction with stakeholders? First, discuss the organization with your advocate. Next, hold preliminary, preferably informal meetings with the key stakeholders. Ask them about their concerns.

Once you've done this, it's time to pitch.

How Do You Pitch Your Study to Stakeholders?

Book authors, filmmakers, entrepreneurs, and graduate students are very different people, but they all share one important thing; they have to learn how to pitch. By pitch, I mean make a short argument that connects the audience's needs with the pitcher's project.

For instance, a filmmaker who wants to pitch her film might talk to a producer at a film festival. Since producers are busy, she might have an elevator pitch—a spoken, 30-second description of the film—just long enough for an elevator ride. She might also have a production package, covering basic information about the film, such as a synopsis. The filmmaker knows that the producer won't want to read her entire script unless she can get him interested in the film first.

You're in a similar position. You may have developed a research proposal, consent forms, a protocol, and other documents. But a stakeholder won't want to pore through all these documents—at least not yet. They're incredibly busy, and in fact, if they have a lot of problems in their organization which you could help them understand and solve, they ironically have less time to consider your study! So, like the filmmaker, you'll have to develop a pitch.

Your pitch should have the following components:

A 30-second elevator pitch. This should be a spoken pitch consisting of one to three sentences that bottom-line your proposed study. Examples include:

"Internet marketing is changing constantly, so your people have to learn new techniques constantly and communicate these techniques to each other rapidly. I'd like to find out how they manage these complex projects in this rapidly changing environment. I also want to find out if and when the process breaks down. If it does, I'll recommend ways to address those problems."

"I'd like to build a picture of how information flows in Unit X and where communication lines break down. To do that, I would observe people at work in Unit X, interview them briefly, and pick up copies of their texts with their permission. Within six weeks, I can recommend improvements to their work."

"You have problems with your reimbursement system. I would like to study those problems and develop recommendations for solving them."

A three-minute pitch. If the stakeholder seems interested once you've delivered your 30-second pitch, you can elaborate on the study for about three minutes. Like the 30-second pitch, the three-minute pitch is spoken. It should give them greater details about your proposed timeframe, your methods, and your main deliverable: the recommendation report.

A study description. If the stakeholder seems receptive, hand him or her the one-page study description. This description should be a written version of your three-minute pitch (see example at end of chapter).

How Do You Modify Your Study?

Often, stakeholders will be receptive, but they will want you to modify your study. Sometimes those modifications can be slight:

"If you're studying the reimbursement process, you should see what the accountants are doing too."

Sometimes they can be deeper:

"We do have problems with the reimbursement process, but you'll have a hard time watching our people process reimbursements, because they

usually do it on the road. We can have them walk through the process with you."

And sometimes they can be extreme:

"Our reimbursement process is confidential. We can't let you near it. But we can have you study an adjacent process."

Under these circumstances, consider how deeply the proposed changes will affect your study design.

- Revisit your research design matrix: are all the slots still covered?

- Revisit your research question: are you still getting to an interesting question? Does the new approach allow you to genuinely study the work, or does it push you toward the stakeholder's conclusions?

- Is the study still reasonable and doable, given your time and resource constraints?

Preparing for Data Collection

Now you're almost ready to begin your field research. But before you start, put together a *research kit* that you'll bring to each site visit.

What's a research kit? Think of it as your toolkit, full of all the tools you need.

You'll need to bring that kit every single time you visit the organization. Believe me, you don't want to get there only to find that you forgot your consent forms, your batteries, or some other vital resource that you absolutely need for your research.

So in this chapter, you'll assemble a research kit. In the sections below, I detail the items your kit should contain.

Paperwork

You've developed a lot of paperwork in previous chapters. Make sure to bring it! Bring plenty of copies of the following paperwork for managing your interactions on site.

Research description. Bring at least one copy per participant.

Consent forms. Bring at least two copies per participant, since you'll want to leave a copy with them.

Research proposal. Even though participants won't necessarily want to look at this, you might use it to consult your methodology or discuss the research process with a skeptical site contact.

Site letter. Similarly, bring a copy of the signed site letter. If people don't communicate well in the organization, the signed site letter might go a long way toward addressing confusion.

Protocol. Bring one copy for yourself. This is your "to do" list.

Data Collection Tools

Data collection tools may vary, based on research design. I typically observe, interview, and collect artifacts, so I use these tools (but see your research design matrix to help you develop a more specific list).

Notepads. Bring these, even if you plan to type notes on your laptop. Laptops die sometimes.

Pens. Bring lots of pens. You'll need people to sign forms, and you might also need them to take field notes. I usually carry at least two different colors—black or blue for field notes and red for circling unusual things I want to ask about later.

Voice recorder. Bring these for interviews.

Batteries and/or charger. Bring these for the voice recorder and other devices.

Digital camera. Bring these for snapping quick pictures of the workspace layout and of specific artifacts.

Note: An all-in-one data collection device can handle most of this work. For instance, a phone can take photos and record interviews.

Coordinating and Organizing Tools

Beyond the resources above, make sure to bring tools that help you to coordinate and organize your site visit. You may be gathering a lot of data in each visit, especially artifacts, and these tools will help you to keep those data straight.

Sticky notes. These have many uses, especially for labeling artifacts you pick up.

Folders or plastic document envelopes. Use these for carrying your documents and for storing copies of information resources you pick up on site. Create separate folders/envelopes for artifacts and for signed consent forms.

Calendar or list of participants and dates. These will allow you to reschedule on the fly if you need to (can be paper or electronic).

Contact information. At minimum, keep a site contact name and phone number in case you're delayed. Preferably, keep contact information for every participant you're planning to visit (also, can be paper or electronic).

I suggest putting your research kit in an accordion folder or bag and label it on the outside, so you know at a glance what it is.

Since your kit will contain sensitive information (i.e., signed consent forms, contact information, calendar, etc.), keep it in your sight or lock it up.

Maintaining Confidentiality

As you assemble the kit, remember, it may contain sensitive information. You promised in your research proposal that you would keep this information confidential—so make sure you follow through on that promise.

Before the Visit

Before the visit, you haven't collected any data, so you may think that the kit is safe to leave out. But your kit may already contain sensitive information. For instance, you've promised to keep the names of research participants confidential; if you have a list of research participants to contact, you can't leave it out. Similarly, if you've told the company that you won't use their name, the site letter itself should be kept confidential. So keep the research kit locked away, not on the coffee table.

After the Visit

After the visit, the research kit will contain highly confidential information, such as signed consent forms, raw field notes, raw recordings of interviews, and artifacts. Clear these out as soon as possible, process them, and lock them away.

Rehearsing Your Materials

So now you have the toolkit of materials you'll need. But like any good toolkit, this one will help only if you know *how to use the tools*. That means rehearsing.

In Chapters 6-10, I'll talk about how to prepare to meet participants and collect various kinds of data. But before you actually do these, make sure to rehearse:

- Rehearse the elevator pitch in spare moments.

- Go over your research protocol, imagining what it will be like to move through the different parts.

- Conduct mock interviews with the mirror, with your friends and roommates, and perhaps with acquaintances who match the target audience.

- Practice conducting observations and taking notes.

- Anticipate possible contingencies: participants who are friendly, hostile, or suspicious; observations that are interrupted by emergencies; voice recorders that cut out during the interview. These contingencies won't ruin your study if you can anticipate them.

Now that you've assembled the kit and rehearsed your materials, you're ready to conduct the study.

Exercises

- Develop a study description, based on the example below.

- Develop a 30-second pitch and a three-minute pitch based on your study description. Practice these in front of a mirror, then with a partner.

Examples

On the next few pages are a study description, a 30-second pitch, and a three-minute pitch.

Study Description

To the supervisor:

Project Management in High-Tech Organizations: A Field Study

Dr. Clay Spinuzzi, University of Texas at Austin

INTRODUCTION

Internet marketing is changing constantly, so your people have to learn new techniques constantly and communicate these techniques to each other rapidly. I'd like to find out how they manage these complex projects in this rapidly changing environment. I also want to find out if and when the process breaks down. If it does, I'll recommend ways to address those problems.

To accomplish this, I propose a field study of project management at SEObrate. In this study, I would spend approximately three hours each with up to five people in the department, observing their work (especially their project management work), interviewing them about it, and examining the tools and texts they use to get it done. At the end, I will submit a recommendation report in which I analyze their current way of working and suggest ways to improve the communication and coordination aspects of their work. I'm interested in the following questions:

- **Project management.** How do workers manage their time and projects?

- **Collaboration.** How, and to what extent, do they collaborate in management?

- **Communication.** How do workers share information with each other?

- **Training.** What training have they received in project management?

I would also plan to publish a paper based on the study. In the paper, the staff, the department, and SEObrate would all be represented anonymously.

HOW WOULD I STUDY PROJECT MANAGEMENT?

I would study office work from April 1-July 1, 2016. On separate days, I will visit different workers and use the following methods to study their work:

- **Observations.** I will visit participants at work and conduct two-hour observations of their work. During the observations, I'll note anything I see them do that relates to the categories above.

- **Interviews.** After the observations, I will interview participants for about half an hour, focusing on these categories. I'll start by discussing things I observed them doing, then I will ask further questions about these categories. I'll ask them to walk me through how they perform activities that I didn't get a chance to see.

- **Artifact collection.** I will collect copies, photos, and screen shots of any tools they use, texts they write, and software they use to perform these activities.

Once I collect these data, I'll analyze them to develop an ecological view of the work, including breakdowns and bottlenecks.

How Does This Study Help SEObrate?

The study will provide a systemic view of project management at SEObrate, allowing workers to examine how they manage projects and to see issues such as redundancies and breakdowns. It will also generate specific recommendations directed to [supervisor] for dealing with these issues.

How Does This Study Help the Researcher?

I perform studies such as these to gain new insights on work. Benefits for me include a published study of project management.

Example

To the participants:

Dear ___:

I specialize in studying how people communicate at work. Right now, I'm very interested in how you and other workers at SEObrate manage your projects. So I'm hoping that I can come visit you for a couple of hours over the next month, observe you at work, and ask you some questions.

Speaking of questions, here are a few you might have. Please consider participating in this study.

WHY CONDUCT A STUDY?

The idea is to provide a systemic view of how project management happens at SEObrate and to get your feedback about how it's conducted. The feedback and observations are anonymous; I'll be summarizing my findings, but I won't be reporting on your individual comments or things that I see individuals doing at work. The findings may result in more insights into how you manage projects and in ways to improve project management among your group.

DO I HAVE TO BE INVOLVED IN THIS STUDY?

No—your participation in the study is completely voluntary.

DOES [THE SUPERVISOR] KNOW ABOUT THIS?

Sure, [supervisor] has approved the study and understands that results are completely anonymous.

Because they are anonymous, results will not be used in evaluating individual achievement, although they might lead to improvements in how project management is supported at SEObrate.

This research is approved by my university's Institutional Review Board.

WHAT DO I NEED TO DO NEXT?

See the attachments, which explain the study and your involvement in more detail. Contact me to let me know if you're willing to participate. We'll set up some times for me to visit you at work at your convenience.

Questions? Please ask. Looking forward to hearing from you.

30-Second Elevator Pitch and Three-Minute Description

"Internet marketing is changing constantly, so your people have to learn new techniques constantly and communicate these techniques to each other rapidly. I'd like to find out how they manage these complex projects in this rapidly changing environment. I also want to find out if and when the process breaks down. If it does, I'll recommend ways to address those problems."

If the listener seems interested, continue:

"To accomplish this, I propose conducting a field study from April 1-July 1. In this study, I would spend approximately eight hours each with up to five people in the department, observing their work, interviewing them about it, and examining the tools and texts they use to get it done. At the end, I will submit a recommendation report, in which I analyze their current way of working and suggest ways to improve the communication and coordination aspects of their work.

In the study itself, I'd do three things.

First, I'd shadow some of your workers—with their permission. Basically, I'd hang out with them at their workspace, watching what they do and taking notes. This helps me build a picture of what they do, how they communicate, and what challenges they face. We're talking about a few hours per person, but I would not be interacting with them or interfering with their work.

Next, I'd interview these workers. I typically interview people right after the observation so I can get their perspective on what happened. Interviews take 15 to 30 minutes.

Finally, I'd pick up copies of some of the information resources they use. For instance, if they write a report, I'll ask for a copy of the report. Of course, I respect your company's confidentiality, so they can redact anything before they give it to me. I'm mostly interested in the types of information resources they use and the patterns they follow when they use these resources.

Once I've observed and interviewed participants a few times each, I'll provide an interim report with some tentative conclusions. Then, a few weeks later, I can supply a thorough analysis and some recommendations for improving information flow."

Example

Conducting the Study

Now that you've designed the study and put your kit together, it's time to take the plunge and get some data. In this section, we'll answer these two questions:

- How do you follow through on the study you've planned?

- How do you push past obstacles and get your data?

CHAPTER 6

Introducing Yourself to Participants

In Chapter 4, we discussed consent forms, and in Chapter 5 we discussed how to persuade stakeholders, including research participants. Now, it's time to actually begin collecting data. And you might be ... nervous. Especially if this is your first time to conduct a study.

But remember that the participants might be nervous too. In fact, as we saw in the last two chapters, they might have a lot more at stake than you do. Your findings could affect their job. Even though you've built safeguards into the consent forms, they might worry that you are going to evaluate them. Think about the other experiences with visitors that they may have had or heard about:

- **Job evaluations,** which could go in their file and affect raises and promotions.

- **Efficiency evaluations,** which might result in demands to work faster or harder.

- **Client visits or regulator visits,** which require them to be on their best behavior.

Any of these perceived roles can cause participants to act differently and to regard you with suspicion. In fact, the very sorts of problem solving that might interest you most—the little workarounds and tricks, the corner-cutting and step-skipping that build flexibility into the work—are often the sorts of things that participants will avoid doing when they are being observed.

I've faced this issue in my own research. For instance, in my first study, participants would sometimes greet me with, "So you're the efficiency expert." In a later study, one participant characterized me as, "Jane Goodall, studying the chimps." Needless to say, that's not the sort of relationship I was trying to cultivate.

So how do you deal with this issue? You have most of the tools already. But now you need to put them into practice. You need to introduce yourself to participants in a way that establishes your actual role: someone who wants to know what challenges they face at work and wants to recommend improvements that can improve their work.

Below, I'll discuss three ways to establish and affirm your role.

Introducing Yourself and Establishing Your Role

The first way comes when you actually introduce yourself to each participant. Notice that I say *introduce yourself.* Although someone may introduce you to participants at the site, they may not completely understand what you're up to; you need to be able to control the impression you give to each participant—and that starts with your elevator pitch.

The Facilitated Introduction

For instance, suppose Sheila is planning to study report writing in a large office. The unit's manager, Alex, offers to show her around. He takes her to one desk.

ALEX: Bob, you have a minute? This is Sheila. She's going to be studying our office to see what kinds of problems we have.

Bob looks at Sheila suspiciously.

SHEILA: Hi, Bob. I'm interested in how people move information around the office here, not just what doesn't work, but also the things that work well. Once I build up a picture of how information is circulated, I'm hoping to identify best practices across the office.

BOB: Hi, Sheila. Well, I can sure think of some places where we can learn from each other!

Okay. Not every exchange will be like the one between Sheila and Bob. Bob might be cautious or even hostile, especially if he distrusts Alex or others in management. But Sheila has the right idea:

- She makes sure that she characterizes *herself*. This helps her to provide a more accurate understanding to Bob, but it also shows that she is her own agent rather than Alex's employee.

- She draws from her 30-second elevator pitch, focusing on getting Bob to see how the study will benefit him.

- She is ready to launch into her three-minute pitch, if Bob expresses interest.

Alex introduces Sheila to others in the office. After a couple of introductions, typically Alex will either start to provide a more accurate introduction or will just allow Sheila to run the introductions herself.

After the introductions, Sheila will be ready to revisit some or all of the people in the office, this time with consent forms. As she does,

- she makes sure that Alex doesn't simply assign participants to her because she doesn't want them to be coerced; and

- she approaches the most receptive-seeming people first, knowing that if she can get one or two people on board, she can win the trust of the others.

The Cold Introduction

On the other hand, perhaps Alex has just emailed everyone in the office, letting them know that Sheila will come by. Or perhaps, the office is full of independent contractors. In this case, Sheila needs to introduce herself. She'll follow the same basic template:

- Let them know that she's conducting the study with Alex's approval, but is not working for him. (This is important—if she doesn't do this immediately, workers might think that she's just wandered in off the street.)

- Use the 30-second elevator pitch to describe the study, focusing on demonstrating how the study will benefit the potential participant.

- Be ready to launch into the three-minute pitch, if the potential participant expresses interest.

- Pull out the consent forms.

Presenting the Consent Forms

The 30-second and three-minute elevator pitches help Sheila to describe her project so that potential participants can understand it. But to convince them to take part in the study, she'll also need to present and explain the consent forms to them.

Think of the consent forms as the "contract" between the researcher and participant.

Although people will often do business with just a handshake, when people don't know each other well, they tend to sign a contract spelling out their agreement. Later, if they have a dispute, they can pull out the contract and see what they agreed to.

Similarly, your potential participants might think that the study good, but they may be unclear on the details—and they may not be sure what they're getting into. So you might introduce the consent form as similar to a contract. In this case, the contract spells out what you'll do, how much time it will take, and how you'll protect their confidentiality.

In this case, once Sheila describes the study and the potential participant expresses interest, she pulls out two copies of the consent form:

- She hands one copy to the potential participant so that he can read along.

- She covers the basic parts of the consent form, paraphrasing and summarizing so that the participant gets the gist of its terms (especially the confidentiality terms), the fact that she isn't working for or reporting directly to the manager, and the fact that the participant can drop out at any time.

- She also emphasizes any confidence-building measures that are built into the consent form (see Chapter 3).

- She lets the participant read the consent form thoroughly, being present to answer questions.

- If the participant is willing, she asks him to sign both copies then signs both copies herself.

- She keeps one copy for her files and gives the participant the other one for his records.

During this process, Sheila can correct the participant's misapprehensions. She can also get a sense of what might concern participants at this site; as she approaches the next potential participant, she can proactively address those concerns.

Affirming Your Role

The first two steps allow you to establish your role at the research site. But people's impressions can change, so you'll need to be alert for characterizations of your research and to look for opportunities to reestablish your role. I suggest two techniques.

Introducing Yourself to Nonparticipants

As you're observing a participant, he or she will often encounter nonparticipants, and they'll wonder why you're there. Are you a new employee? A friend? An evaluator? Your participant will likely introduce you, but since impressions drift, he or she might mischaracterize what you're doing. Be ready to jump in with your 30-second elevator speech.

Why? You do this, partly, to answer the nonparticipant's question; partly, to lay the groundwork for adding new participants, if you need to; but most importantly, to reaffirm the role for your current participant. If their understanding of your role drifts, their attitude might as well. So, even though you're speaking "to" the nonparticipant, you're also reminding the current participant that they should see you as a researcher rather than an evaluator.

Bending the Rules

You may also have to bend the rules a bit to reaffirm your role.

For instance, sometimes you may find that when you interview people or take observational notes, they seem to be holding something back. But once you turn off the voice recorder or put down the notes, they may feel freer to *confidentially* discuss issues with you.

Yes, they know that you've assured them of confidentiality, but they still don't want their voice recorded as they level criticisms against management or the company (you might think of this as their decision to opt out of part of the protocol). At the same time, they want you to know about these criticisms—otherwise, they wouldn't tell you at all.

If this happens, respect their confidentiality even further:

- *Don't* take notes or try to turn on the voice recorder.

- *Do* wait until you've left the building, then write down notes as well as you can remember them.

- *Don't* include the participant's name or identifying characteristics when you write these notes.

- *Absolutely do not* source or quote the criticism in the report. Use it in your analysis, but skeptically, and see if other pieces of data tend to confirm it.

You might find that, at certain points in an interview, the participant says, "Can we turn the voice recorder off for a minute?" Or, during an observation, the participant might make a remark and then say, "Don't put that in the notes!" If possible, accommodate them. Maybe even make a show of accommodating them by exaggeratedly turning off the recorder or scratching out your notes. Make sure that these traces don't show up in the interview transcript or observation notes. If you write down notes later, keep them in a separate file so you don't confuse them with your other data.

CHAPTER 7

Observing

Observing involves, basically, following people around and writing down what they do. As you can imagine, observing can feel a little weird at first, but it's usually a good idea. In this chapter, I'll discuss why it's a good idea and how you can do it well.

Observations can be weird—and problematic

Let's come out and say it: observing people at work can be weird. That's true for at least two reasons.

Sometimes people change their behavior: the Hawthorne Effect. People are often very nervous when they know they're being observed. They act differently. They think about what you might be seeing rather than what they're trying to accomplish. They become self-conscious. Sometimes they begin to narrate everything that they do. Or they try to chat with you about something else: "Did you see that football game last night?" Or they clam up. If a stranger were following you around and writing notes on everything you do, wouldn't you be nervous too?

In fact, there's a famous effect called the *Hawthorne Effect*. Long story short, the Hawthorne Effect is the phenomenon in which people change what they do simply because they know they are being observed (see Appendix A for more on this effect). This effect, obviously, poses real problems when you're trying to build up a picture of how an organization works.

Sometimes people *don't* change their behavior. On the other hand, some people may be completely unconcerned by your observation. In one observation, for instance, a participant took a phone call from his wife. When he called her "love monkey," I decided to go take a break.

Beyond this weirdness, observing can be problematic in at least two other ways.

Sampling. Sometimes you can't tell if an observation is representative. For instance, suppose you spend a day observing three different people in a workplace. You find out that earlier in the day, the fire alarm went off, temporarily disrupting work. Are you going to see normal work, or is everyone still on edge due to the fire alarm? How typical is this observation?

Similarly, if you observe three of the ten people in a unit, are these "typical" people? If you've accidentally picked the newest people, or the most motivated people, or the nicest people, your view of the work may be skewed.

Scope. Finally, you may not be able to tell to what extent your observations apply to the organization as a whole. For instance, everyone you observe may privately tell you that the organization is poorly run; does this mean it really is poorly run, or that just this unit thinks so? Similarly, you might notice that people ignore the company's central database and use their own folder-based system instead; does this mean that no one in the company uses the central database? (This actually happened in one of my studies, and the answer was no—this unit was a special case.)

Why should we observe people?

If it's so weird and problematic—and potentially uncomfortable for everyone involved—why do it? Why should you go observe people when you can just ask them about what they do? It would be a lot faster and easier—but unfortunately there are a lot of things that people can't tell you about their work. Those things include:

Tacit knowledge. Tacit knowledge is what people know without explicitly knowing it. Think in terms of habits and expectations that have become second nature. For instance, suppose you interview a supervisor about how she communicates with her subordinates. She tells you that she prefers face-to-face communication, but emails if she has to have a record of the conversation. That sounds reasonable. But if you observe her, you may find that her choices are a lot more complex: she tends to tell people good news face-to-face, but uses email when she has to deliver bad news; she sends complex information as email attachments, but uses instant messaging to coordinate with people. And she texts with her immediate reports, but tells them not to give her number to *their* reports. She may follow these patterns without being consciously aware of them—but once you can see them, you can bring them to her attention and get better answers in your interviews.

Contingencies. When you interview people about how they work, they tend to tell you how they think things usually work. But work is often filled with *contingencies*, or special cases that require different strategies—such as a fire alarm going off (and notice that this is the flip side of the sampling problem mentioned above). Understanding these contingencies can help you to better understand why people do what they do. And, truthfully, some contingencies happen more often than your interviewees realize.

Interactions. As they're being interviewed, people tend to think about ideal cases: "Here's how I do my paperwork." But in practice, they often have to interact with other people to complete even their solo tasks. It's rare for an interviewee to wind through the different sorts of interactions they often have to pursue in order to complete a task.

Patterns in tool use. When people do their work, they typically line up a lot of different tools to help them out. For instance, once I observed how people in a telecommunication company's Accounts Receivable department handled payments that had been sent through the mail. In their interviews, they mentioned opening mail and sorting out types of payments; in my observations, I got to see how they arranged different stacks of paper (always in the same places), how they saved their place when they had to get up from the desk, and how they used tools that they hadn't previously mentioned (such as letter openers and sticky notes) to help their work along.

Environment. Finally, people sometimes take their work environment for granted and can't really talk about it in an interview unless they are prompted. For instance, if I were to interview someone about their work, they might mention that they try to keep document printing to a minimum. Why? If I've observed them first, I might be able to guess at the answer: The workplace has just one printer, and it's on the opposite end of the building.

So, yes, observations can be weird and problematic. But if you can get past the weirdness, observations can be an incredibly useful way to gather data on an organization.

Conducting Observations and Taking Field Notes

By *observations*, I mean data collection incidents in which you systematically follow people in the organization and record what they do. As you may remember from Chapter 2, observations provide *your* perspective on the work; think of them as your side of the story.

Observations are not the same thing as dropping in and gathering a few impressions. That is, you're not just putting together a few anecdotes. Instead, you're closely recording certain aspects of your participant's work environment, actions, and tools so that you can spot and investigate patterns.

How do you do that? You might set up video cameras and take hours of video to analyze later. But often, it's less intrusive and easier to take *field notes*: detailed notes on what you see during a given observation.

Different qualitative research traditions advocate different approaches to field notes. For instance, many researchers think that you shouldn't take notes in front of a participant; you should participate yourself, like anyone else, then excuse yourself during breaks and write down what you can remember. That approach works well for long-term ethnographic studies in which researchers are studying cultural and social norms. In that approach, the researcher tries not to be seen recording what people do—rather, she or he tries to participate fully in normal interactions. Later, when she or he is alone, the researcher writes detailed notes.

But we are not conducting long-term ethnographic research meant to understand a culture. Rather, we are conducting short-term case study research meant to explore a bounded case (an organization or a unit within that organization). Consequently, we approach our research more as observers than as participants (although, granted, we are always participants at some level). We take notes openly so that we can capture micro-level events as well as meso- and macro-level ones (see Chapter 2). So, in this book, we'll approach field notes as something you write throughout the observation.

Taking Field Notes: General Advice

The idea of taking field notes might be daunting. For some people, the challenge is to write enough. Everything seems boring! Nothing seems significant! And at the end of the session, they find that they only have half a page of notes. For others, the challenge is to avoid writing too much. They notice *everything*!

Here are some guidelines for you as you begin your observations:

Set your focus. Base it on the research question/concern. Out of the universe of possible things you could note, decide what subset will attract your focus. For instance, if you're interested in collaboration, focus on events when people interact with each other or each other's artifacts. If you're studying self-mediation, look at how people arrange and use artifacts for themselves. If you're observing a meeting, consider whether you'll be observing how one individual handles the meeting or how leaders have organized the meeting's structure and flow.

Survey the surroundings. Take a moment at the beginning of the session to get a sense of the workspace. How is it arranged? Where does the participant face? What resources are in arm's length? Out of the research focus, which of those resources are most important? Record these (e.g., write a description, take photos or video, sketch, etc.).

Develop a shorthand. You'll be taking lots of notes; you probably won't even pause once you get in the flow. Using abbreviations and symbols, will help you get the most of the session. For instance, I typically use the symbols > and < to indicate when the participant is communicating or being communicated with.

Commit to the observation. Is it better to take the time to write that exact quote or quickly paraphrase it so you can write more field notes? Should you lean over and copy what the participant is typing on the screen or lean back and note the entire scene? You'll have to make many such decisions. Trust your instincts, commit, and don't second-guess yourself.

Write constantly. It's easy to convince yourself that what the participant is doing *right now* isn't important or relevant. But you don't necessarily know what is important or relevant, and when you don't write, you don't gather data. Find things to write about. If the participant is speaking, write quotes. If the participant is sitting immobile and staring at the screen, describe what's on the screen or sketch out how the participant has arranged the items on her desk. Capture as much detail as you possibly can, because you never know what might be important later.

Be sensitive to similarities (repeated patterns) and differences (deviations). Patterns show you the general flow of the work; deviations indicate unusual conditions. The more observations you conduct, the easier it will be to see both of these.

Be sensitive to the totally expected and the totally unexpected. It's easy to see things that you don't expect, because they stick out, but it's also easy to dismiss them as anomalies. Note them. It's sometimes hard to see things that you totally expect to happen, but those things are headline news as well, since it takes a lot of work behind the scenes for something to happen reliably. Note them too.

Be sensitive to stereotyping. By "stereotyping," I don't specifically mean pernicious racial and gender stereotyping (although that can certainly be a problem). I mean the general set of time-saving stereotypes or expectations that we all tend to carry around in our heads: the kindly mentor, the sullen teen, the kindly grandfather, the restless audience. It's easy to project our expectations on the people we observe. Be careful about short descriptors of the people you observe, and if you find yourself stereotyping them, try looking for disconfirming evidence. For instance: How do you *know* the audience is restless? Can you see any evidence that some members of the audience aren't restless?

Beyond these general guidelines, you can also follow guidelines for getting good field notes at all three levels you're investigating. You might work these guidelines into your protocol so that you can remember them.

But if you lose track, don't worry. Writing field notes takes practice, just like any other complex activity.

Taking Field Notes at the Meso (Human) Level

The meso level is where the participants "live"—where they are focusing their attention. And because of that, it may be where you're focusing most of *your* attention. Thus most of your field notes will likely describe the meso level.

But what should you specifically note at the meso level?

Information resources. Note any information resources you see—especially resources that you see them read, compose, or annotate.

Relationships among information resources. Note how the participant relates resources, especially in terms of

- *juxtaposition* (two resources attached to or overlapping each other);

- *placing* (two resources placed side by side, in a stack, or in regular places);

- *annotation* (writing or altering a resource);

- *transfer* (using one resource as source for filling in another);

- *modeling* (using one resource as a model for another);

- *reference* (using one resource to interpret or operate another).

Discoordinations. Look for points at which people seem to have trouble relating two resources—or points at which an unexpected, informal resource (like sticky notes) is substituted for another resource.

Handoffs. Note any communication "handoffs"—resources you see the participant give to or receive from other people.

Repetition. Look for repetition in communicative events. Does this participant follow the same general sequence each time?

Divergences. Look for points at which the participant diverges from the sequence. These divergences might include restarting the sequence, taking a detour, or abandoning the task.

The meso level is the easiest level to observe and discuss, since it's the level of conscious goal-directed actions. So most of your notes will likely be at this level. Make sure to get as much detail on paper as you can.

Taking Field Notes at the Micro (Habit) Level

At the micro level, participants are constantly drawing on habits to help them do their work. Most of the time, these habits are practically invisible, and sometimes they're too fast to record. For instance, you probably don't have the time or ability to write down every detail about how the participant types.

But you can look for breakdowns, points at which the participant's habits fail her or him, breaking the flow of work. When they encounter breakdowns, participants must consciously retrace steps. As we'll see in Chapter 20, breakdowns can be very important analytically. So how do you record them? Look for and write down instances:

External indications of breakdowns. Listen to your participant. If she says, "Huh?", "Uh oh!", or utters an unprintable word, she may have encountered a breakdown.

Points at which participants retrace steps. Look for incidents in which the participant repeats a piece of work.

Points at which participants undo work. Look for incidents in which the participant deletes a piece of text he has just written, hits the Cancel button, or uses his eraser.

If the meso level is the easiest to record in your field notes, the micro level is the hardest. That's because the micro level is the level of unconscious habits and reactions. We can't capture all of these in field notes, and it wouldn't be that useful if we could. So focus on the most useful things to capture: the breakdowns.

Taking Field Notes at the Macro (Organization) Level

The macro level is the level of culture and history. Participants are usually unconscious of it, and for the most part, you'll have to figure it out in the analytical stage. But you can still record some macro-level details:

Objective. Watch for points at which participants explain or express the organization's overall objective or mission.

Tools. Look at how they come across the tools and information resources they use. Do they make these themselves? For instance, does your participant write a document from scratch, or use a template from somewhere else? Do they customize their tools? When do they reach for a certain tool? Do all participants use the same tools? What tools correspond to certain job descriptions?

Actors. What roles do certain participants take? What do they touch? What do they pile or stack or arrange on their desks? What do they draw on? What do they attach to other things? Most importantly in knowledge work—what do they write on, annotate, type, or share?

Community stakeholders. You may also be able to see communities through participants' interactions. Do certain people group together? Do participants identify themselves as part of a group? Do they identify others as part of other groups? Do they distinguish themselves from other groups by work style, dress, language, or other ways?

Rules. How do people conduct themselves? What seems unusual to you as an outsider? Do people change their conduct when dealing with people in different communities? Do people have rules, procedures, or guidelines posted in their workspaces?

Division of labor. Observe how people handle information and artifacts at the site. Does an individual or group always give a certain information resource to another individual or group? Does an individual or group characterize another individual or group in a certain way, such as "they always do things that way"?

You may find that you won't be able to capture macro-level details in your field notes until you've lived at the meso level for a while. For instance, the first time you see someone passing a report to a coworker, you may not have enough context to realize that this action represents a specific division of labor. But as you continue your observations, you'll begin to see patterns. Note these as you do.

Example Reading

> McCarthy, J. E., Grabill, J. T., Hart-Davidson, W., & McLeod, M. (2011). Content Management in the Workplace: Community, Context, and a New Way to Organize Writing. *Journal of Business and Technical Communication*, 25(4), 367–395.

In this article, the authors examine how a new content management system (CMS) is introduced to an office. Rather than just *interviewing* the office staff, they also *observed* how the staff used the CMS over time and collected *documents* and *meeting notes* to get several perspectives on the change.

The researchers noticed that the new CMS actually changed work practices. By examining the genre (or information resources) and activity of the site, they found that the CMS actually introduced new incompatibilities into the office's workflow. Consequently, the office staff had to use the CMS in ways that the CMS designers didn't anticipate. By observing the office staff, the researchers were able to pinpoint problems in the CMS design and recommend ways to better support the office work.

Exercises

- Go to a public place and observe a cyclical activity again. This time, try taking detailed notes. How much detail did you capture? Were you writing constantly, or waiting around for something to happen?

- Look at your field notes the next day. How much can you reconstruct of the scene? What's missing?

- As you look through the field notes, circle the information resources and tools people used and underline the actions they took. What patterns do you see?

- Finally, as you look through these field notes, you might find yourself wondering about details that you didn't capture. Using a different color of pen, mark those questions in your field notes.

Examples

The next page shows an example of field notes from the SEO case.

Field Notes

These field notes represent a small part of an observation from the SEO case. Notice the scene-setting, the reported speech, and the conventions and abbreviations I use so that I can shorten writing time and get in more detail. (SEObrateMax is a pseudonym for the company's in-house analysis software.)

9:00am Dani

Dani came in just before I did. Says she has a 10am meeting and a brief 11am. We'll try to fit in an interview after that. Cubicle is next to Craig's. Nobody in adjoining.

She explains: usually uses headphones. Puts them on.

Cubicle L top: books on analytics, mysql, php, javascript, etc.

Cubicle L desk: books – "Becoming a successful manager"; "Managing for results"

Cubicle R desk: "Competitors"; "Competitive Strategy"; "Competition Intelligence"

She's looking at videos. (Company blog featured an interview w/her yesterday re video and search options.)

logged into YouTube

External screen showing Outlook.

>Outlook:Email: agrees to meeting, sends

>Outlook:Email: ?? (Going through these quickly)

Outlook:Cal: Looks

Chrome: Moves win to right screen. Googles "mobility scooters" then "power wheelchairs"

FF:SEObrateMax: window to left. "Client Natural Search Rankings" (incl kwds she just used)

>IM(Lindy). Hey, what do we need for the meeting with Clara?" [Lindy is acct mgr]

<>IM: converse re mtg.

FF:SEObrateMax: rankings

FF: [client website] (tab)

<>IM: more on meeting

Outlook:Email: Looking at email from Lindy re meeting

<IM(Lindy). continue talking re status and mtg needs

Above monitors: 2 sheets – "seomoz.org The Web Dev's SEO Client Sheet"

Above monitors: Printed calendar

Above monitors: Names and phone extensions

>Outlook:Email. Creates new folder. Drags messages into it.

Desktop: Finds file.

Excel: Opens it.

>Outlook:Email: Thanks, promises to look through.

Excel: Scrolls. Creates line graph. Cols (therefore lines) for SEO, PPC search revenue. Changes to bar graph. (very granular). (Deletes? No, goes to other sheet?)

Excel: Hovers over graphs, then (re)creates line graph. Adj colors. Messes with this a while.

Excel: Creates graph - just SEO revenue. Adjusts.

On other side of cubicle wall, coworkers talk about overturned car on highway.

Excel: Adjusts data sources.

Coworkers joke about poor driving. One talks about how he ran into a cyclist on Guadalupe and Fifth. Dani snorts. Apparently, can hear this despite headphones.

Excel: Titles chart. Daily SEO Revenue vs. Email

Example

108   Topsight 2.0

L of desk: notepad with To Do 10/27. A neatly numbered list in black ink

>Excel. Continues adjusting. Fills in col Email Sent? - a few highlighted cells that she fills with numbers xxxx.xx. These show up as red points on graph. Unclear where numbers come from - oh

Excel: Title is now Daily SEO Revenue vs. Email Blast Dates.

>Excel: Adds marker at low point. 10/9/2008

>Excel: Selects all data, copies to sheet 2. Renames sheet 1 -> SEO Graph. Sheet 2 -> "PPC Graph." Very quickly reviews spreadsheets.

>Excel: Copies and pastes graph from SEO to PPC, then changes data source.

Excel: PPC tab: reviews Daily PPC Revenue vs. Email Blast Dates.

We hear a tone. Her mobile phone, in purse.

>Excel: Del an SEO graph. Renames Sheet 3-> Both (Pastes data?) Adjusts data. adds graph. Line graph as seen earlier - SEO vs. PPC data.

Phone again. She turns it off. (Blackberry.)

Excel: changes graph type a couple of times.

<>IM: discussing coworker's need for coffee.

Excel: Other color schemes.

<>IM:

Excel: Selects colors. Adds col: Average". enters a formula (?) pastes down entire col. Accidentally enters date range in graph, resulting in straight line. Changes; title "Average" graphs average.

<>IM: ??

Excel: deletes graph? Selects entire data range. Now 3 lines (PPC, SEO, Avg). Adj colors (gray scale).

<>IM: ?? [just looks like casual conversation there]

Excel: More adjusting.

<Outlook:Email: email alert.

Outlook:email. Looks. "Bizarre scooter video"

Excel: looks. changes "average" in heading to "SUM." reformulates looks at graph. Adj colors.

Excel: another column. copies "SUM" retitles "Email Sent." Dels all figures that don't corr. to highlighted dates.

>Excel: Drags chart upwards. Chgs data src. Markers for email sent. Title: "Total PPC and SEO Revenue vs. Email Blast Dates."

>Outlook:Email. explains that she added charts. "See what you think. Things get all muddy and it's hard to read." Sends.

Outlook:Email: reviews

Grabs todo list, looks.

Desktop: Opens file

Excel: (on left screen) "XYZ - need to change." Cols "campaign specialist" ?? "Anchor URL" ...

FF: (on right screen) SEObrateMax. scrolls. tab: "SEObrateMax Link Marketing by Text-Link Ads." Looks thr list of ads. Searching in page for domains (from Excel). when checked

>Excel: changes cell for "Campaign" to green. (a sort of checklist.) Next up: [client name]

FF:SEObrateMax: (rt scr) looks at SEO links for [client]. hangs.

Outlook:Email: skims

FF:SEObrateMax: still hung

Chrome:SEObrateMax: fills out info for [client]. hangs. cancels, hits Try Again. Does this a few times. Info - keywords?

Outlook:Email: glances

Example

> Excel: in rows between clients, enters SEObrateMax

unplugs laptop. Head down to the meeting.

CHAPTER 8

Interviewing

In Chapter 7, I acknowledged that sometimes observing people at work can be weird and problematic. Interviewing can be uncomfortable too—especially if you're not sure what to ask. But for the most part, your participants will *want* to be interviewed. It's a chance for them to tell their side of the story, to explain their innovations and solutions, to brag a little about the areas in which they excel, and to downplay their mistakes. If they trust you enough, they might also share their complaints about their work, their managers, and their fellow workers.

As we saw in Chapter 3, interviewing allows you to get the participant's perspective on what's going on. Although we might think that interviewing is the perfect way to get the inside story, as I point out above, every participant has their own perspective, their own blind spots, their own interests, and their own gripes. They have plenty of reasons for emphasizing certain things and minimizing others. They also have their own interpretations: If they call a coworker "lazy," that could simply mean that the two of them have different priorities. If they call him a "foul-up" (or worse), they may only be able to see how he handles the one task that inconveniences them. And when you ask them a question about their own actions, they may not know the answer—and they may make things up rather than admit that fact.

In other words, they're *people*.

So how do you get these people to give you good information?

Types of Interviews

Let's start with the types of interviews you might conduct. Qualitative researchers typically use three types of interviews.

Structured Interviews

Structured interviews are simply interviews that involve a fixed set of questions. Suppose you are part of a team, interviewing a large number of people about the same thing. All the team members need to gather the same kind of information, so they're given a list of questions. Every interview involves asking the exact same questions in the exact same order.

Structured interviews are essentially a spoken version of a questionnaire. They're great for gathering very large data sets, but they're not so great for the kind of research described in this book, because they don't provide enough flexibility for researchers to ask about incidents they've seen. In fact, structured interviews are typically used in research that doesn't even involve observations.

Unstructured Interviews

Unstructured interviews, on the other hand, don't involve a specific set of questions at all. For instance, suppose that you're following someone around as she does her work. As you do, you constantly ask her questions: "What are you doing now?"; "Why did you write that note?"; or "Who are you about to call and why?"

Unstructured interviews are great for getting into the micro level of people's work, and you may find uses for unstructured interviews in your own study. On the other hand, they have drawbacks. For instance, some work takes a lot of concentration or involves communication. You can't perform an unstructured interview if your participant is performing brain surgery or making phone calls. In addition, some participants may feel shell-shocked by all of these questions. On the other hand, as I mentioned in Chapter 7, some participants may actually feel more at ease if they narrate their work to you. So you'll need to carefully consider whether you should use unstructured interviews.

Unstructured interviews happen during the observation.

Semi-structured Interviews

Semi-structured interviews are basically what they sound like; they involve a list of questions, but they also give you a lot of flexibility to ask follow-up questions or add questions based on things you saw during an observation. They are guided conversations that you have with participants, and because they are conversations, they tend to be easy to conduct. People usually like to talk about themselves and present their side of the story.

In a semi-structured interview, you'll come to the interview with a short list of interview questions. These questions, which will be in your protocol (see Chapter 3), should relate to your research question. But they don't come in a specific order, so you can ask them at any point during the interview, and you don't have to read them verbatim from the protocol. In fact, semi-structured interviews work best when you can ask them as part of a conversation with your participant.

Semi-structured interviews also give you the flexibility to ask further questions. For instance, suppose you observe your participant calling people from a call list then putting a checkmark or an X beside each name. You might note this in your field notes then ask about it during the interview.

Because semi-structured interviews have this kind of flexibility built in, they are well-suited to the kind of research described in this book.

Semi-structured interviews can happen *before or after observations,* but they can also happen in research designs that don't involve observations at all. Typically, if you perform an observation, you will want at least a post-observation interview so that you can get the participant's perspective on what happened.

Questions for Semi-structured Interviews

Interview questions are there to help you get to your research question or concern. (As we discussed in Chapter 3, research questions are like the detective's question: who committed the murder? Interview questions are like the questions that a detective asks witnesses; they are not the same as the research question, but they should help you answer it.) So as you develop your protocol, you'll need to formulate some appropriate questions. Make sure they're *in* the protocol so that you have them in front of you as you conduct the interview.

Opening Questions

Since interviews can be tense for the participant, open the interview with questions in the participant's comfort areas. These questions can be asked in a pre-observation interview or a post-observation interview. They mostly focus on who the participant is, what she does, and how she sees things.

By the way, it's surprising how often participants will relax and open up when you invite them to talk about themselves. Partly that's because they get to characterize themselves, and if you express nonjudgmental interest, they start to see the interview as a dialogue with someone who is genuinely interested in what they think.

Typically, opening questions cover areas such as these:

Background. You'll often want to find out how participants got into their current position, as well as what sort of experience and education they have.

Experience and attitudes. Participants have opinions—often very strong opinions—about their organization and how it runs things. Ask them how they feel about their job.

Their job description. I've found that one of the most rewarding ways to begin an interview is to simply ask a participant, "So, tell me what you do?" You may have a formal job description for them already—in fact, you may have a very good idea of what they do—but ask the question anyway. Not only is it an icebreaker, it can tell you how they see themselves and where they disagree with their formal job description.

Their unit's description. Similarly, you can ask the participant what her unit or group does. You'll often find that they tell stories about how they themselves learned about the unit on the job. For instance, once I asked a participant, "So, you're in Long Distance Provisioning. What does that involve?" She not only described it, but told me about how she once discovered key differences with CLEC Provisioning during a meeting, including vocabulary differences that had caused multiple misunderstandings between the two units.

Other people or units with whom they work. Sometimes people work entirely within their own unit, but often, they have to interact with others—others in the company, but also partner organizations, clients, customers, and competition. Ask whom these people or units are, what they do, and how they mesh.

Today's work. Another rewarding question—one that gets directly at the meso (human) level—is "Tell me what you're doing today."

Observation-Based Questions

Whereas openers can be asked either in a pre-observational or a post-observational interview, *observation-based questions* naturally have to be asked in post-observational interviews. These questions zero in on things you saw during the observation.

Why ask observation-based questions?

First, *you might not have understood what happened.* For instance, during one observation, I caught one end of a telephone conversation in which a new employee gave someone extensive directions on how to use software. How, I wondered, did this new employee get this expertise? So I asked her about it during the interview; it turns out that the caller was from her previous job. I would have never been able to figure that out just from the observation.

Second, *you might think you have understood what happened, but you need to confirm it.* An example comes from my very first study in which I observed software developers working with code. During one session, I saw a software developer reading through and editing a piece of code. Like other pieces of code, this one had a lot of embedded comments (i.e., notes that a software developer leaves in the code so that others can understand what it does). So I assumed that, like the other software developers I had observed and interviewed, this guy was reading the comments.

But when I asked him about it during the interview, he told me he never read the comments. They were 10 years out of date! He did *use* them, but only as "landmarks"; if he saw a four-line comment, for instance, he knew that it was close to the piece of code for which he was searching. If I had just relied on my outsider's (etic) view of the incident, I wouldn't have gotten to the insider's (emic) view.

So what are some good observation-based questions?

Tell me about this incident. As you observe the work, you'll notice certain things (see Chapter 7). These things might be highly unusual things that you've never seen anyone else do or things that seem irrational. On the other hand, they might be things that the participant does over and over with an amazing degree of skill. Find out how they learned this approach and what they think of it.

Tell me about this document/tool. You'll also notice documents and tools—often lots of them, strung together in complex ways.

Ask about them, especially ones that seem nonstandard, ones that are heavily annotated, and ones that they use a lot. Find out where they got these, how they create or read them, and how they connect to other documents and tools—especially ask when they have trouble using a particular document or tool. As you discuss these, you may notice that participants have actually forgotten all about those tools until you ask them.

Tell me about this team member. Ask whom the participant's team members and collaborators are. Ask how and why they interact with others in the workplace. Ask about who's on the other end of the phone calls, emails, IMs, and texts in which they engage.

Tell me about your conduct. You may see incidents of context-switching in the observation. For instance, you may notice that your participant jokes a lot with others in her office, but turns serious when a particular person walks in. How do they conduct themselves in different situations? How do they expect others to conduct themselves? Do they follow rulebooks, procedural manuals, or other standards?

Tell me about your team's roles. People take on different roles in their organizations. Sometimes these roles are formal. For instance, doctors and their administrative staff have different credentials, training, and even outfits; one generally can't substitute for another. Sometimes they're more informal. Maybe, one person habitually makes the coffee for the office. What roles do you see? Ask about these, where they come from, whether they are formal or informal, and whether they've always been done this way.

Tell me about this sequence. Organizations tend to involve a lot of cycles. Some of these are very short (e.g., an office worker has to read and approve a stack of timesheets). Others are longer (e.g., a team works for six months on a software release). Look for these sequences and ask about them, especially in terms of who is involved, what information resources they circulate, and where things go wrong.

Asking observation-based questions can be tricky because participants can be self-conscious about their work, especially if they've made a lot of mistakes during the observation. They can easily become defensive. So formulate these questions in ways that are non-judgmental. Sometimes this can be as simple as using second-person plural:

- **Second-person singular.** "I noticed today that you seemed to have a lot of trouble finding the total balance in the report. Do *you* often have a lot of trouble with that?"

- **Second-person plural.** "I noticed that you *and others in your group* seemed to have a lot of trouble finding the total balance in the report. Do *you guys* often have a lot of trouble with that?"

To someone who's on the defensive, the first question might sound like a personal criticism; the second sounds more like you're trying to figure out why the report's format trips everyone up. The first question invites the participant to be defensive; the second one invites the participant to criticize the report.

Closing Questions

Finally, you will probably want to end with at least one closing question that allows them to have their say—especially following the observational questions, which can make participants tense or defensive. Closing questions should provide a safety valve.

But closing questions aren't just there to make participants feel better. They can also alert you when you're tending to ask the *wrong questions*. For instance, perhaps you've obsessed about the particular sequence this participant has followed, but when you give her a chance, she offers that she doesn't usually do this sort of work!

By their nature, closing questions are very general. Here are a few closing questions I've used:

- What else do I need to know about your work?

- Is there anything that we haven't talked about that we should?

- What other questions do you think I should ask?

- Do you have any questions for me?

These questions are all variations of a simple statement, *it's time to have your say*. They're a way to remind the participant that this is a conversation, that they have some control over it, and that you're interested in their perspective and insights.

Sometimes participants will shrug and say, "No, I think we've covered it pretty well." That may or may not mean that they're satisfied with the interview.

But sometimes they will grab hold of the wheel and start driving. A few times, I've asked a closing question with my thumb on the voice recorder's stop button, then found that the participant has 20 minutes' worth of remarks about his work, his coworkers, his boss, and his company. Sometimes it's a rant, but it's always valuable.

The Interview Performance

Up to this point, we've focused on what sorts of questions to ask. But conducting an interview involves more than just asking questions. It involves giving a performance.

By *performance*, I don't mean that you have to act like someone you're not, but you do have to clearly signal your interest in the participant's perspective.

Think about it this way:

Suppose someone is interviewing you—maybe for a job, maybe for a story in the local paper. You're not sure what they think of you, or even whether they are interested in you as a person. Maybe they're just interviewing you because they have to. Maybe their time is really valuable and they have a lot of other interviews lined up.

So when he starts the interview, you pick up on his cues. And everything he does seems to signal boredom. He leans back in his chair. He reads from a piece of paper instead of making eye contact with you. In fact, you can tell he's just reading questions verbatim. He sounds bored, with that flat voice that you remember people using when they had to read out loud in elementary school. You catch him looking at his watch.

Well, he obviously doesn't want to be here, and neither do you. So— maybe without even thinking about it—you make the interview quick. You give short literal answers, but you don't elaborate. You provide information that he could have gotten from reading your resume or job description. When he asks you questions that might be uncomfortable for you, your answers become even shorter, and maybe you even over-simplify or fudge your answers a little. When he finally asks his closing question, you don't believe he's actually interested, so you don't respond meaningfully. When the interview is over, you feel relieved. After all, no one likes to be interrogated by a bored bureaucrat.

In fact, the interviewer might have been genuinely and intensely interested in what you could tell him, but he wasn't able to *convey* that, and consequently, his poor performance has seriously compromised the information that he could have gotten from you.

How do you convey interest? This might sound weird, but you should rehearse it. Here's how I *convey* my real, genuine interest in the participant.

Have a Conversation before Turning on the Recorder

Once you switch on the voice recorder, the participant knows she is on record. That's not an optimal time to begin developing a relationship. So, long before turning on your recorder, try to start a conversation. Chat about what they're doing today. If you notice that they have a novel on their desk that you've read, talk about that. If they went to your university, point that out. In other words, find ways to connect with them on other levels. Get to know them as a person.

Pretend You're Not Nervous

You might not be nervous, but most people who are about to do their first interview are. I certainly was; I'm not an extrovert, and I don't make a habit of talking to strangers, so it was hard for me to approach my first participant and conduct my first interview.

How did I get over it? Here are some simple techniques:

Pretend that you are someone else. Imagine that you are someone who is more confident, someone who has conducted many interviews before.

Practice in front of a mirror. Practice with your research questions. Imagine the participant reacting in different ways.

Practice with someone else. Interview your friend, roommate, or spouse about what they do.

Whatever approach you take, you do need to keep a lid on your nervousness. If participants think you're nervous, they might behave in different ways. Sometimes they want to help you out—by keeping their answers short and getting the interview out of the way. Sometimes they become impatient. Sometimes they try to hijack the interview and steer it toward their own complaints. Although there's a place for that, it shouldn't constitute the whole interview.

Use Body Language

We're often unaware of our body language, but it speaks volumes. Use it to convey your interest.

Lean forward. When you lean back, people will read it as disinterest. Leaning forward toward the interviewee conveys interest in what they're saying.

Use eye contact. I'm not talking about *continual* eye contact, which comes off as creepy. But frequent eye contact conveys interest. For this reason, I encourage people not to take extensive notes when interviewing (that's what the voice recorder is for), and I also tell them to just glance at the interview questions rather than reading them verbatim.

Pause and Nod

When a participant answers your question, she will often give you a short answer and stop. That's not necessarily because she's done; she wants to see if you're satisfied with a short answer or not. If you accept that short answer and go on, she'll tend to tailor her other answers similarly. You don't want that. So when your participant gives a short answer, nod encouragingly and wait for her to say a little more. Usually, she will.

React with Your Face

Think about how people react when you tell an interesting or funny story. During the story, their eyes might narrow or widen, their eyebrows might go up, or their jaws may drop. If you describe something ironic, they might scoff and shake their heads. If you say something funny, they might laugh and say, "Oh no!"

You should do these things. Encourage the participant. Egg her on. Be an active listener.

Ask Follow-Up Questions

Although asking follow-up questions is part of a good interview in any case, it's specifically a way of demonstrating your interest. You're showing that you were actually listening to the participant and you want to know more.

Example Reading

> Propen, A. D., & Schuster, M. L. (2010). Understanding genre through the lens of advocacy: The rhetorical work of the Victim Impact Statement. *Written Communication*, 27(1), 3–35.

In this article, the authors investigated *Victim Impact Statements*: short statements that a victim makes in court to a criminal, describing how the criminal has impacted her or his life. VISes are presented after the criminal has been convicted, but just before he or she is sentenced. The researchers wanted to know what rhetorical work this genre did.

The researchers were able to interview 28 judges and 16 advocates about their experiences with VISes (in addition to examining examples of the VISes themselves and observing court hearings). By carefully examining these interviews, they were able to understand how the VIS interacted with other genres and how judges and advocates perceived its role. Based on this systematic analysis, they conclude that although VISes do not officially impact sentences, "Judges certainly share, however, stories of cases in which direct contact with the victim inspired them to consider alternative conditions of a sentence." (p.27)

Exercises

- Observe a friend doing something familiar, such as studying, buying a cup of coffee, or taking the bus. Based on that observation, write up some opening questions, observation-based questions, and closing questions.

- Rehearse the interview questions in a mirror. Practice your body language.

- Observe your friend again as he or she does the same thing as in the first observation. Then interview her or him.

- After interviewing your friend, debrief. Ask your friend:

- How comfortable were you being interviewed?

- What seemed false or weird?

- What worked well?

- Have your friend assign you a "grade" and tell you how you can improve.

Example

The next page shows an interview transcript from the SEO case.

Interview

Below is the first half of my initial post-observational interview with Dani. It came immediately after the observation described in the observation notes from Chapter 7. Note how I address the questions from the protocol; rather than following a particular order, I pull them into an actual conversation with Dani.

Dani, 10/29

CS: You're still in natural search, right?

Dani: Yes.

CS: I understand that ... you've kind of taken a management role or leadership role in your group, which is new, right?

Dani: Yeah. Yeah.

CS: Last time we talked, you'd done a little bit of training, but now you're calling meetings and things.

Dani: Right, the structure is, just of the department has changed, so now we've got three sort of managers to—and then we each over see one to two people.

CS: And this is based on seniority or ...?

Dani: To some extent seniority, seniority based on knowledge, results—

CS: The first thing I noticed—

Dani: Not total seniority.

CS: The first thing I noticed is in your cubby, you have all these Javascript books, and then over to the left you have management books—how to manage people. Then to the right you have all these books on competition.

Dani [laughs] Yeah.

CS: So there's your three areas. How's that working out? Has that been an easy transition for you?

Dani: Pretty much. Kind of busy the past two to three weeks getting things organized. Have taken over some of financial stuff, looking at financial accountability. Like okay, we have a system where we put how much we're spending. Does that match the invoices we're getting from the people we're buying the links from? Does that match? So we've been trying to do some of that. And that's been really time consuming. Other than that, it hasn't been too big a change at this point. I think because I was training people already, so just the feel, the attitude of it hasn't changed a whole lot. And next month we'll probably get more into—this month is still, since we changed things this month, everything's still kind of okay, keep doing what you're doing this month. And next month we'll see, do my people need to help? They'll probably need to help some with my clients, and do I need to look and see what you're doing with your clients? Just stuff like that. So next month may be more of a change, I don't anticipate a huge change...

CS: ...So I'm reading the company blog yesterday, and they interview you— [about Dani's work on SEO in YouTube videos]

Dani: My lovely video, yes. [laughs]

CS: So is that a big focus on what you're doing? I noticed you had videos up when I came in.

Dani: Oh. Um, it's kind of an emerging thing in SEO natural search. Yesterday, I just happened to optimize some of the videos for [a client]. And so I was kind of looking at them again today. I wouldn't say its a huge focus, although actually Bram, one of the other kind of managers in the department and I today spoke at [conference] about video optimization—I think that's why they chose video optimization for my little video. And yeah, it's kind of one of the little hot topics that people are looking for. So—

CS: ... it's all so emergent, so it's easy to be a leader ...

Dani: It really is. I've only been doing this a little over a year. But things are moving so fast. There are some basics ... like web coding ... and those hold, but you have to keep up with it. But then new stuff ... yeah, i probably know about it just as much as people who have been doing SEO for a long time because it's so new. And there's lots of topics like that.

CS: And there's so many question marks around it too. For instance, you're talking to a client today, and she's talking about two different analytical tools and they're having a lot of trouble interpreting them. And she was talking about this internal infighting because people just grab the most unfriendly numbers.

Dani: Exactly!

CS: Wow. So I guess it makes it difficult to show how well you're doing, or even if you know how well you're doing. To be able to convey that to other people.

Example

Dani: Yeah, you have to think about which of those analytics— not even just systems, cause most of our clients just have one. So they don't have the comparison. But—yeah, all of them measure stuff in different ways. But even just choosing which of those metrics to use, because there's a lot of them out there. And okay, which do they even care about? Which of them even means something? So.

CS: ... the first part of the observation you were messing with this Excel graph, and you keep creating these different graphics. And are those for customer consumption?

Dani: The one that I was working on on my desk? That was one that we were—it's for ... one of our e-commerce clients, and they send out email blasts. I can't think of a better word for it but [drums on desk] and so we were trying to see, cause they have some spikes in their sales, really abnormal spikes every so often. So we were trying to figure out exactly why, if that's related to the emails. So how do you make a graph with the SEO sales and the paid search sales and the email dates that they—and I think I figured out that you couldn't do it all. When you put the SEO and—I don't know, the numbers were so simple that the line was like a big jumbled disaster. So -

CS: So this isn't the kind of graph you would do every month ...

Dani: No, and probably only for big important clients. Yeah, probably wouldn't do it all the time. We will probably send them—I don't know if we will send them the graph itself— well I hope we do. I tried to make it look nice. [laughs] But at least show them, okay, these emails really do spike the revenue, keep doing 'em, or this one totally worked, this one didn't do anything. Or something to help figure out what went on.

CS: Well, this is really jumping out at me. Because my impression has been that you get the clients in, you do some planning on the front end, and then you get them in kind of a cyclical mode where you fill out a report month after month and things don't change too much.

Dani: Right.

CS: But then I start seeing, every once in a while there's this kind of specialized analysis.

Dani: And I think that's kind of ... a difference in I would say like my position vs. like Craig's position. I mean Craig still does that some especially on the front end of the campaign. And even with some of the small clients, once they get going we're like, OK, there you go. But with the big important clients, yeah, we do more of that ongoing analysis. And I like to do that, so I think I have the tendency to do that, like the graphs and the numbers and so forth, more than some other people. But—

CS: That makes a lot of sense. Part of the reason you got into this is that you like problem solving.

Dani: Yeah, definitely.

CHAPTER 9

Artifacts

"Artifacts" might sound like an exotic term to you. Maybe you think of mysterious items used by some unfamiliar culture. But most of the artifacts you examine will look familiar, so familiar that you'll have to work hard to understand why they are mysterious and what insights they can give you into this unfamiliar culture.

What are Artifacts?

"Artifacts" is a catch-all term that covers the information resources, tools, and other physical materials that participants use in the organization. For instance, here are a few artifacts I have encountered during my many studies:

- A sticky note that a participant used instead of a cumbersome map

- A word processing form that a customer service representative filled out to order phone service

- A heavily annotated list of past due accounts, used as a checklist by a collections worker

- A decorated mannequin head that served as a trophy in an inter-departmental competition.

- A set of three bed-sheet-sized pieces of paper taped to a wall, listing company values and the team members working on them

- A handbag that an administrative assistant used to transport files between north and south offices

- A LinkedIn page describing a participant's background

- A printer hidden away in the closet of a freelancer's condo

What do these artifacts have in common?

They're designed. Even the sticky note was "designed" in the sense that the participant used its unique properties to address specific aspects of her work. In this case, the sticky note could be stuck on the bezel of her monitor so that she could read numbers from it and type them into her computer.

They're persistent. People use artifacts to offload effort. For instance, the word processing form provided ready slots for the customer service representative to type customer information. When she emailed the filled-out form to a second person, that person could easily interpret it and enter it into a database.

They're (mostly) shared. The mannequin head, for instance, was meant to be displayed; other teams could see that this team had won an award, and visitors (like me) were almost guaranteed to ask about it.

They're (more or less) integrated into the workflow, and thus tell us something about the work. When someone sees a deficiency in their workflow, they usually look for artifacts to address it. In fact, in highly literate societies, texts are the default solution. For instance, collections workers needed to keep track of each person they had called, whether they had spoken to the person or left voice mail, and whether the person had promised to make payment or cancelled the account. To deal with the issue, they developed an elaborate set of annotations that they would write directly on the past due list.

They often come from outside the organization. For instance, the administrative assistant knew that the office could use interdepartmental mail, but it was slow and unreliable. Her handbag—despite the fact that it was never meant to hold files—was just the right size to carry files. Why not use it?

There's something else about artifacts. Often—more often than you might expect—individuals in the organization will look for a solution to some sort of problem, find the solution in the form of an artifact they have used elsewhere, and adopt it temporarily. It then becomes part of the organization's workflow. But since it came from somewhere else, it may have different assumptions and expectations embedded in it.

For instance, let's take the list of past due accounts. This list was generated by off-the-shelf software, so it included various types of information. It also sorted the output by the customer's last name. Naturally, when the collections workers treated this output as a list, they worked from top to bottom—after all, that's what we generally do with lists. But why should they call customers in alphabetical order rather than, say, by how long the account had been past due? And why did the printout include information that the collections workers didn't need? For the reason you might imagine; when you're using an off-the-shelf tool, you end up dealing with its logic and limitations. The collections workers did this in a very visible way—by annotating the heck out of the list.

In practical terms, when a person adopts an artifact from somewhere else, he has to deal with the logics and assumptions for which that artifact was designed. Of course, people tend to borrow from lots of different places, so the artifacts often don't share the same logics and expectations. They "fight." If you've ever had to fill out multiple forms for a doctor's visit, each of them asking essentially the same things but in a different order, you know what I mean.

So we can learn a lot about an organization from looking at its artifacts, but we have to be aware of how people use and modify those artifacts, how they connect the artifacts together, and where they got the artifacts in the first place.

Of course, any organization will be littered with artifacts, and they can't all be studied. How do we decide what to collect?

Artifacts in Observations

First, when conducting your observations, keep track of what the participant touches, reads, writes, and uses. Especially look for artifacts that they use repeatedly, customize, modify, coordinate with each other, or hand off.

For instance, if you're studying how your participant gathers information for a report, you might not spend a lot of time looking at her chair, the greeting cards she's pinned to her cubicle, or the paperweight that sits on her desk. But you'll probably zero in on the previous month's report, which she spends considerable time annotating; the website where she is gathering information; the Instant Messaging window, which she's using to ask a colleague some questions; and the massive headphones that she puts on every time she starts to write.

You can probably collect some of these artifacts. For instance, she might let you have the marked-up report when she's done with it, but she won't let you keep her headphones. So how do you collect artifact data?

Collect the original when possible. You might even scoop sticky notes out of the trashcan, if they give you permission.

If you can't collect the original, try getting a photocopy or electronic copy. Especially for documents, getting a copy might be your best bet.

If you can't collect a copy, try getting a photo. You can usually take a decent copy of a document, artifact, or even an office layout.

If you can't collect a photo, try sketching it. In some cases, it'll be too difficult to collect the artifact any other way: either physically impossible (e.g., an office layout) or impossible under terms of confidentiality (e.g., a confidential document). In this case, you can at least sketch the artifact so that you can remember the gist.

Collecting artifacts during observations does the following things for you:

It lets you coordinate the field notes with the artifact. Not only have you seen them use the artifact; you also can examine the artifact in more detail.

It lets you look for traces of the participant's process. For instance, you can closely examine the annotations on the document or compare two different drafts of the same document.

It lets you examine relationships among information resources. You might see people working with two different resources during the observation. But you can also examine the artifact to investigate, for instance, where they have copied information from one information resource to the other.

Artifacts Mentioned in Interviews

Next, when conducting interviews, your participant will likely discuss other artifacts that you haven't seen him use. For instance, he might explain that the work you saw today was just preliminary work for writing next week's report.

So, you might ask, can I see that report too?

Keep alert for these possible artifacts during interviews:

Other parts of the process. If they note that their work is part of a larger process, see if you can collect artifacts that they use for other parts of the process—especially the final product.

Tools and information resources that they report modifying.
People frequently modify their tools and information resources.
They add new parts to reports. They introduce new innovations.
They replace printed lists with spreadsheets. Often they are proud
of these innovations and will be flattered if you say, "Can I see
that?"

Traces of changes. Looking at static artifacts is great, but you can
learn even more if you can get a "time lapse" view. For instance, if a
participant mentions that they've recently changed forms, ask for
copies of the old forms too. If she says she always leaves the Track
Changes function on in Word, ask for a recent Word file so you can
see how the document was modified. If she files multiple drafts,
see if you can look through the stack.

Artifacts in the Background

Finally, be alert for other sources of artifacts, especially those that
can provide insight into context or history.

Context

In terms of context, look for clues that demonstrate how the
organization represents itself, how others represent it, and how
participants represent themselves.

How the organization represents itself. Organizations must
represent themselves, and they do so in a number of ways: mission
and vision statements, charters, annual reports, press releases,
brochures, and of course websites. You don't have to collect all of
these, but see if some of them relate to your research question.

How others represent the organization. You can also look for
indications of how the organization is perceived by others. For
instance, if the organization is customer-facing, you might look at
Yelp and Google Places reviews.

How participants represent themselves. Participants represent themselves in different ways, including resumes and social media. I've interviewed participants about their experiences, then looked at their LinkedIn pages to verify and amplify details.

History

In terms of history, see if you can find archives that can shed light on how the organization has changed over time.

For instance, in one study, I examined how the Iowa Department of Transportation used traffic accident statistics over 40 years. I couldn't go back in time and observe workers in 1973, but I could go back into the archives and look at their annual reports, collection materials, and punch cards. Among other things, I discovered that punch cards from 1973 were the templates for all the subsequent interfaces!

Example Reading

> Teston, C. B. (2009). A grounded investigation of genred guidelines in cancer care deliberations. *Written Communication*, 26(3), 320–348.

In this article, Christa Teston investigated deliberations at a Midwestern community hospital's Tumor Board meeting—a meeting in which different medical professionals (oncologists, surgeons, case managers, radiologists, pathologists) came together to go over cases of tumors at that hospital. They were guided by a particular genre, a *Standard of Care* document. "At this particular hospital's Tumor Board meeting, one or two patients' cases are discussed during each weekly meeting. In addition to past experiences, expertise, published studies, statistics, and visual displays of anatomical and cellular information as evidence, medical professionals also invoke Standard of Care documents as evidence" (p.324). Teston was able to contextualize this genre's use through her observations and interviews, but she also closely analyzed the documents themselves. Through this work, she was able to understand the rhetorical work that each part of the Standard of Care genre did—and she was able to demonstrate how this genre pulls together an argument that can speak to different specialists, both through its text and through its extratextual features: "hyperlinks, footnotes, and explicit linguistic features afford conceptual links between medical professionals' scientific understanding of, or experience with, the patients' disease and the profession's expectations as a whole" (p.344).

Exercise

- Observe people in a public place. Then collect artifacts involved in their activity. For instance, if you observe them at the coffee shop, you might take pictures of the coffee shop layout and menu. You might also buy a cup of coffee and keep the receipt and the paper cup on which the barista has written your order.

  NOTE: *Don't* try this in a high-security area. If you do this in an airport, don't tell Homeland Security it was my idea.

- Get online and find out more about the history and mission of the public place you observed. For instance, if it was a coffee shop, look at the website of the chain.

CHAPTER 10

Other Data

In Chapters 7-9, we covered the three major ways of collecting data. But data are supposed to be clues to help you unravel a mystery. Sometimes you can't get those clues through collecting observations, interviews, and artifacts.

Adding a Method to Get to a Research Question

Sometimes, you have to add a method simply because the other methods won't answer your question.

Example: Drawing Pictures

For instance, in her famous study of automation, Shoshanna Zuboff (1988) wanted to know how workers felt when they had to switch from the familiar manual systems to the new automated ones. So, in addition to interviewing them, she asked them to draw pictures showing how they felt, then explain the pictures. Through these pictures, Zuboff was able to find out much more about the workers' feelings than she might have through more conventional methods.

Example: Prototyping

Another example comes from participatory design. Researchers in the UTOPIA project partnered with workers to develop a usable interface for laying out newspapers. But the workers had never used computers and were reluctant to give feedback on completed interfaces. So the researchers came up with the idea of paper prototyping; they would sketch out an interface on paper, present it to a participant, and have the participant pretend to use it. The participant could then suggest changes, sometimes grabbing a pen and writing directly on the prototype. (We will cover prototyping in more detail in Chapter 29.)

Example: Diary Studies and Systems Monitoring

A third example comes from William Hart-Davidson (2003), who has used diary studies and system monitoring in his research. In diary studies, the participant keeps a "diary" of his work, periodically writing down what he's doing; this technique allows the researcher to see a general work pattern over days or weeks. In system monitoring, the participant allows the researcher to install a program on her computer; after a set period, the researcher can come back, download the data, and see the patterns that the participant follows in using her computer.

Substituting a Method

Beyond that, sometimes you simply can't use one of your existing methods, so you need a substitute.

Example: Social Media

For instance, in one study, I was planning to observe people at a certain type of workspace. But due to the nature of the workspace, people were not available long enough or regularly enough for me to observe them. So, instead, I turned to other sorts of data. For instance, I read people's Yelp reviews of the workspaces, examined what they said on the workspaces' Facebook pages, and looked at people's remarks as they checked into these spaces on Foursquare and Gowalla.

You might similarly think of other data that could provide you with insights into your site. These could include:

- **Advertisements**. Print, online, Craigslist

- **Reviews**. Yelp, Google Maps

- **Social media**. Twitter, Facebook, Instagram interactions and comments

- **Traffic flow**. Counting how many people walk in and where they go

- **System logging**. Collecting use data from computers or hits on digital assets

We've already seen a list of several data collection methods in Chapter 2. In the Resources appendix at the end of this book, you'll see more resources on methods you might use. I can't cover them here, but if they sound appropriate, read up on them and try them.

Example Reading

> Spinuzzi, C. (2012). Working Alone, Together: Coworking as Emergent Collaborative Activity. *Journal of Business and Technical Communication*, 26(4), 399–441.

Above, I mentioned my study in which I substituted other sorts of data for observations. This study was of *coworking spaces* in Austin: open-plan office spaces in which independent people can rent desks by the month. As mentioned, I drew on several different pieces of data to better understand why people worked in these spaces.

One significant thing about this study was that most of the data were emic rather than etic: they provided me with the participants' perspective rather than letting me see their work from my own perspective. For instance, when I interviewed people, read their Foursquare reviews of a coworking space, and looked at their Facebook comments, I was seeing how *they* characterized the space and their interactions within it. Since I was short on etic data, I had to be careful when writing up the study: Rather than saying "People work at coworking sites for these reasons," I had to emphasize that they *reported* these reasons.

Exercise

- Review your research design matrix. Come up with at least one other data collection technique. Justify it in terms of an additional view on existing data or an entirely new view.

CHAPTER 11

Member Checks

Once you collect data, you may find it useful to conduct *member checks*—points at which you run your work by your participants so they can tell you if they think it's accurate and reasonable. The point isn't to make them do the work, but rather to identify weaknesses in your developing analysis. This feedback loop can help you to strengthen your argument at each stage.

Member checks aren't always necessary. But if you use them strategically, you can often develop a better analysis *and* your participants may feel more involved.

Why Conduct Member Checks?

As mentioned above, member checks can give you the participants' perspective on your work. There are several advantages to setting up this kind of feedback loop.

It reinjects the emic perspective. Recall that the *emic* perspective is the insider's perspective. If you conducted interviews, you largely got their emic perspective; if you conducted observations, you largely got the etic (outsider's) perspective. If you allow them to see your field notes, you can get further emic perspective on what you saw.

It lets them correct misunderstandings. In one study I conducted, I asked participants to look at the transcripts of their own interviews. The transcripts had been produced by a transcription service, and unfortunately one of the transcriptionists had done a poor job. The interviewee was able to read the transcript, identify mistakes, and give me a little more background.

It allows them to make repairs. Sometimes participants will make strong comments that they later wish they hadn't made. Or they will make a joke that, in the transcript, looks like a straight statement. Or they will report an incident, then find out later that things didn't happen the way they thought. A member check can let the participant correct, walk back, or moderate earlier statements.

The Different Kinds of Member Checks

I'm discussing member checks here because data collection is the first point at which you can conduct a member check. But you can conduct member checks at different points in your investigation:

After collecting data. After you transcribe an interview, you may want to run it past the participant. Does it seem accurate? Is there something they want to add or elaborate on? Similarly, you might share your observation notes with the participant so they can give you feedback on what you thought you saw.

After coding your data. After you code your data in Chapter 12, you may see certain themes or patterns emerging. But are you interpreting them reasonably? You could bring the coded data back to participants and see what they think.

After building models. In Phase IV, you'll build several different models to represent patterns that you're seeing in your data. Once these models are built, you can try running them by participants to see whether they agree.

After writing up your findings. In Phase V, you'll use your models to help you develop findings; these will describe systemic issues that affect the organization. As you draft these, you might show them to participants to see whether they think your arguments are reasonable. Doing so will help you identify alternate explanations, but it will also tell you where you may need to include concessions, rebuttals, or more evidence.

Member checks are feedback loops (see Chapter 28). And you probably won't need feedback loops at every single stage. In fact, if you tried to use several member checks, you would likely burn out your participants; they simply don't have the time or interest to look at every stage of your work! If you do deploy member checks, do it strategically, at the point where it can do the most good.

Deploying a Member Check Wisely

Perhaps the best point at which to deploy member checks is after you collect a round of data. In fact, the more concerned a participant is about your fieldwork, the more helpful a member check might be.

For instance, I once conducted a study of independent contractors in the Austin area. It turns out that independent contractors are very concerned about their image: since they are in business for themselves, their image is crucial for attracting clients. Something that they say in an interview, between two people, might not reflect the image that they are trying to project. And even though I had put the usual measures in place to protect their privacy and confidentiality, they were still concerned.

When I shared a transcript with one of the contractors, he discovered that he did not come across the way he wanted to. He became very concerned—concerned enough that he asked to strike some of the interview. I worked closely with him to develop an acceptable paraphrase that fairly represented his answers while taking off the edge of the original comments. In the process, I was able to maintain his confidence and keep *our* relationship in good working order.

Conducting a Member Check of Data

So how do you conduct a member check well? Here's how I have typically handled it.

Present the data. I select the data that I want member-checked. Typically that's just the participant's own interview, but it might also include observation notes of the participant. It should *not* include others' data.

To present the data, I usually email it as an attachment with a short explanation. Specifically, I want them to know that the transcript is not considered final; I want the participant's feedback to make it as accurate and representative as possible.

Discuss. In most cases, participants have simply accepted the data. But in some cases, they see points that they would like to amplify, explain, or even delete. If these are minor, you can likely accept them over email; if they aren't, you may need to arrange a meeting.

Incorporate feedback. Sometimes the participant's feedback will be simply corrective. (For instance, one young student transcribed the name of an operating system as "DAAS"; elderly people like me know that it's actually "DOS," for "Disk Operating System.") If it's corrective, and if you can verify it, correct the transcript.

Other feedback might be elaborative or interpretive ("I was joking there, I didn't mean that") or even suspicious ("No way did I say that!") *Under no circumstances* should this feedback change the original transcript. They said what they said, and if it's in the original recording, your job is to preserve it. Instead, include it as an annotation that helps you better understand what they were trying to say.

Example Reading

Spinuzzi, C. (2014). How Nonemployer Firms Stage-Manage Ad-Hoc Collaboration: An Activity Theory Analysis. *Technical Communication Quarterly*, 23(2), 88–114.

In this article, I conducted member checks after collecting interviews and again before submitting the article for publication.

During the first member check, one participant asked to elaborate on his interview. The interview had been far-ranging, and the participant was unhappy with some of his answers. He also spotted some transcription problems. I corrected the transcription problems (listening closely to the interview as I did). For the answers, I developed paraphrases that allowed me to keep the important part of the answers while moderating the tone and concealing the specifics, then vetted these with the participant before proceeding.

During the second member check, a different participant identified an answer that she felt needed to be clarified. I indicated the clarification in the final article with this phrase: "In her member check, Sophie added..."

CHARACTERIZING DATA

At this point, you should have a lot of data. In fact, you may be wondering how you'll turn all of these details into a big picture. In this section, we'll answer two questions:

- How do you start fitting the data together and start seeing relationships?

- How do you characterize the data you've collected?

CHAPTER 12

Triangulating Data

In Chapter 1, I described research as being like a mystery you're trying to investigate by gathering clues. The detective has to gather these clues *systematically*. That is, the detective might have hunches, but can't just rely on those hunches—she has to actually prove the case.

To prove your case, you'll need to learn how to triangulate your data.

Data triangulation involves confirming your impressions across different data—that is, making sure that you have more than one piece of evidence pointing to your conclusion. (It's different from *investigator triangulation*, which involves using multiple investigators, and *theory triangulation*, which involves using different theories.)

To give you an idea of how to triangulate data, let me tell you a story from my own research (Spinuzzi 2008).

In 2000, I found myself sitting in the Network Control Center (NCC) of a regional telecommunications company. The NCC is where this company processes reports of service interruptions and coordinates repairs. If someone in Oklahoma City accidentally digs up a cable with a backhoe, or if a tree branch falls on a telephone line, the NCC finds out about it and dispatches a tech to make repairs.

What was I looking for in the NCC? I wasn't sure, to be honest. I had talked this company into letting me study its employees over a period of 10 months in exchange for reports on the company's "communication problems." Whatever they turned out to be. So I started with Customer Service, moved to Customer Service Data Entry, and then to the NCC, simply to see how people were communicating with each other. I would spend two hours shadowing each individual, then observe them again a couple of weeks later, interviewing them after the second observation. I would also pick up artifacts (e.g., printouts, sticky notes, or anything else that looked interesting and related).

The NCC was a big room with a screen on one wall, seats facing it on tiers, kind of like a small movie theater or the bridge of a starship in *Star Trek*. Specialists hot desked in the NCC, and the phones were always ringing; the NCC was where you were transferred when you reported some sort of network problem, like lost or interrupted service, crosstalk on the line, and so forth. If a falling branch snapped a customer's overhead line, or if a customer accidentally dug up an underground cable with a backhoe, the incident would eventually make its way to the NCC. There, a specialist would create a trouble ticket, assign it to a technician—usually a technician working for the dominant telecomm provider in the area, which we'll call BigTel—and communicate with the technician until the problem was resolved.

The NCC was busy. Even though individual phone service is rarely interrupted, strands of the telecomm network break all the time. So specialists would be working three tickets on the screen, typing up a fourth while talking to a customer about the fifth. It was quite incredible to watch.

So one day I was sitting in the NCC, waiting for all these incidents to form patterns, when a specialist, Nathaniel, leans over to the guy I'm shadowing, Donald. Nathaniel said:

"BigTel let somebody's dog out and it got run over. Nothing mentioned in the ticket about it."

Donald nodded and listed the tickets he was to work for that day.

A few minutes later, the NCC's assistant manager sternly told the story again, this time to the entire NCC.

"There was nothing about a dog on the ticket," he said. "You *must* note that."

This intrigued me. It was a mystery, and as I discussed in Chapter 1, sometimes I think of myself as a detective gathering clues to solve a mystery. So of course I asked people about it. Long story short, treating this incident like a mystery helped me to understand how Telecorp communicated internally and externally.

But like a detective, I found that witnesses sometimes give conflicting stories. *This frequently happens in field research.* So when I drew conclusions, I had to source each claim by *triangulating*. I also had to make uncertainties clear through *hedging*.

Fortunately, if you've followed your research design matrix (Chapter 3), you're already set up to do data triangulation because you have repeatedly collected different types of data. There are at least two types of data triangulation: across *data types* and across *data instances*.

Triangulating Across Data Types

In a qualitative study, you should have at least a few different *types* of data—such as interviews, observations, and artifacts—and these should give you different views of the phenomenon. You can't rely on just one. If you just rely on observations, you'll only have your (etic) perspective; you will be able to describe what happened, but not why or how it connects with their goals. If you just rely on interviews, you get their (emic) perspective—their story—but sometimes people recall incorrectly or are just flat wrong. So as much as possible, you have to build a story by looking *across* the data to see what the different data types are telling you. In this case, people from the NCC were blaming the other units for the problem, and if I hadn't crosschecked their stories with the other data, I might have told a more simplistic, less accurate, less interesting story (See figure 12.1).

Figure 12.1. Triangulating across data types.

Triangulating Across Data Instances

I also had to make sure to triangulate across *instances*. For example, it wasn't enough to just compare Nathaniel's statements with observations and artifacts pulled from his sessions. I also had to compare his statements against the statements of others; his observations against observations of others; his artifacts—well you get the drift. Doing this allowed me to ask:

- How representative is this incident?

- How representative are these views?

- Am I talking to an outlier, or does everyone see things this way?

This sort of data triangulation helps you to ensure that the most interesting or extreme views don't take over the argument (see figure 12.2).

Figure 12.2. Triangulating across data instances.

Hedging

Finally, unlike a mystery writer, we don't get to take a bird's-eye view. We don't see everything. For instance, in his ethnography of a research center, sociologist John Law recounted how he always seemed to be missing the action. Like Law, when you didn't see an incident, didn't get that interview describing it, or didn't pick up the artifact that would confirm it, you have to straightforwardly acknowledge that gap. When you acknowledge and work around those limitations, you are *hedging*. When done appropriately, hedging makes your work more credible because it demonstrates honesty and confidence.

Here are examples of hedging I used when describing this case:

- "I did not witness the original complaint being filed, of course, but I did observe customer service clerks dealing with similar complaints."

- "We can't rule out Customer Service entirely, but their culpability seems less likely than Donald suggested."

- "I did not observe any sales reps asking about pets and locked gates. But ... sales reps had developed no self-regulative genres, no scripts or checklists or forms, to remind them to ask about pets and locked gates."

Letting Triangulation Do Its Work

Triangulation is supposed to help you confirm or disconfirm what you think you're seeing or hearing. If you saw someone skip a step, did they make a mistake or is this a workaround? If someone tells you that they always check the official checklist, is that true or do they sometimes forget? If you notice that people always start their meetings ten minutes late, you may assume that that's a problem; do *they* think it's a problem?

Triangulation can also help you to question what you think you know. For instance, when I started the Telecorp study, I was working within a standard theoretical framework, activity theory. Even my interview questions were constructed around the parts of an activity system. But soon I realized that the data were not fitting activity theory well. I was thrilled; that meant that my theoretical preconceptions were not shaping what I saw. I wasn't just repeating the story that other activity theorists had told me; I was actually recounting my own story, based on the data I had collected.

Finally, as you triangulate, you'll find that your early hypotheses (i.e., claims) often won't be complex enough to account for the data. Great! Let the claims simmer a bit, working in the data, deciding which claims to abandon, which ones to hedge, and which ones to make more specific. Often the early claims are not nearly as interesting as the ones that you've let simmer, just as a two-dimensional character isn't as interesting as a three-dimensional one.

When we get to Chapter 18, we'll learn a second level of triangulation, which takes place during the analysis stage.

Example Reading

> Teston, C. B. (2009). A grounded investigation of genred guidelines in cancer care deliberations. *Written Communication*, 26(3), 320–348.

Earlier, we discussed Christa Teston's study of how a Cancer Board discussed cases to determine whether and how to intervene medically. This case involved a lot of perspectives—after all, the Cancer Board was made up of different specialists, and each had to lend expertise to the discussion. Teston triangulated data in two ways: (1) by systematically comparing the observations to each other and (2) by comparing individual observations with the documents being used during those observations. Consequently, she could (1) determine which parts of the observation were routine and repeated and (2) understand how a given observation was guided by a given set of documents.

Through this approach, Teston was able to conclude that (a) the documents were too inflexible: they didn't cover everything that they really needed to cover. But (b) that flexibility was reintroduced through the deliberations. In other words, the documents and deliberations had to be taken together in order to solve problems.

Exercises

- Earlier you observed a friend then interviewed them. Compare the observation and interview. Do you see points at which the two confirmed each other? Do they contradict each other in any way?

- Now look at the sample observation and interview at the end of chapters 7 and 8. Do you see points at which the two confirmed each other? Do they contradict each other in any way?

CHAPTER 13

Coding Data

You've collected a lot of data at this point, and it might start to seem insurmountable. There's just so much detail. How will you make your way through it? How do you spot trends and patterns?

One way is through *coding*.

Coding is Like Hashtagging

Suppose that you are interested in an event, such as a conference (South by Southwest) or a sporting event (the World Cup). What's going on there, and what do people think of it? One way to find out might be to go to Twitter and look at applicable *hashtags*.

A hashtag is a phrase with a "hash sign" (#) in front of it. It could be any phrase. For instance, someone who tweets about the 2018 FIFA World Cup could use hashtags such as

- #WorldCup2018

- #2018WorldCup

- #FIFA18

or some other descriptive phrase.

In practice, when people want to tweet about the same topic or event, they tend to converge on a small set of hashtags. Searching for one hashtag, such as #WorldCup2018, brings up every tweet with this hashtag (Figure 13.1):

Figure 13.1. #WorldCup2018.

Some tweets might have more than one hashtag, meaning that the person tweeting them want to make them part of multiple conversations. For instance, the 2018 World Cup is to be held in Russia, so some tweets also include #Russia.

When people include hashtags, they're doing several things:

- They're *categorizing* their tweet with an emergent label. A hashtag could be any phrase; over time, people tend to converge on a phrase that helps them find tweets about the same topic. As they converge on the phrase, they are developing a durable label that they can use to describe a particular type of information.

- By converging on a label, they are *distinguishing* between topics. They might even distinguish subtopics by stringing together different hashtags (such as #WorldCup2018 #Russia).

- They are thus *filtering* complex, overwhelming information. If you're interested in a particular topic, you can't get a good overview by reading every single tweet, because most of them have nothing to do with your topic. But if you click on the right hashtag, you see only tweets on the topic you want.

Hashtagging turns out to be a good way to inductively organize a large amount of information. And that's wonderful, *because that's exactly what we need to do* with our field notes, interviews, artifacts, and other data. We have collected a very large amount of data. Now, we need to tag it so that we can make sense of it—to categorize it, to distinguish it, and to filter it.

When qualitative researchers tag data, we call it *coding*. And we do it systematically so that we can carefully build up an understanding of the relationships among data points.

But since we're doing research, we will approach our tagging a little more systematically than most Twitter users do. We will code to reach the following objectives:

- characterize data

- see relationships in the data

- see patterns in the data—and confirm those patterns

- quantify patterns

To understand how we'll do these, let's talk about types of codes.

Types of Codes

Consider using three kinds of codes:

- *Starter codes,* for things you expect to find. These tend to come from your research questions and your expectations.

- *Open codes*, for things you find along the way. These emerge from repeated readings of the data.

- *Axial codes,* for connections you find across the codes. These come from seeing repeated clusters of codes.

In the Topsight approach, we use *nonexclusive* coding, which means that you may use multiple codes (or tags) for each data point.

Starter Codes

Starter codes are descriptors representing things you expect to find—things that you expected to look for when you designed the study. These could include phenomena, tools, or roles. If you use starter codes, you'll want to use a fairly small set drawn from your research proposal. You will tend to have a small number of starter codes, and they will probably be abstract.

Of course, even if you look for something, you won't necessarily find it.

For instance, in the SEO case, I decided to code interactions by categories such as "TIME & PROJECT MANAGEMENT", "UNDERSTANDING", and "TRUST", all of which are mentioned in the research proposal.

Table 13.1. Starter codes.

PROJECTMANAGEMENT	Keeping projects on track. Allocating time and labor, coordinating and delegating work, and holding clients accountable for agreements on how projects are scheduled and executed.
UNDERSTANDING	Learning about others' work, business. Discovering and applying knowledge about clients' and subcontractors' disciplinary languages, fields, activities, and work styles.
TRUST	Expressing, extending, building, or losing trust in someone. Assurance that a collaborator or client will consistently behave in a way positive to the ongoing relationship.
STRATEGY	Strategic plans and moves: Selecting projects, pursuing clients, selecting collaborators with a long-term agenda in mind. Particularly includes growing and positioning business.
TRAINING	Training for this particular job. Receiving and providing knowledge and procedures needed to perform work appropriately.

As I went through my transcribed interviews and my observation notes, I wrote the appropriate code next to each line of text. For instance, when coding my observation notes for Dani, I saw that she had books on business strategy, so I coded that line with STRATEGY:

Cubicle R desk: Competitors"; "Competitive Strategy"; "Competition Intelligence""	**TOOLS_BOOKS** ****STRATEGY**** **TEAMS_LEADERSHIP** ***NETWORKS***

As I coded the whole data set for all participants, I coded lots of data on each of these categories—except "TRAINING". It turns out that this organization does not provide much formal training for its workers; they generally learn through mentoring and figuring things out.

Open Coding

Open coding is the type of coding you'll be using most. These are descriptors representing things you start to see in the data as you go through it. They're most like the free-form hashtagging that you see in Twitter and Instagram.

Identifying. As you begin open coding, think about mapping parts of the data that you'll want to look at later. These might include

- Things (such as tools and furniture)

- Actions (such as creating or planning)

- Attitudes (such as frustration or optimism)

- Routines (such as starting the day or closing down)

- Relationships (such as dependence or autonomy)

Reconciling. After coding a few pieces of data, you'll start *reconciling* these codes. That is, you'll make sure that you're using the same codes for the same phenomena. It's easy to code one incident as "teams_leadership" and the next as "teamleadership", but if these two codes mean the same thing, they should have the same name!

Defining. Also after coding some pieces of data, you'll start *defining* the codes. That is, write a short description for each code you've used. For instance, if you've tagged eight instances of "teams_leadership", what do those eight instances share? The more you can define each code, using definite criteria, the more easily you'll be able to code similar instances in your other data.

For example, suppose that you start coding field notes and observations and quickly realize that much of the project leadership is shared. People agree on a small set of steps at the beginning, but day-to-day, they decide their own tasks and keep in contact via

IM. So you tag these interactions with the starter code "PROJECT-MANAGEMENT", but you also tag them with an open code, (e.g., "AUTONOMY").

Below are some of the open codes I developed for the SEO case.

Table 13.2. Open codes.

ACCOUNTABILITY	Measures to ensure that collaborators and clients lived up to their implicit or explicit agreements.
AUDIENCE	Expressions of concern about how end users would select keywords or understand content.
AUTONOMY	Working with operational autonomy, such as choosing particular tasks and how to execute them. Includes subcategories: isolation, lone wolf, and mobility.
CLIENTS	Discussion of or communication with clients. Subcategories included client compliance with recommendations, client infighting, and client tiers based on types of service contracts.
CYCLES	Indicators of SEObrate's work cycles. Subcategories included recurrent cycles (daily, weekly, monthly, yearly) and project stages (launch, maintenance).
FLUX	Examples or discussions of organizational, automation, and market changes.
HIRING	Discussions of hiring policy or strategy.
KEYWORDS	Discussions or examples of keywords; subcategories included selection, measurement, and deployment.
MEETINGS	Discussions or examples of meetings in which workers assembled in person, either informally in hallways or formally in brown bag meetings and reporting parties.
REACTIVE	Discussions or examples of organizing work around triggers, both cyclical incidents and contingencies, rather than planning work tasks in advance.
SCOUTING	Discussions or incidents involving individuals discovering potentially useful tools, services, or procedures, then sharing them with others on their teams.
SEARCH	Discussions or incidents involving enacting, explaining, or understanding components of the search business.
SNAKE OIL	Discussions or incidents involving deceptive SEO practices, including "gray" practices, false positives, and search engine detection of SEO gaming.

STABILITY	Measures for enacting stability, including subcategories: automation, reuse.
STATUS	Discussions or incidents in which team members communicate or request status on a project or client.
TALK	Incidents in which team members communicated orally rather than via texts (such as Instant Messaging, email, reports) or tools (phone).
TEAMS	Discussions or incidents involving teamwork. Subcategories include types of teams; team roles; team behaviors; experience; and scaling.
TOOLS	Discussions or incidents involving tools, broadly speaking, including texts, images, and software.
UNIQUE	Discussions or incidents involving contingencies that participants indicated were unique, resulting in customized analysis or reporting.
WRITING	Discussions or incidents involving writing, including the forms of writing listed under TOOLS.

Axial Coding

Axial coding is a way to indicate relationships that you see emerging across codes—connections that start to jump out at you because the codes appear together so frequently. Axial codes describe persistent connections between some of the existing codes.

Typically, you'll develop axial codes only after applying starter and open codes across most or all of your data.

For example, perhaps you notice that when you code "ACCOUNTABILITY", you often also code "TRUST". Perhaps there's a stable relationship between the two, based on developing trust through a history of accountability? You can develop an axial code, "ETHOS", to express the connection, and you see how often that connection exists. Below, you can see this code along with other axial codes.

Table 13.3. Axial codes.

AUDIENCE ANALYSIS	Discussions of, or incidents involving, building a structured picture of how end users search for content or what end users the clients want to attract. Based on codes: audience, understanding, search_keywords, search_analytics, search_local.
ETHOS	Discussions of, or incidents involving, building authority and trust. Based on codes: snakeoil, accountability, trust, clients_compliance.
FLEXIBILITY	Discussions of, or incidents involving, making work and work organization flexible in order to rapidly react to flux. Based on codes: flux, stability_automation, scouting, autonomy, reactive, clients_infighting, hiring.
NETWORKS	Discussions of, or incidents involving, recombinant networks of team members organized around a project. Based on codes: teams, tools_im, meetings.
TRANSFORMATIONS	Discussions of, or incidents involving, enacting and using standing sets of transformations. Based on codes: stability_reuse, stability_automation, tools_templates.

How to Code

Early qualitative researchers would code their field notes by numbering them, cutting them apart, then sorting them into different piles. This process took a lot of time and effort—to put it mildly.

How should you code your data? For your first few research studies, you might consider the following alternatives.

Coding on Paper

This is the easiest technique to perform. Simply print all of your data (e.g., field notes, interview transcripts, artifacts, etc.) and write codes in the margins.

However, coding on paper has problems as well. For larger data sets, you may find it difficult to search for specific codes, and if you're interested in finding out how frequently a code appears, you'll have to do that by hand. Finally, it's hard to keep track of codes and easy to accidentally use two codes for the same thing.

Coding with a Spreadsheet or Word Processor

Coding with a spreadsheet is also fairly easy, once you drop all of your data into a spreadsheet.

With this approach, you copy your data (e.g., field notes, interview transcripts, etc.) and paste it into the spreadsheet. Typically you'll use a cell for each paragraph in the field notes or transcripts. Drop in columns on the left to indicate the participant and date, a column on the right for your codes, and then type in the codes.

On the other hand, you could also code with a word processor. If you typed your observations or interviews, you can insert the codes directly into the text or in comments. Then you can use the word processor's search function to find the codes.

Either approach lets you code quickly and search for codes. If you know enough about spreadsheets, you might even be able to automatically count frequencies of each code.

Coding with Qualitative Data Analysis tools

You may have heard of dedicated qualitative data analysis (QDA) packages. I don't recommend these unless you are working on a massive data set, such as a dissertation. Personally, I use custom MySQL databases rather than purchasing QDA packages (see Appendix B for more on this system).

Autocoding

Finally, if you are using a database or QDA, you might cautiously try *autocoding* or automated coding. Essentially, this means assigning codes automatically based on keywords. For instance, you could tell a database to search for the term "email" in your observation notes and assign the code "EMAIL" to each line that has that term.

Autocoding can get you started quickly, but it has definite limitations:

- Autocoding won't catch instances that don't include the keyword. For instance, it won't code a typo ("emial") or a variant ("e-mail").

- Autocoding won't work for concepts, just keywords.

- Autocoding can yield false positives. For instance, if you try to autocode "IM," you may accidentally catch any word in which those two letters appear (such as "**im**patient" or "a**im**s").

So if you use autocoding, make sure to check your results by hand.

Example Reading

> Spinuzzi, C. (2010). Secret sauce and snake oil: Writing monthly reports in a highly contingent environment. *Written Communication, 27*(4), 363–409.

The code examples in this chapter come from the above article, which lays out the coding scheme and choices in detail.

Exercises

- Develop a list of starter codes based on your research question and research proposal.

- Apply the starter codes to one set of field notes. Which are easy to apply and which are difficult? Which seem to give you guidance and which don't?

- Apply the same starter codes to one interview. Do you find yourself using the same codes as you did for the field notes? What similarities and differences do you see?

- Apply open coding to the same set of field notes. What codes do you come up with?

- Apply open coding to the same interview. What codes do you come up with? Are they the same ones?

- Develop axial codes for both the field notes and the interview.

Examples

The next couple of pages show a coding scheme for the SEO case, plus an example of how some of these codes were applied to field notes.

Coding Applied to Field Notes

In this example from the SEO case, I'm applying codes to different lines from my first observation with Dani—the same observation that appears in the example at the end of Chapter 7. Here, I've put each set of codes directly underneath the line to which they apply. Notice that starter, open, and axial codes are all represented here.

One more thing: notice that I surround each code with asterisks. I explain why in Appendix B, but you don't have to follow this convention as you code.

Table 13.4. Coded observation notes.

Observation notes	Codes
9:00am Dani	
Dani came in just before I did. Says she has a 10am meeting and a brief 11am. We'll try to fit in an interview after that. Cubicle is next to Craig's. Nobody in adjoining.	**MEETINGS**
She explains: usually uses headphones. Puts them on.	**AUTONOMY_ISOLATION** **AUTONOMY_MOBILITY** **MUSIC**
Cubicle L top: books on analytics, mysql, php, javascript, etc.	**SEARCH_ANALYTICS** **TOOLS_BOOKS** ***AUDIENCE_ANALYSIS***
Cubicle L desk: books—Becoming a successful manager"; "Managing for results""	**TOOLS_BOOKS** **STRATEGY** **TEAMS_LEADERSHIP** ***NETWORKS***
Cubicle R desk: Competitors"; "Competitive Strategy"; "Competition Intelligence""	**TOOLS_BOOKS** **STRATEGY** **TEAMS_LEADERSHIP** ***NETWORKS***
She's looking at videos. (Company blog featured an interview w/her yesterday re video and search options.)	**SEARCH_VIDEOS** **TOOLS_BLOG**
logged into YouTube	**SEARCH_VIDEOS**
External screen showing Outlook.	**TOOLS_OUTLOOK**

>Outlook:Email: agrees to meeting, sends	**TOOLS_EMAIL** **TOOLS_OUTLOOK** **MEETINGS** **TOOLS_OUTLOOK**
>Outlook:Email: ?? (Going through these quickly)	**TOOLS_EMAIL** **TOOLS_OUTLOOK**
Outlook:Cal: Looks	**TOOLS_OUTLOOK**
Chrome: Moves win to right screen. Googles "mobility scooters" then "power wheelchairs"	**TOOLS_CHROME** **TOOLS_GOOGLE** **SEARCH_KEYWORDS**
FF:SEObrateMax: window to left. "Client Natural Search Rankings" (incl kwds she just used)	**TOOLS_SEObrateMax** **SEARCH_KEYWORDS** **TOOLS_FIREFOX** **CLIENTS** **SEARCH_NATURAL** **SEARCH_ANALYTICS** ***AUDIENCE_ANALYSIS***
>IM(Lindy). Hey, what do we need for the meeting with Clara?" [Lindy is acct mgr]"	**MEETINGS** **TOOLS_IM** **TEAMS_ACCT_MGR** **TEAMS_ACCT_MGR** ***NETWORKS***
<>IM: converse re mtg.	**TOOLS_IM** **MEETINGS**
FF:SEObrateMax: rankings	**TOOLS_SEObrateMax** **TOOLS_FIREFOX** **SEARCH_ANALYTICS** ***AUDIENCE_ANALYSIS***

CHAPTER 14

Reporting Progress

At this point, you have collected and characterized the data. But you haven't analyzed it yet. That's next. Therefore, you can't tell us what it means. Even though you have the data, you're not yet able to achieve topsight.

At the same time, the research site deserves to find out what's happened. They have opened up their work to you, and they may be eager to find out what happened. In fact, they might be asking you, "What did you find out?" or "Have you learned anything yet?"

But you don't want to give them your impressions at this stage. For one thing, those impressions are very incomplete at this stage. And they could be wrong; you may have seen a lot of *symptoms*, such as consistent errors, but you haven't yet detected the *underlying problem*. Giving away too much could lead the people at the site to make changes before you're sure those changes would do any good.

You're in a dilemma. What do you do?

The Jobs of the Interim Report

The answer is to provide an *interim report*. This report has four jobs:

- It provides continuity in your overall argument.

- It covers the progress that you've made so far.

- It gives them an idea of what happens next.

- It tells them not to act until you've finished your analysis.

Although the example I provide here is of a written report, you could also deliver it as a slide deck. Either way, the principles are the same.

The Interim Report Provides Continuity in Your Overall Argument

You originally approached this organization with planning documents in hand:

- The research description

- The site letter

- The consent forms

Depending on how you approached the organization, they might have also seen your research design matrix and your research proposal.

As discussed earlier in the book, all of these documents work together to present an overall argument for your research; and the interim report continues that argument. It connects your earlier planning documents with your later document—the document they're most looking forward to seeing: the recommendation report.

Not only does it *connect* those documents, it must also *reinforce* the argument you're making through these documents. That's important because your readers have a lot of other things on their minds, so they may not remember the argument you're making. You need to remind them here.

As you read the following sections, flip to the end of the chapter to see the sample interim report.

The Interim Report Covers the Progress That You've Made So Far

Suppose you've decided to take a long road trip. At the beginning of the trip, you plan your route: You'll start here, take these highways, stop in these towns, and end up at your destination on this day. During the trip, you probably check your progress against this plan. You might trace your route on the map or watch the glowing dot on your GPS, you might compare your actual arrival at each town to the schedule you put together, and you might watch out for landmarks to give you an idea of how close you are to your destination.

Similarly, the interim report gives your readers an idea of what progress you've made relative to your plan. It lets you remind the audience of the plan, explain any changes you've had to make, and show how far you have to go.

For instance, in the sample interim report, the first full paragraph provides the following sentence:

> Below, I cover three findings, then discuss our next steps.

In this simple sentence, the readers see the structure of the rest of the interim report. They know that you'll talk about the three findings, then move on to the next action. With a longer report, you might need a more detailed statement.

The Interim Report Gives Readers an Idea of What Happens Next

Although you gave your readers a research description at the beginning of the study, they might not have gotten a clear idea of what would happen at each stage. In fact, you yourself might have been fuzzy on the details, especially since exploratory studies tend to be full of contingencies. But at this point, you've collected and characterized your data. You can give them—and yourself—a much clearer idea of what is coming up next.

In the sample interim report, the last section—headed "Next Steps"—covers the next actions:

NEXT STEPS

I plan to conduct a more thorough analysis of the existing data over the next two weeks. Specifically, I plan to generate several analytical models to detect any patterns I've missed. At the end of those two weeks, I should be able to provide a more rigorous analysis.

The Interim Report Tells Readers Not to Act until You've Finished Your Analysis

This is perhaps the most important message that the interim report must convey. Often, people in organizations, especially managers, want to change things for the better. If they can see a possibility for making their organization more productive or efficient, for making their employees happier or more amenable to management, or for making their own bosses happier; managers will want to take action right away.

The problem is, as we'll see in the next section, that up to this point you have been detecting *symptoms* rather than analyzing the *systemic issue* toward which those symptoms point. Until you've conducted the analysis, interventions might actually do more harm than good. So, although you should give readers a good idea of what you've seen, you should also clearly state that they shouldn't take action until the analysis is in.

The sample report contains this message throughout, especially in the introduction:

This is an interim report on my research at SEObrate. I have finished data collection, but I have not rigorously analyzed the data yet, so please regard it as a summary of my initial impressions, not a final report.

And the conclusion:

Please don't hesitate to contact me with questions. I'm restricted in terms of specific details, due to confidentiality, but I should be able to discuss the basic trends I've seen at SEObrate.

So how do we put together the interim report?

The Structure of the Interim Report

I recommend a simple interim report with these components:

- Introduction

- Findings

- Next steps

Each component has its own job.

Introduction

The introduction of the interim report should do three things: forecast, remind, and hedge.

Forecast. Provide a sentence that previews the structure of the document.

Remind. Remind readers that you did the study, what you did, and when (you can do this in one sentence).

Hedge. Make clear that these findings are tentative and will be followed up with a formal analysis later.

Notice that the sample report accomplishes all this in one paragraph.

Findings

In this section, you'll describe one to four findings, with subheadings for each. Here, findings are general insights about the organization that you or the audience might not have known otherwise. As you'll see in the sample interim report, it's a good idea to summarize each finding in a subheading.

Findings can be negative (i.e., some problems) or positive (i.e., things they are doing well). For instance, the sample interim report contains one positive finding:

> Internal communication channels appear robust.

And two findings that can be considered challenges:

> Work organization is changing rapidly at SEObrate.

and

> Tools and documents are also changing rapidly.

Since this is an interim report, hedge your findings. Make clear that these findings are preliminary.

> I'm not sure how the organization will look in the next month or two. My impression is that it will remain very loose, for a while, as analysts become more comfortable with their roles.

For each finding, make sure that you include:

- a finding (i.e., claim) in one sentence, highlighted;

- one or more reasons why you believe this claim to be true; and

- at least two pieces of evidence per reason.

Make sure these reasons are triangulated—that is, that they come from different places and confirm each other.

Evidence can be quotes, incidents, or artifact features. Remember: don't include evidence that can reveal participants' specific identities.

Next Steps

In this final section, do the following things:

- Let them know what you'll do next (i.e., analyze).

- Give them a timeframe.

- Hedge.

Example

The next page shows an interim report based on the SEO case.

Interim Report

Tim—

This is an interim report on my research at SEObrate. I have finished data collection, but I have not rigorously analyzed the data yet, so please regard it as a summary of my initial impressions, not a final report.

Below, I cover three findings, then discuss our next steps.

FINDINGS

Work organization is changing rapidly at SEObrate. During my first visits, analysts worked autonomously, reporting results to account managers, but not taking direction from them. Training and direction happened primarily through mentoring. I suspect this was true, in large part, because search analysis is a fairly young field with few established procedures. Analysts, therefore, tend to be self-directed and to develop solutions to novel problems. In their interviews, all three of the analysts reported that they worked in this way, and the observations bear that out. Working independently has worked well in the past.

However, as SEObrate takes on more clients, this system doesn't scale up well. The analysts report separating clients into different types; SEObrate is developing new services for these different types; and the company is taking on more employees as well. So, in my later visits, I saw a more hierarchical organization emerging: analysts were assigned to teams and certain senior analysts were designated team leaders. This more hierarchical organization is still very loose, based on my interviews, but it appears to be developing rapidly. I'm not sure how the organization will look in the next month or two. My impression is that it will remain very loose for a while as analysts become more comfortable with their roles.

Tools and documents are also changing rapidly. Like your industry, and like SEObrate's internal organization, tools are a moving target. Partly that is because SEObrate is rapidly developing new internal tools, though analysts report that they are not always sure what these tools do or how to integrate them into their loose workflows. Analysts tell me that they know it's critical to integrate these new tools properly into their workflow, but they have had trouble doing so, partially because the workflow is so rapid. They are also continually developing new ways to perform SEO—such as new techniques for using YouTube videos and Quora comments—and that makes it difficult for them to concentrate on development in any particular direction. One analyst told me that it feels like he's always chasing down new solutions and SEObrate's tools just aren't keeping up with his needs.

Analysts often create their own documents as well. Although they are provided with several templates for different types of reports and analyses, they often face novel situations in which they had to perform complex analyses that they haven't done before. These situations typically involved upcoming meetings with large clients who deserved special attention. In one observation, for instance, an analyst struggled to create an Excel graph that showed several relationships; after spending a good deal of time on it, this analyst abandoned the task. She later explained that the relationships may not be relatable in an Excel graph. In another case, an analyst developed a novel chart to demonstrate that keywords nominated by a new client were not as suitable as ones the analyst had identified. Such documents were invented on the spot; served as reactions to upcoming presentations, usually, scheduled for later that day; and appeared to be one-off inventions (i.e., analysts did not plan to use them again or share them with others). These suggest, again, that the work, and workflow, of search analysis is still developing rapidly. As the field matures and as SEObrate further defines the parameters of its services, these documents will become more regular.

Internal communication channels appear robust. Most analysts and the account manager are on IM constantly and appear to use it appropriately to communicate throughout the day; they ask questions, give answers, redirect inquiries, and follow up with face-to-face meetings when appropriate. IM also serves as a roster of available team members, which was important given the loose schedules of some team members. Finally, it serves as a way to conduct private conversations about potentially sensitive topics, such as how to stage-manage the introduction of new tools in a meeting.

The physical separation between account managers and search analysts is obvious, but both parties communicate over IM and by crossing over to the other's section, so I don't think the physical separation poses a communication problem. That separation also allows each team to mentor its own members. The analysts report that they prefer being in their own section, where they can ask each other questions day-to-day. Interestingly, I saw more crosstalk with the account managers than with the analysts.

Email functions, as it often does, as an archival resource as well as communication. For instance, an account analyst filled out her timesheet by looking at the emails she sent the previous day. Account managers in particular are conscious of how they wrote emails to clients, and they consult others in the company on email drafts before sending them out.

NEXT STEPS

I plan to conduct a more thorough analysis of the existing data over the next two weeks. Specifically, I plan to generate several analytical models to detect any patterns I've missed. At the end of those two weeks, I should be able to provide a more rigorous analysis.

Please don't hesitate to contact me with questions. I'm restricted in terms of specific details, due to confidentiality, but I should be able to discuss the basic trends I've seen at SEObrate.

ANALYZING THE DATA

Now that you've collected and characterized the data, it's time to develop topsight. To do that, you'll analyze the data at different levels, cataloguing the symptoms, then using them to diagnose the illnesses—the systemic issues—affecting the work. In this section, we'll answer two questions:

- How do you make sense of the data?

- How do you work inductively to discover and understand the systemic issues in the work?

CHAPTER 15

Analytical Models

In one *Simpsons* episode, the Simpsons are reflecting on recent events. Marge proposes several morals to the story, but Homer concludes that there was no moral, "It's just a bunch of stuff that happened."

At this point, you might feel like Homer. You've designed a study, gathered data, and characterized it. You may have seen some patterns emerging. But you're probably having a hard time getting the big picture; you're not yet able to develop topsight. Do the data tell you anything? And if they do, how will you know?

Generally they do. If you've carefully collected data, you can find patterns to people's work, including patterns in their mistakes and difficulties. That's because work is generally set up in cycles and managed with relatively stable information resources and work patterns. Because that's the case, even mistakes and difficulties tend to cluster around specific parts of the work.

Understanding Disruptions as Symptoms: What's the Disease?

Let's call those mistakes *disruptions*. Disruptions happen at different levels: macro, meso, and micro levels. As you may remember from Chapter 3, these are the same levels that you designed your study to investigate (see table 15.1).

Table 15.1. Levels of activity and disruptions.

Levels	Models	Time scale	Disruptions	Essential Questions
Macro (Organization)	Activity systems Activity networks	Days, weeks, months, years	Contradictions	Why?
Meso (Human)	Resource maps Handoff chains Triangulation tables	Minutes, hours	Discoordination	What?
Micro (Habit)	Breakdown tables	Seconds	Breakdowns	How?

Remember what I said in Chapter 1: You can think of these disruptions as *symptoms*. They aren't the underlying illness, but they point to the illness.

For instance, imagine that you're not feeling well, so you go to see the doctor. "What symptoms do you have?" the doctor asks. You list the symptoms: a bad headache, a high fever, a sore throat, and you feel weak. As the doctor listens, she makes notes.

You've been trying to treat the *symptoms*. For instance, you've taken aspirin for the headache, you've been drinking coffee to raise your energy levels, and you've been popping cough drops for your sore throat. But treating the symptoms isn't useful because you haven't addressed the underlying *illness*.

What's the illness? Your doctor should be able to figure it out just from listening to you and examining you. That is, she sees the relationship among the symptoms and determines the underlying illness—in this case, the flu. With that information, she can recommend a course of action that actually attacks the illness, not just the symptoms.

In your study, you've been compiling data on the symptoms—in this case, the way people work and the disruptions they encounter at each level. But in the next several chapters, you'll begin to pinpoint the relationships among these disruptions. By Chapter 23, you'll be able to diagnose the underlying illnesses in the organization that are causing these symptoms. That is, you'll achieve topsight.

To do that, you'll be learning several different analytical *models*. Below, I'll explain what analytical models work, then introduce you to the models you'll use to achieve topsight.

Identifying Relationships: What are Analytical Models?

By *models*, I mean visual representations that help you to pull out and investigate aspects of your data. And you need to be able to do that, because you are faced with an intimidating, maybe even overwhelming amount of data: hours and hours of interviews, pages and pages of observation notes, stacks of artifacts. With this much data, it's hard to see the forest for the trees, and it's easy to say, like Homer, that "it's just a bunch of stuff that happened."

But it's not just a bunch of stuff. You should be able to find patterns in the data. Coding helps because it lets you begin to map some of the patterns out. But there are certain patterns that we can expect to find, and if we represent them visually, we can learn a lot about our data. We can get out of the trees and start to see the forest.

Qualitative researchers usually draw on three major types of models: flow, network, and matrix models.

Flow models show sequential relationships. For instance, in a flowchart, boxes show steps and arrows show how one steps leads to the next. Even better, you can show decision points—points at which the results of one step determine what the next step will be.

We usually see flowcharts in technical documentation. But you could also use a flow model to describe actions you're seeing in the data. For instance, if your observation notes describe several different people taking similar actions, you can use flow models to *just* show the actions they take. Do they follow the same sequence? If they don't, is it because they hit a decision point? How similar is their workflow?

Network models show nonsequential relationships. In a network model, almost anything can be a *node* (usually represented as a circle) and their relationships can be represented as a *link* or *edge* (a line between the circles). Developing a network model lets you map out relationships and test how consistent they are.

For instance, you may notice that when your participants are processing their timesheets, they tend to consult other texts: their calendar, their emails, sticky notes on their desk, and so forth. What are the major kinds of texts they need in order to process their timesheets? One way to find out would be to write the name of each text in its own circle, then connect texts with lines when you see the participant using them together. Does every participant use the same texts together? Or do they substitute different ones? A network diagram can help you cut through the details and look at just this aspect of your data.

Matrix models, or tables, allow you to make ordered comparisons. They let you compare *things* (in rows) using the same *criteria* or characteristics (columns). If you've ever used a *Consumer Reports* article to compare different laptops, phones, or headphones, you have used a matrix to compare different products using consistent criteria.

Similarly, in a field study, you can use matrixes to compare characteristics. For instance, you may notice differences in how the morning crew and the night crew do their jobs, even though these are supposed to be the same job. Using a table can help you to verify these differences and further identify patterns.

Flow, network, and matrix models are the major models used in qualitative research studies; they give you a way to represent three major types of relationships. But other models are possible, and you may even find yourself inventing models to get at interesting parts of your data. We'll discuss some possibilities in Chapter 22. But for the most part, you'll use *seven specific models* to get to topsight.

Integrating Models: What are the Topsight Models?

In the Topsight approach, we use flow, network, and matrix models, just like other field research approaches. But the difference is that we use specific variants of these models, and these specific variants are *integrated* (fitted together). If you build these seven models in order, they should lead you to topsight.

The seven topsight models all share the following characteristics:

- **Triangulated**. You can use models to demonstrate mutually confirmatory evidence.

- **Patterned**. You can use models to see patterns in the evidence.

- **Leveled**. You can use models to see patterns across levels of activity (once the patterns are completed at each level).

The models are at meso, micro, and macro levels.

Meso-Level Models: The Human Level

As you recall, the meso level is where we usually "live"; it's the level of goal-directed actions.

Suppose one of your participants is writing a report. When you ask him what he's doing, he probably won't respond, "I am typing the letters 'R-E-P-O-R-T'." Nor is he likely to say, "I'm creating shareholder value." He is, however, likely to say, "I'm writing a report." The report is a goal that he's consciously trying to achieve, which is why semi-structured interviews tend to yield a lot of insights at this level. He achieves that goal in minutes, hours, or—perhaps—days.

In fact, part of the data collection in your study is geared toward gathering this meso-level data. You observe people in real time and write notes about what you see them doing. You ask them about their goals. You examine the information resources—in this case, the draft report—to learn more about them. And you repeat these data collection measures across different instances and people so that you can see general patterns.

As you do, you might see common disruptions. In particular, you might see points at which people have trouble coordinating their resources. For instance, perhaps a participant has trouble finding the right information to put into the report.

In Chapters 16-18, we'll learn three models that will help us examine meso-level work and the disruptions involved in that work:

Resource maps (Chapter 16) are network models that help us to examine the *information resources* that people use as they do their work and the disruptions they encounter as they try to coordinate those resources.

Handoff chains (Chapter 17) are flow models that help us to examine the *patterns of communicative events* that people use as they convey information resources to each other and the disruptions that sometimes force them to restart these patterns.

Triangulation tables (Chapter 18) are matrix models that help us to put together the insights of the two models, allowing us to compare and contrast how individuals and groups do things and to spot innovations that may allow some people to avoid disruptions.

After using these models, you'll have a good idea of what people are doing at the organization: how they marshal their resources, how they follow sequences, and how different people or groups use innovations.

Micro-Level Model: The Habit Level

While the meso level is where participants "live," we're also interested in the micro level. If you ask your participant what he's doing, he probably won't respond, "I am typing the letters 'R-E-P-O-R-T'," but at the micro level, that's exactly what he's doing.

The micro level is the level of habits and reactions (a.k.a. operations). When we touch-type, click a mouse, or shift gears in a manual-transmission car without thinking, we are generally performing operations. We do these second-by-second in reaction to regular events. And for the most part, those operations are so automatic that we perform them without problems.

 But sometimes we do have problems. We miskey; we click the wrong thing; we grind the gears. These disruptions are called *breakdowns*. When they happen, we have to become conscious of, and focus on, what we are doing.

Breakdowns happen all the time, and often they are by happenstance. People make mistakes. But sometimes you'll find that lots of operational breakdowns cluster around the same place—the same information resource—the same part of the process.

As you recall, your research design involves data collection at the micro level. Ideally, you would be able to collect second-by-second data to examine operations and breakdowns. Realistically, you might have to rely on field notes and interviews to get to this level.

In Chapter 19, we'll learn a micro-level model:

Breakdown tables are matrix models that help us to map out incidents at the level of unconscious habit, specifically incidents involving breakdowns and the ways that participants recovered from these breakdowns.

After using this model, you'll have a good idea of how people recover from micro-level breakdowns and where these breakdowns cluster.

Macro-Level Models: The Organization Level

The macro level is the level of culture, history, and organizational activity. We're not generally aware of it because we're not generally focused on big-picture issues. For instance, when you ask your report-writing participant what he's doing, he's unlikely to say, "I'm creating shareholder value." But at some level, he is; through his report writing, he's contributing to the overall objective of the organization, which, in a publicly held company, includes creating shareholder value. Yet, few of us are thinking about these sorts of macro-level objectives, which happen on the scale of years or decades.

At the macro level, organizations develop to address such macro-level objectives. They acquire people and tools; they develop rules and divisions of labor; and they establish relations with community stakeholders. This is a complex, long-lasting, and cyclical process. It's no surprise that such organizations develop macro-level disruptions called *contradictions*—points at which the parts of the activity just don't fit well together.

For instance, perhaps the report your participant is writing is an annual requirement—that is, every year, the participant must report on how his employees perform on their assessments. The reporting requirement was set up in 1983, when the organization had several layers of middle management and employees tended to stay in the organization their entire careers. But in 2013, most of the middle-management layers are gone, and many of the participant's employees are contract workers. Consequently, parts of the report aren't even relevant, but the participant has to write them anyway. A contradiction has built up between the genre of the report and the actual division of labor within the organization; the two motives or "whys" don't match.

As you recall, part of your data collection involved macro-level data.

In Chapters 20-21, we'll learn two models that will help us examine macro-level work and the disruptions involved in that work:

Activity systems (Chapter 20) are network models that help us to examine the specific organization in which your participants work, including its objectives, actors, tools, rules, community stakeholders, and division of labor, as well as the contradictions that have built up within and across those elements.

Activity networks (Chapter 21) are network models that help us to examine how this organization interacts with other activities, as well as the contradictions that have built up across activities.

After using these models, you'll have a good idea of why organizations work the way they do, what they accomplish, and where macro-level disruptions occur.

Looking Across the Models

Earlier, I mentioned that the Topsight models are integrated: not only do they *individually* give you insights, they fit together to provide *broader* insights.

At this point, we've been able to use the different models to examine work and disruptions at each level. That is, we've pinpointed all the different symptoms, seeing how thy individually affect the work. But how do we see how these symptoms interrelate? How do we diagnose the illness?

In fact, diagnosing the "illness" in an organization can be complicated since organizations can have more than one "illness"—more than one systemic issue that is manifested in disruptions at each level. For instance, maybe your report-writing participant is encountering disruptions related to the report, but *also* disruptions related to the organization's record-keeping system.

To sort out the systemic issues, in Chapter 22, we'll turn to our last model:

Topsight tables are matrix models that help us to see relationships among the disruptions at each level. Using this table, we will examine the evidence and determine which contradictions, discoordinations, and breakdowns are related to each other; we will then name the systemic issue that relates them.

After completing this table, you will be able to pinpoint one or more systemic issues in the organization, and be ready to move toward recommending a solution.

Now that we have this overview, let's get started modeling our data. The first step: Building resource maps.

CHAPTER 16

Resource Maps

Suppose that you've observed several people at your research site, interviewed them, and collected copies of information resources that they use in their work. These information resources range from complex interfaces to improvised sticky notes. As we saw in Chapter 1, these information resources tend to be in recognizable types.

You know that they are all interconnected, and you are pretty sure that certain resources make the work a lot easier. But how can you tell for sure? How do you get a handle on this complex set of resources?

In this chapter, we'll get at these aspects of the work by developing *resource maps*. Resource maps are network models that focus on the meso level of the workers' activity. That is, they focus on *workers' conscious actions* and how they use different information resources to help them complete these actions.

Resource maps help us to answer questions such as these:

- What information resources do people use?

- How do people actually use these resources, in what combinations?

- Which resources are established parts of the work, and which are workarounds or innovations?

- How do the resources work together?

- How do people use different resources to accomplish the same things?

Because resource maps let you map out the resources that people are using at your site, they also help you to see important aspects that you might have otherwise missed:

- Where people consistently have trouble coordinating two or more resources

- Where people have improvised new resources, such as sticky notes, to improve how the resources interrelate

- How resources interrelate

To get to these aspects of the work, we'll follow these steps:

- Identify the resources involved in the work.

- Identify relationships among the resources.

- Develop a resource map.

- Detect discoordinations among the resources.

As you try out your first resource map, start with just the data from just one observation with one participant. Start small. Once you complete that resource map, *then* you can verify it with other data from the same data set (interviews, artifacts), adding to the map as you go.

Once you've created resource maps for different visits, you can compare them, note differences, and create an overall resource map for your entire set of observations.

1. Identifying Information Resources

Description

As we saw in Chapter 1, information resources are relatively stable responses to recurrent situations. Usually, these are instantiated in texts or speech. Since they're regular and recurrent, we can recognize them, share them, and use them in predictable ways. They're a way to mediate our own work and the work of others. Consequently, examining information resources tells us a lot about how people understand their work.

For instance, when we talk about a shopping list, we have a basic idea of what it might look like, based on what it's supposed to accomplish and on how similar resources have looked in the past. Shopping lists tend to be very different, as you'll see if you watch people shop at a grocery store, but they are similar and predictable enough that strangers could swap lists and probably do a pretty good job of filling each other's orders.

More specialized information resources might be harder to understand and might take a bit more time to learn. Think about learning a new software interface, doing your taxes, or filling out a travel request.

As you analyze how people accomplish things at your site, you'll look for the information resources they use. Think in terms of

- resource types that participants identify as types and

- resource types that are repeatedly used at the same site to accomplish the same things.

Sources

To identify information resources, look for any sort of text or exchange that participants used, composed, or placed: interfaces, forms, documents they wrote, calendars they consulted, notes they wrote on scraps of paper, checkmarks they made on a printout, or even greeting cards that they have posted in their cubicles.

Observations. Note any resources you see, especially resources that you see them read, compose, or annotate. You might use highlighters to highlight these in your field notes.

Interviews. Ask participants about those resources. When do they use them? Why? Where did they get them? Don't be shy about asking about apparent mistakes or issues. And see if they make the same distinctions about resources as you do; if they refer to both handwritten lists and printed lists simply as "lists," that might tell you that they don't draw a distinction between the two.

Artifacts. Examine the resources. Get copies of the resources your participants worked on or with. Get photos of their workspaces so you can see how resources are placed.

Now we have a good idea of the information resources involved. Let's go to the next step: figuring out how they relate.

2. Identifying Relationships Among Information Resources

Description

As you look over your field notes and interviews, you'll notice that these information resources are rarely, if ever, used on their own.

- One participant might use a printout of customers as a checklist when calling them, checking off the people they've called, then entering customer data into a spreadsheet.

- Another participant might consult documentation to understand how to fill out an unfamiliar form, and at the same time look through their email to get the content that they use to fill in the form.

- A third might pull information from several databases in order to write a report for customers, using IM to ask the account manager questions and a calendar to estimate how long she has before the report is due.

All of these scenarios are based on what I've seen in my own research; they're typical. If anything, they're a little simple. Knowledge work involves a lot of resources. We tend to use these resources in complex combinations. In fact, a set of resources lets us do things that individual resources won't let us do.

- The combination of a printout of customers *plus* a checklist *plus* a spreadsheet yields a system for tracking overdue accounts.

- The combination of documentation *plus* a form *plus* email yields a fairly accurate report.

- The combination of databases *plus* a report *plus* IM *plus* a calendar yields information that the customer needs, delivered in time and with the right level of detail.

Sources

When it comes to information resources, the whole is greater than the sum of its parts. So we need to track the mediational relationships among information resources—the ways that they work together to guide or enable people's work.

Observations. Note how the resources interact, especially in terms of

- *juxtaposition* (overlapping two resources);

- *placing* (spatially situating two resources, such as placing them side by side or in a stack);

- *annotation* (writing on or altering a resource);

- *transfer* (using one resource as source for filling in another);

- *modeling* (using one resource as a model for another); and

- *reference* (using one resource to interpret or operate another).

Interviews. Ask participants about those resources' relationships. Why do they use these resources together? Why do they stack these sheets in this way? Where did they learn to make these sorts of marks? Where did they get the idea to use this printout as a checklist? Do other people do the same thing?

Artifacts. Examine how resources are juxtaposed, placed, annotated, transferred, modeled, or referenced. Again, get copies of the resources in their relationship. If you can't get these copies, try to get photos of them.

At this point, you have enough information that you can describe the resource map—the interrelated set of information resources that are brought to bear at the research site.

3. Developing a Resource Map

Now that you have documented the information resources at work and the relationships among them, you can depict these in a resource map. In a resource map, you map these resources, drawing lines between the ones that are used together— the ones that co-mediate each other. Once you have this maps, analytical possibilities open up:

At the individual level, you can compare how a participant uses resources in their work. At this level, you can examine how people marshal different information resources to get things done, especially how they bring their own innovations to their tasks. You can also map out the most central information resources—the ones that link most densely to other information resources; these tend to be heavily used and important for coordinating work.

At the group level, you can compare how people in the same group, or in different groups, use resources. At this level, you can compare their resource maps to see how different people or groups tackle similar tasks with different sets of information resources. These comparisons can help you detect different innovations, especially when different groups respond to the same issue with different solutions.

To construct a resource map, start with a single set of field notes, artifacts, and interviews.

- Get a single sheet of paper. In one corner, write the participant's name and the observation date so you can remember which participant you're describing.

- In the center of the paper, write the name of the most used information resource. Circle it.

- Starting from there, write names of other information resources that are associated with it (e.g., through juxtaposition, placing, annotation, transfer, modeling, or reference). Circle them too, and draw lines to connect each information resource with the first information resource. Make sure you can point to at least one piece of evidence for each link.

- Repeat the process for each of these information resources.

At the end of the process, you should have a resource map that looks something like figure 16.1.

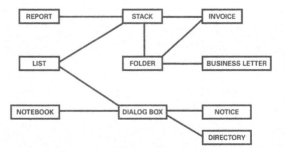

Figure 16.1. A resource map.

You can repeat this process across a participant's observations, across the group, or across the organization. Consider generating separate resource maps whenever you see significant differences. These might include

- one participant who does things significantly differently from others;

- two different roles (e.g., account managers and web developers in the same unit);

- two different sections (e.g., two different units); and

- two different offices or branches (e.g., the uptown and downtown branches).

At this point, you should be able to show how people coordinate their resources, and how that coordination does or does not differ. Now, let's look at the discoordinations you may have detected.

4. Detecting Discoordinations

Description

Often, resource maps suffer from action-level disturbances called discoordinations—points at which two or more different information resources just don't "fit."

For instance, in my book *Tracing Genres through Organizations*, I examined how traffic safety workers used a database of traffic accidents and a set of 3'x3' maps to find patterns in traffic accidents. Unfortunately, the workers had a lot of trouble coordinating the two information resources. The database could only search for intersections designated by six-digit "node numbers," which were printed on the maps, and "links" between those nodes. To find information about a particular intersection, the worker would have to look up the intersection or stretch of road on a map, find the appropriate node number(s), and type them into the database. They encountered all sorts of problems—they had a hard time finding the node numbers; they would transpose the numbers when typing into the database; and they would even have a hard time finding a large enough flat surface to spread out the map. Since they ran these searches only a couple of times a year, they weren't able to familiarize themselves with the system through repetition.

But some people didn't have as much difficulty. One police officer, for instance, didn't even bother with the node map. Instead, she simply took out a folder, opened it, and used sticky notes with node numbers written on them. She had to look at accidents for the same intersections each year, so years ago she had simply written the node numbers on the sticky notes. Now she didn't have to even glance at the map; she could put the sticky note next to the dialog box, juxtaposing the two information resources and typing the node numbers in much more accurately.

In this case, workers encountered a discoordination between the two information resources; they represented the roadway in entirely different ways (i.e., maps vs. nodes), with different logics and conventions, and workers had a hard time getting them coordinated. The police officer's innovation routed around this discoordination.

Sources

When you look for discoordinations, look for these characteristics in the data:

Observations. Look for points at which people seem to have trouble relating two resources or points at which an unexpected, informal resource (e.g., sticky notes) is substituted for another resource.

Interviews. Ask participants about these resources. Why do they think they're having trouble relating the resources? Why do they go "off-script," using an innovation or workaround rather than the official resources?

Artifacts. Examine resources that are involved in discoordinations. What are their characteristics? Where did they come from? Do they represent different logics or conventions?

When you detect a discoordination, mark it in a different color of ink—I suggest red—on your resource map.

5. Aggregating Resource Maps

- At this point, you have a resource map for one visit. Try following this process for each visit, creating separate resource maps. As you do, you'll likely notice many similarities, but also some differences.

- If the resource maps are fairly similar, you can *aggregate* them. That is, you can create a single resource map with all the resources from all the visits. Doing this allows you to get an even bigger picture of the resources people are using—and where they are collectively having trouble coordinating those resources.

Exercises

- Starting with just one dataset—an observation, interview, and set of artifacts for a single participant—follow the steps above to develop a resource map. What pattern of interconnections do you see?

- Based on your dataset, label the connections among information resources. Is each connection a juxtaposition, annotation, model, or something different? Remember to identify a piece of evidence for each connection.

- Now grab a red pen. Based on your dataset, label any discoordinations in your resource map. Which connections do your participants have trouble making or sustaining?

- Repeat steps 1-3 for your other datasets. Do you see patterns emerging?

- Develop a single resource map that consolidates the other resource maps. You should see a broad set of information resources and the way they are connected.

Example

Figure 16.2 shows a resource map for the SEO case.

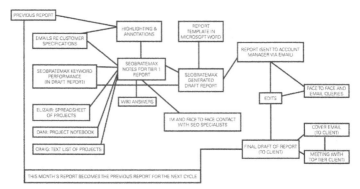

Figure 16.2. A resource map for the SEO case.

CHAPTER 17

Handoff Chains

Now that you have a resource map for your worksite, you have a good idea of the information resources people have and the ways they are connecting those information resources. But you don't have a good idea of how those information resources are strung together to achieve specific actions. That's the job of our next model, a flow model called the *handoff chain*.

Like resource maps, handoff chains focus on the meso level of the workers' activity. Whereas resource maps mapped out connections among information resources, handoff chains identify "handoffs"—points at which one person conveys a resource to another. That is, they focus on regularly occurring chains of communicative events. In doing so, they help us to answer questions, such as:

- What communicative events do people encounter in their work? That is, when do they hand information resources to others?

- Which communicative events are common to a particular group? Which are idiosyncratic? Which represent recoveries from disruptions?

- What chains of communicative events exist?

- In these chains, where are decision points?

- Do people use different chains of communicative events to accomplish the same things?

Handoff chains let you map out the chains of communicative events that people use at your site, allowing you to detect common patterns, or scripts, and divergences.

To get to these aspects of the work, we'll follow these steps:

- Identify communicative events

- Identify sequences

- Develop a handoff chain

- Detect discoordinations

As you try out your first handoff chain, start with just the data from just one observation with one participant. Start small. Once you complete that handoff chain, *then* you can verify it with other data from the same data set (interviews, artifacts), adding to the handoff chain as you go.

Once you've created handoff chains for different visits, you can compare them, note differences, and create an overall handoff chain that describes a process across your entire set of observations.

1. Identifying Communicative Events

Description

Communicative events are events in which one actor "hands off" a communication to another; emails, phone calls, document handoffs, and "do not disturb" signs on doors could all be considered communicative events. Usually, these "handoffs" are instantiated in texts or speech.

Communicative events tend to follow patterns, and these patterns tend to cycle within the larger activity at the research site.

- A proposal writer receives a *call for proposals*, meets with her team to distribute tasks, writes her *section*, and then circulates the *draft* to the rest of the team.

- A telecommunications worker receives a *list* of past due notices from his manager, calls a customer, and then makes a *note* in the *database* for his fellow workers.

Since these communicative events involve identifiable transactions, we can detect them, especially if we ask the participants to help interpret them. In most cases, these events follow regular and recurrent patterns; people tend to develop or learn a sequence for communicating, and they tend to stick to that sequence unless other circumstances intervene. So examining communicative events tells us a lot about how people understand their work and how they handle disruptions.

One way to represent the communicative "handoffs" is through Communication Event Models—also known as handoff chains (see Hart-Davidson 2002, 2003). Handoff chains provide a simplified, easily comparable description of event sequences—a description that can help us detect patterns in people's work, compare patterns, and see sequential divergences. Any given action is a contingent choice made in response to situational constraints. In the handoff chain, these contingent choices are essentially portrayed as strings of verbs and nouns. If we were to apply handoff chains to longer segments of work, we should be able to formally detect consistent patterns, identify larger units of interaction, and consistently explore places where sequences diverge across workers or conditions.

In a handoff chain, you record communicative events—events in which actors exchange information by exchanging texts, speech, or other signs. To find these communicative events, start with the information resources you identified in the resource map. Which ones are handed off? Based on the information resources you identify, define symbols for frequently occurring events, such as face-to-face meetings, emails, and phone calls (see figure 17.1).

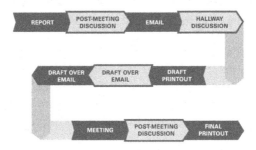

Figure 17.. A handoff chain.

Sources

As you analyze how people accomplish things at your site, you'll look for their chains of communicative events. Think in terms of

- conversations (face-to-face or through telecommunications);

- synchronous-online communication, such as IM; and

- information resources that are sent to others, including paper documents and email.

To identify communicative events, examine your data for any sort of direct exchange that participants had with other people.

Observations. Note any communication "handoffs": resources you see them give to or receive from other people or conversations they have with other people. You might use highlighters to highlight these in your field notes.

Interviews. Ask participants about those "handoffs." When do they hand off information? Why? How do they characterize or name that "handoff"? Don't be shy about asking about apparent mistakes or misunderstandings. See if they make the same distinctions about these events as you do; if they characterize face-to-face conversations and IM conversations as "updates," that might tell you that they don't draw a distinction between the two.

Artifacts. Examine the resources. Get copies of the resources your participants handed off. Get photos of their workspaces so you can see where these handoffs occurred.

Now we have a good idea of the communicative events involved. Let's go to the next step: figuring out sequences.

2. Identifying Sequences

Description

As you look over your field notes and interviews, you'll notice that these communicative events often form patterns.

- A proposal writer receives a *call for proposals*, meets with her team to distribute tasks, writes her *section*, and then circulates the *draft* to the rest of the team.

- A telecommunications worker receives a *list* of past due notices from his manager, *calls* a customer, and then makes a *note* in the *database* for his fellow workers.

If you observe people who do fairly structured or repetitive work over a short amount of time—such as calling customers whose accounts are past due—it's easy to spot sequences in communicative events. On the other hand, when people do work over longer cycles, such as proposal writing, sequences might be harder to spot. But in most work, you'll find sequences of communicative events. That's because people tend to create structure in their work. That structure helps them to make better estimates, to make better guesses about what their collaborators are doing, to optimize their work, and to recover from disruptions.

Sources

So, to get a better understanding of why people do what they do, we need to determine how people chain their communicative events into sequences.

Observations. Look for repetition in communicative events. Does this participant follow the same general sequence? Do others in her group? Do others in different groups?

Interviews. Ask participants about those communicative events. Why do they follow this sequence? Where did they learn it, or if they developed it themselves, why? Why did the sequence vary at these spots? Why is their sequence different from others'?

Artifacts. Examine how information resources and conversations are conveyed. Again, get copies of the resources and, if possible, conversations; if you can't get these, at least get photos.

At this point, you have enough information that you can develop a handoff chain.

3. Developing a Handoff Chain

Now that you have documented sequences of communicative events, you can depict these in a handoff chain. In a handoff chain, you map these events, showing regular patterns and divergences. Once you put together the handoff chain, analytical possibilities open up:

At the individual level, you can examine a participant's workflow. At this level, you can see how people hand off different resources, with whom they communicate, and especially how they bring their own innovations to the sequence. You can also map out the people they contact the most, and see how their sequence changes as they face disruptions and recover from them.

At the group level, you can compare how people in the same group, or in different groups, follow communicative sequences. At this level, you can compare their sequences to see how different people or groups accomplish their goals with different sequences. These comparisons can help you detect different innovations, especially when different groups respond to the same issue with different solutions.

To construct a handoff chain, start with a single set of field notes, artifacts, and interviews.

- Get a single sheet of paper. In one corner, write the participant's name and the observation date so you can remember which participant you're describing.

- At the top left corner of the paper, write the name of the first communicative event.

- Starting from there, write names of subsequent communicative events. Draw arrows to show the sequence. Make sure you can point to at least one piece of evidence for each arrow. (If you run out of room, draw an arrow down to the next line and start at the left.)

- Repeat the process for each of these events.

At the end of the process, you should have a handoff chain that looks something like figure 17.2.

You can repeat this process across a participant's observations, across the group, or across the organization. Consider generating separate handoff chains whenever you see significant differences. These might include

- one participant who follows a significantly different sequence;

- two different roles (e.g., account managers and web developers in the same unit);

- two different sections (e.g., two different units);

- two different offices/branches (e.g., uptown and downtown).

At this point, you should be able to show how people follow event sequences and how those sequences do or do not differ. Now let's look at the discoordinations you may have detected.

4. Detecting Discoordinations

Description

Often, work suffers from action-level disturbances called discoordinations—points at which two or more resources just don't "fit". At these points, the sequence is interrupted, and the participant has to find a way to repair the coordination before she can continue the sequence.

Sources

When you look for discoordinations, look for these characteristics in the data:

Observations. Look for points at which people diverge from the sequence. These divergences might include restarting the sequence, taking a detour, or abandoning the task.

Interviews. Ask participants about these events. Why do they think they had trouble with the sequence? Why do they go "off-script"?

Artifacts. Examine resources that are involved in discoordinations. What are their characteristics? Where did they come from? Do they represent different logics or conventions?

When you detect a discoordination, mark it in a different color of ink—I suggest red—on your handoff chain.

5. Repeating and Aggregating

Now that you've created a handoff chain for one observation, you can see and verify information flow—and the discoordinations that participants encounter during that process. Now, make handoff chains for other data sets. As you do, you may see new things: new information resources (which may include innovations and workarounds); new processes; and new disruptions.

Once you have several handoff chains depicting the same process, you can overlay them and systematically examine differences. Who hands off which information resources? Who encounters disruptions?

Exercises

- Starting with just one dataset—an observation, interview, and set of artifacts for a single participant—follow the steps above to develop a handoff chain. What sequences do you see?

- Now grab a red pen. Based on your dataset, label any discoordinations in your handoff chain. Which sequences do your participants have to restart or repeat?

- Repeat steps one and two for your other datasets. Do you see patterns emerging?

- Develop a single handoff chain that consolidates the other handoff chains. You should see a broad sequence of communicative events and the way they are connected.

Example

Figure 17.2 shows a handoff chain for the SEO case.

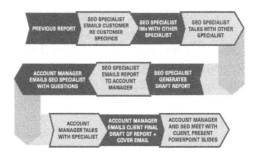

Figure 17.2. A handoff chain for the SEO case.

CHAPTER 18

Triangulation Tables

At this point, you've developed resource maps and handoff chains—that is, you have been able to visualize the sets of resources that your participants use, and you've also visualized how they use those resources in particular sequences. But that's not quite the whole picture.

Think of your research site as a football game. In handoff chains, *the camera follows the ball*, tracing through the series of handoffs and tosses that move it downfield. In resource maps, *the camera follows the game*, watching systemic dynamics and tactical changes as players and artifacts all over the field continuously reconfigure themselves.

Can we follow the ball and the game? Can we find a way to coordinate these two models? Yes: that's what we use the *triangulation table* to do. In the process, this matrix model allows us to triangulate data. Using the first two models as inputs, the triangulation tables lets us systematically compare the stories from different sets of data, helping us to see where these stories agree and where they don't (see also Chapter 11).

Better yet, the triangulation table also helps us to detect differences in the roles people take in different groupings and units.

To get to these aspects of the work, we'll follow these steps:

- Understand triangulation tables
- Build triangulation tables
- Detect discoordinations

1. Understanding Triangulation Tables

Triangulation tables come from work done by sociologist Bruno Latour and collaborators on what they called *socio-technical graphs*. Latour and his collaborators compared participants' statements about technology, looking at these statements along two dimensions: syntagmatic and paradigmatic. Think of these as "AND" and "OR" dimensions. By graphing the statements along these dimensions, they could examine how participants chained together elements in their statements. They could also see how different participants might substitute elements in these chains.

In our implementation, triangulation tables are tables in which

- **columns** represent communicative events from the handoff chains;

- **rows** represent different points of comparison—different data sources, participants, roles, groups or locations; and

- **cells** contain information resources that are used for a given communicative event within a given point of comparison.

For instance, table 18.1 shows a triangulation table in which the researcher examines a single participant's work, using two different data sources: field notes from the observation and the post-observation interview. Notice that this triangulation table helps us relate communicative events from the handoff chain to the information resources from the resource map. And it helps us to see how our field notes differ from the participant's account. It helps us to triangulate the two data sources; we can see how closely they line up and where they disagree or are partial. See the italics in each cell; these are resources that are mentioned in just one account.

Table 18.1. A triangulation table for a single participant.

	Prepare for call	Contact customer and discuss bill	Record notes on call
Arnold: Field notes	Collections list, annotations on collections list, database *screen for customer, database screen for customer's collections information*	Phone call to customer, *collections list, database screen for customer's collections information*	*Database screen for customer's collections information, fax cover sheet, sticky note,* collections list
Arnold: Interview	Collections list, annotations on collections list, *bankruptcy notices, spiral notebook, phone calls from coworkers*	*Bills*, phone call to customer	Collections list, *annotations to collections list, database notes, database screen for customer*

Now, suppose we do the same thing for multiple participants. We can collapse the list of resources from both data sources into one list for each participant then compare the participants. We begin to turn up similarities and differences in how individual participants work. Triangulating at this level helps us to do the following:

- Figure out which resources are "core" resources—the bare minimum for executing each communicative event.

- Spot innovations that one participant uses and others don't.

For instance, in table 18.2, Clara uses a resource that the others don't use: a log of previous customer interactions. Does this log function as a substitute for some of the resources that others use, such as Arnold's spiral notebook? The triangulation table helps us to spot differences and reexamine our data—including our copies of the spiral notebook and the log—to answer questions about how participants work differently. Through this triangulation, the triangulation table helps us to catch innovations and workarounds, showing how these substitute for other resources.

Table 18.2. A triangulation table for multiple participants.

	Prepare for call	**Contact customer and discuss bill**	**Record notes on call**
Arnold	Collections list, annotations on collections list, database screen for customer, database screen for customer's collections information, bankruptcy notices, *spiral notebook, phone calls from coworkers*	Phone call to customer, collections list, database screen for customer's collections information, bills	Database screen for customer's collections information, fax cover sheet, sticky note, collections list, annotations to collections list, *database notes, database screen for customers*
Bill	Collections list, annotations on collections list, database screen for customer, database screen for customer's collections information, bankruptcy notices	Phone call to customer, collections list, database screen for customer's collections information, bills, spiral notebook of call log	Database screen for customer's collections information, collections list, annotations to collections list, phone call to supervisor
Clara	Collections list, annotations on collections list, database screen for customer, database screen for customer's collections information, *log of previous customer interactions*	Phone call to customer, collections list, database screen for customer's collections information, *log of previous customer interactions*	Database screen for customer's collections information, collections list, annotations to collections list, *log of previous customer interactions*

If the organization is large enough, you may triangulate to spot differences in how groups do their work. Groups can be

- participants doing the same work at different locations;

- participants taking on the same role at the same location and in the same workflow;

- participants at the same location, working in the same role, but with different characteristics (e.g., training, experience, access).

For instance, if a company has two offices, it's common for the offices to develop different ways of doing things due to different technologies, training, backgrounds, expectations, or innovations. A group-level triangulation table can help you spot those differences as well. Table 18.3 shows how two offices might handle the same communicative events differently, and how the second office has managed to use one resource to substitute for many.

Table 18.3. A triangulation table for different groups.

	Prepare for call	**Contact customer and discuss bill**	**Record notes on call**
Group A	Collections list, annotations on collections list, database screen for customer, database screen for customer's collections information, bankruptcy notices, spiral notebook, phone calls from coworkers	Phone call to customer, collections list, database screen for customer's collections information, bills	Database screen for customer's collections information, fax cover sheet, sticky note, collections list, annotations to collections list, database notes, database screen for customer
Group B	Collections list, *customer folder with contact information and last bill*	Phone call to customer, *customer folder with contact information and last bill, calendar*	*Customer folder with contact information and last bill, Word template, email*

2. Building Triangulation Tables

To build triangulation tables, you'll determine what you want to compare or triangulate—data sources for one participant, accounts for individual participants, or accounts for groups—and use your resource maps and handoff chains to build the table.

A. Choosing What to Compare

First, decide what you want to compare.

- If you have few participants and your data sources (i.e., interviews, observations, etc.) don't seem to overlap much, build a triangulation table for one participant at a time.

- If you have many participants and data sources seem to agree, or if you've already built triangulation tables based on data sources, build a triangulation table for multiple participants.

- If you notice strong similarities within groups and dissimilarities across groups, or if you've already built triangulation tables for participants, build a triangulation table for groups.

Your comparison categories will provide your *row headings*: the cells in the left column. See tables 18.1-18.3.

B. Choosing Events to Examine

Next, choose events to examine. The events will come directly from your handoff chains, especially events that are often repeated. These events become the column headings: the table cells in the top row. See tables 18.1-18.3.

C. Filling in the Resources

Now you can methodically compare the resources used by each comparison point. Consulting your resource maps, fill in each of the remaining cells with information resources that are involved in each communicative event for each comparison point. See tables 18.1-18.3.

Make sure that each resource you mention is backed up with at least one piece of evidence, preferably more. For instance, see the resources listed in table 18.2. If challenged, you should be able to demonstrate from your field notes, interviews, and/or other research data that each of those resources was used by that participant to complete that communicative event. Don't guess. Don't assume. Prove!

D. Mapping the Differences

Finally, we are ready to examine differences across the triangulation table. The previous steps have helped you to join your resource maps and handoff chains, yielding a triangulated, confirmable, systematically generated map of resources used to mediate events. Now, you should be able to easily detect the core resources that everyone uses together, as well as substitutions that allow individuals and groups to work differently. Such substitutions often include innovations and workarounds.

Highlight these differences, perhaps using italics (see tables 18.1-18.3) or a highlighter.

At the end of the process, you should have one or more triangulation tables that look something like tables 18.1-18.3.

3. Detecting Discoordinations

Finally, recall that you used handoff chains and resource maps to detect discoordinations—points at which two or more resources just don't "fit".

- In resource maps, you detected these by looking for points at which people had trouble relating the resources, especially when they resorted to workarounds.

- In handoff chains, you detected these through interruptions in the sequence and repairs that got participants back on track.

Use triangulation tables to map these discoordinations in the appropriate cells. To do this, look at disruptions you have already identified in resource maps and handoff chains.

1. For each cell, note whether it involved one or more disruptions. For instance, in Table 18.2, how many disruptions did Arnold encounter when preparing for a call? Once you

tally up the number of disruptions, insert that number in the cell—in red.

2. Once you've done that for each cell, stand back and look at the whole table. Where are disruptions clustering? Think of the triangulation table as a dashboard. If you see red down an entire column, you know there's something wrong with that step. If you see red across an entire row, you know that Arnold is encountering disruptions across the whole process; maybe his training was different from others'? And if you see that everyone is having trouble with a step except Clara, you know that she's doing something right. Maybe she has developed an innovative workaround that the others could use.

Suppose you review table 18.2, mapping discoordinations from the resource maps and handoff chains of individual participants. Every time you notice a discoordination in your resource maps and handoff chains, you put a red tally mark in the corresponding cell of the triangulation table. When you're done, you notice that Arnold and Bill experience multiple discoordinations when preparing for a call, but Clara only encounters one. That suggests that Clara has found some sort of solution or workaround for the discoordination—an innovation that could provide a starting point for redesigning the work.

What could that innovation be? We can easily compare the resources used by the different participants, so we see at a glance that *only Clara* uses a log. Is that the difference? Go back to the primary data to confirm.

Exercises

- Develop a triangulation table for one person, modeling it after table 18.1. Do you see any differences between the participant's account (in her or his interview and your account in your observational notes?

- If the participant encountered any discoordinations in this session, mark them in the appropriate cell. Where do the discoordinations show up? Are they localized in one part of the process or spread throughout?

- Now, develop a triangulation table that compares participants, modeling it after table 18.2. What substitutions do you see? And where do the discoordinations occur?

In groups:

- Examine the meso-level models (i.e., resource map, handoff chain, triangulation table).

- Based on your data, identify the discoordinations in the resource map and handoff chain.

- Mark the discoordinations on the resource map and handoff chain.

- Compile the discoordinations on the triangulation table.

- Be ready to discuss, using specific evidence from your data.

Example

Table 18.4. A triangulation table for the SEO case.

	Prepare for report	**Write report**	**Deliver report**
Elizair	Previous month's report, highlighting and annotations on previous month's report, emails with client, spreadsheet of projects, IMs and talks with Craig, WikiAnswers	Emails from customers, SEObrateMAX, report template, notes, email to Sonia	Final draft of report, client presentation, PowerPoint slides
Craig	Previous month's report, highlighting and annotations on previous month's report, emails with client, keyword logs, text file listing projects, IMs and talks with Dani	Emails from customers, SEObrateMAX, report template, notes, email to Sonia	Final draft of report, client presentation, PowerPoint slides
Dani	Previous month's report, highlighting and annotations on previous month's report, emails with client, notebook listing projects, IMs and talks with Craig	Emails from customers, SEObrateMAX, report template, notes, email to Sonia	Final draft of report, client presentation, PowerPoint slides
Sonia		Email from Elizair, emails with customers, talk with Elizair	Final draft of report, cover email to client, client presentation, PowerPoint slides

CHAPTER 19

Breakdown Tables

Up to this point, we've been examining work on the meso level: goal-directed actions that participants are consciously trying to accomplish. So far, so good. But we still need to dive down to the micro level—the level of habits and reactions—the level of keystrokes and mouse clicks.

These habits and reactions are called *operations*, and they begin as conscious, meso-level actions.

For instance, suppose you're learning how to drive a stick shift. At first, you have to consciously focus on pushing in the clutch, moving the stick shift to the next gear, then letting the clutch out again. You may even look at the clutch pedal or the stick shift.

After a short while, shifting gears becomes habit. You don't think of it as a long set of steps – you think of it as "shifting gears," and you may even stop noticing that you're taking these steps. The steps have become operations, unconscious and habitual. You're free to focus on other things; instead of pushing in the clutch and moving the stick shift, you focus on driving.

But sometimes you encounter *breakdowns*, points at which your learned, habitual operations don't work as planned. For instance, suppose that you rent a car, and the clutch is firmer than your own car's or, maybe, you're used to driving a four-speed and the rental car is a five-speed. Worse, perhaps your clutch starts going out, so your car won't stay in gear! So your habits don't produce the usual results.

When that happens, you have to refocus on that which is usually habitual. You become conscious of the individual steps, and you have a harder time refocusing on the higher-level tasks you're trying to accomplish, like driving.

We encounter breakdowns all the time. When you hit the wrong key, when you click on the wrong item with your mouse, when you reach for your coffee cup and discover it's not there, those are all breakdowns. When you say, "Huh?" or, "Uh oh!" that's usually a breakdown.

Not every breakdown is important or illuminating to people's work. People make mistakes. But when you find someone encountering the same breakdown repeatedly, or when several people encounter breakdowns dealing with the same artifact; that suggests that you've found a systemic issue or set of issues. You can model these issues with another matrix model, the *breakdown table*.

How do you Identify Operations and Breakdowns?

The ideal way to identify operations and their associated breakdowns is to collect fine-grained observational data. These might include

- videotaping participants;

- using system logging to record all interactions with the computer; and

- tagging and electronically tracking all artifacts in the participant's workspace.

Unfortunately, these data collection methods are hard to pull off; they require special equipment and a high level of cooperation by your participants. You can still do these (see Spinuzzi 2003; Slattery 2007). If you can't manage this level of data collection, though, you can use detailed field notes and look for

- external indications of breakdowns—points at which your participant says "Huh?" or "Uh oh!";

- points at which participants retrace steps; and

- points at which participants undo work – such as deleting a piece of text they have just written, hitting the Cancel button, or using the eraser.

These usually involve diverging from the normal sequence. After all, when your participants encounter breakdowns, they must change focus so that they can recover.

- Look for the regular sequences you've identified through your handoff chains. Find divergences.

- Look up those divergences in the field notes. Do they appear to reflect breakdowns? And how did they recover?

- If you talked with the participants about these instances, examine the interviews. Did they interpret these instances as breakdowns?

- If you collected artifacts related to the breakdowns, examine them. Do they show signs of mistakes, retracing, or corrections? Do they corroborate your field notes and interviews?

- If you collected data logs, diaries, or video; you can code these to map out breakdowns as well.

How Do You Depict Operations and Breakdowns?

You can see examples of operations graphs and matrices in Spinuzzi (2003) and Slattery (2007). But if you're gathering your operations-level data from field notes, I suggest something simpler. Focus on the breakdowns and what people did to recover from them—to refocus from their steps back to their work. Table 19.1, below, is a good format to use.

Table 19.1. A breakdown table.

Participant	Breakdown	Recovery

A breakdown table allows you to

- Catalogue breakdowns and repairs

- Consolidate breakdowns in one place so you can see where they cluster

- Hypothesize relationships to participants, roles, tools, and other parts of the work

Of course, not every breakdown is going to be significant. We make mistakes for all sorts of reasons, some of which are simply happenstance. But this table will alert you to some breakdowns that may or may not be part of larger, more integrated problems.

Exercises

- Look through your field notes for indications of breakdowns. Perhaps your participant restarted the sequence, uttered an unprintable word, clicked the Cancel button, or reached for the eraser. What happened? And how did they recover?

- Examine the interviews for more insight into the breakdown. Did the participant describe it or discuss what happened?

- In groups:

- Look for the regular sequences identified through your hand-off chains. Find divergences.

- Look up those divergences in the field notes. Do they reflect breakdowns? And how did participants recover?

- Examine interviews. Did participants interpret these instances as breakdowns?

- Examine related artifacts. Do they show signs of mistakes, retracing, or corrections? Do they corroborate your field notes and interviews?

- If you collected data logs, diaries, or video, examine these to map out breakdowns as well.

Example

In the office study, Dani encounters several breakdowns from which she must recover. Table 19.2 shows a few of these, taken from the observation notes.

Table 19.2. Breakdowns table for the SEO case

Participant	Breakdown	Recovery
Dani	Excel: Accidentally enters date range in graph, resulting in straight line.	Copies proper range and pastes in Excel.
Dani	Excel: Graph only shows one line.	Deletes graph, selects entire data range, pastes into Excel.
Dani	SEObrateMAX: Fills out info for client. SEObrateMAX hangs.	Cancels, hits Try Again.

CHAPTER 20

Activity Systems

At this point, you've used models to examine work at the meso and micro levels. But there's another level: the macro level, which is the level of organization, culture, and history.

That doesn't mean that we'll thoroughly examine organizational culture with this model—for that kind of work, I suggest using another approach, such as ethnography. Here, our focus isn't culture per se, but how to understand how the organization's macro-level workings impact what we've seen at the meso and micro levels. In particular, we'll look at how the organization has developed over time, what values it has developed, what object it has set for itself, and how contradictions drive innovations in the organization. We will accomplish this goal with a specific type of network model called an *activity system*.

At the macro level, activities are

- strategic;

- long-term;

- objective-oriented; and

- cyclical.

Start with the activity system that is evident in the space(s) you directly observed. The *objective* is the key. Identify it first, and then the rest of the activity system will come into focus.

Developing the Activity System

The activity system is a way of systematically examining the overall activity at your research site. *Why* do people do what they do? How has the site developed to meet its objectives and outcomes? What are the motivations, desires, and values that shape and drive this work?

In this section, we'll refer to the Activity System Components Worksheet (figure 20.1) as we develop an activity system for the research site. The top half of figure 20.1 describes how individuals perform the activity; the bottom half describes how individual work is supported by a larger group.

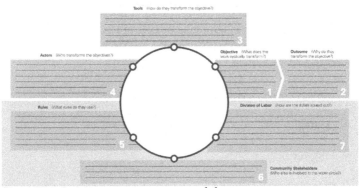

Figure 20.1. Activity system components worksheet.

Right now, we're just generating a systematic idea of how the activity works. Soon, we'll examine how it interacts with other activities and where it has developed contradictions.

1. What Does the Work Cyclically Transform? (The Objective)

Description:

The *objective* is that which the work transforms over and over.

- Farmers transform empty fields into full ones that can be harvested.

- Doctors transform sick people into well people.

- Factories transform raw materials into products.

- Graphic designers transform a company's direction and ideas into an identity system.

The objective is the seed of the activity system. The objective is the recurring issue, problem, or opportunity around which an activity system forms. People, tools, rules, and so forth are aligned to make sure that this transformation happens, whether the transformation is a product, market, or service.

These transformations can and do happen at different scales. For instance, a web development group may form around the objective of keeping a website fresh and accessible. But that web development group might be a unit in a larger organization, such as a mobile phone manufacturer. And their activity might help the manufacturer to continue to market its products: more on that in a moment.

Sources:

To identify the objective, start small. Think in terms of a unit, such as the web development group above.

Interviews. Ask people what their unit does.

Artifacts. Examine the unit's mission or vision statement, plans, and collateral. Sometimes these are vague or overblown, but they will give you ideas about what the unit is doing.

Archives. Look at the history. How has the unit evolved? Look at what has changed and what hasn't.

Now that we have an idea of the objective, let's go to the outcome.

2. Why Do They Transform the Objective? (The Outcome)

Description

We now know what the "seed" of the activity system is—the objective. But why do they keep pouring their effort into transforming it? What's the intended outcome?

When we talk about the outcome, we might think of it as the motivation, but motivation is an individual term. Activity systems are systems of people, tools, and rules. They often last longer than individuals. So what are they set up to achieve?

Think in terms of the activity's strategic direction here: motivations, desires, and values. Understanding these will help you to make sense of why people conduct their activity in a certain way.

- Farmers may want to turn a profit—or maintain a family tradition.

- Doctors may want to build a thriving practice—or make their community a healthier place.

- Factories may aim at higher short-term production—or a more stable business that supports long-term viability.

- Graphic designers may want to help convey a client's message—or generate strong pieces for their portfolios.

Sometimes the activity's desired outcome is not what you might assume, and understanding that outcome is key to understanding why the activity is organized the way it is. For instance, farmers who simply *want to turn a profit* will make different choices about crops, organization, and tools than those who see themselves as *maintaining a family tradition*.

And, of course, sometimes the activity attempts to achieve *multiple* outcomes. As we'll see in the section below on contradictions, interference between these outcomes can lead to systemic destabilizations.

Sources:

To identify the outcome, think big. Think in terms of the unit's values, its strategic direction, and the criteria used to evaluate it in annual reviews.

Interviews. Ask people how they hope their unit is making a difference, and how their unit is evaluated.

Artifacts. Examine the unit's mission or vision statement, plans, and collateral again. Especially look at values, direction, and future projections. If you can get your hands on annual reviews, do so.

Archives. Look at the history. When the unit has evolved, what has been abandoned? How has the unit been evaluated?

3. How Do They Transform the Objective? (The Tools)

Description

Now that you know what is being transformed and why, ask *how* is it being transformed. The answer is usually going to be long, because the typical activity uses many, many tools or mediational means to get things done. In fact, you'll observe an entire ecology of information resources, especially texts, in work.

Watch out for anything that someone uses to transform the objective. For instance, the web developers might use web browsers, web standards, technical references, graphics programs, and testing suites to produce and update their websites. But they may also use communications tools to coordinate their work on the site: IM, texting, writing on printed pages, sticky notes on each other's desks, and whiteboards. They might use hacks, tips, and tricks to deal with different challenges. They might also use specific written or diagrammed processes to get this work done. All of these are mediational means – tools.

Sources:

To identify the mediational means, look around. What do people touch and use? What do they report touching and using? What can't they live without?

Observations. Your key technique will be to observe people as they work. What do they touch? What do they pile or stack or arrange on their desks? What do they draw on? What do they attach to other things? Most importantly in knowledge work, what do they write on, annotate, type, or share?

Interviews. Ask people about the mediational means they used in interviews. They'll sometimes forget what tools they use and why. Prompt them with your list from the observations then ask if you've missed anything.

Artifacts. Examine the mediational means you saw the people using. Especially information resources.

4. Who Transforms the Objective? (The Actors)

Description

You've identified the objective, outcome, and mediational means. Now, for the easy part: who's involved?

Well, sometimes it's not so easy. If you're studying a small unit, such as the web development unit, you can probably find all of the people at their desks or on an org chart. But when you examine larger activity systems, you may find that things get more complicated. Maybe a key team member works off-site, or isn't even part of the official organization. I once interviewed a grant writer for a nonprofit, and found that two key collaborators were her husband and son, who would review her drafts for her!

To identify the actors, look for anyone who is using the mediational means to transform the object.

Sources:

To identify the actors, you'll have to trust your eyes, but also your ears. Watch the people, but also ask them who else is involved. Who does work on the objective?

Observations. Your key technique will be to observe people as they work. Who touches or contributes to the objective? Who uses the mediational means with that objective in mind? Their job titles or positions might give a clue, but look beyond them to how people are actually acting.

Interviews. Ask people whom their collaborators are—who else is working on this objective (i.e., issue, problem, opportunity, etc.). Ask how and why they interact with others in the workplace. Ask about phone calls, emails, IMs, and texts. Ask where their mediational means came from.

Artifacts. Examine the mediational means you saw the people using, and find out who else has touched them, where they came from, and where they go next.

5. What Rules Do They Follow? (The Rules)

Description

We already talked about set processes that people use as mediational means. But when we look at rules, we are more interested in the ways people expect themselves and others to behave in the community or between communities. Think in terms of formal guidelines and protocols, but also dos-and-don'ts, guidelines, unwritten rules, and "the way things are done".

For instance, I once talked with graphic designers about how they conducted themselves with clients. One said, "There are some clients you can cuss with and some you can't." His business partner followed up with an example that is, unfortunately, unprintable. That's an example of an unwritten rule that the graphic designers had developed over time to deal with other communities with which they had to interact.

Sources:

To identify rules, look for standards of conduct that are followed in a community or set of interrelated communities. These might be as binding as a legal code, as rigid as a code of conduct, as explicit as a set of procedures, as idealistic as a manifesto, or as unwritten as the graphic designers' rule about cussing.

Observations. Start with what you see. How do people conduct themselves? What seems unusual to you as an outsider? Do people change their conduct when dealing with people in different communities? Do people have rules, procedures, or guidelines posted in their workspaces?

Interviews. Ask about those differences in your interviews. How do they conduct themselves in different situations? How do they expect others to conduct themselves? Do they follow rulebooks, procedural manuals, or other standards?

Artifacts. Examine any artifacts, especially information resources that indicate written rules. Common resources such as posted guidelines or manuals are great, but you may also find very informal resources, such as a sticky note by the telephone reminding someone to, "Be friendly!"

6. Who Else is Involved in the Wider Circle? (The Community Stakeholders)

Description

People don't just come from nowhere and start working at a job. We're all in different communities—broader, pre-existing groups with shared ideas, values, or characteristics. In the workplace, obvious examples are fields, trades, and disciplines.

For instance, in one study I conducted at a telecommunications company, service technicians worked to establish and maintain service for the company's customers. They had to work with salespeople, switch technicians, the network operations center, provisioners, and others in the company. But they also had to work with service technicians at rival companies—others who were in the same trade, even though they weren't in the same company. Switch technicians shared terms and training background across companies, and they also shared the same viewpoint. They had a set of community stakeholders who intersected the different companies.

That's important, because we get values and viewpoints from our communities.

Sources:

To identify community stakeholders, you'll need to think in terms of professional background. What fields, trades, or disciplines are in the actors' backgrounds? How were they educated and trained, and do they continue to be trained? How do they describe themselves? What are their titles, and what titles and jobs did they hold before now?

Interviews: Here, the key technique is the interview. Ask people about their job history, how they describe themselves, and where they were educated. Ask for their job title. Consider asking for a resume or look at their online portfolio or LinkedIn. Finally, ask them to describe other groups in their unit. Sometimes, they'll come up with surprising groupings that indicate community stakeholders.

Observations: You may also be able to see communities through people's interactions. Do certain people group together?

Artifacts: Examine the organizational chart, if there is one.

7. Spread Out How? (The Division of Labor)

Description

So at this point, you have a good idea of what actors are doing to transform the objective, using certain mediational means, obeying certain rules, and drawing on the values and expertise of certain communities. But how are they dividing up the labor? That is to say, who does what, and how do they decide? How are jobs handed out and broken up? Who do people contact? Who do they find themselves waiting on?

Sometimes divisions of labor are obvious—based on job description or specialty. If you're studying a web development shop with coders and graphic designers, you can make a pretty good guess about how they divide big chunks of their work. But sometimes people develop divisions of labor based on convenience, habit, or strengths. For instance, maybe the coders have an agreement about who works with web forms or who makes the coffee in the morning. Sometimes people adopt divisions of labor based on history. One common example is that of student organizations, which usually include officers such as the president, vice-president, secretary, and treasurer, because those are the officers that most organizations have—even if they don't make sense for a given student organization!

Teasing out the division of labor will give you clues about how and why people split their duties, why people become experts in certain things, and often, why bottlenecks form.

Sources:

To identify the division of labor, start with the communities you've identified. But go beyond that to see how they identify local expertise and how they associate people with tasks. When someone says, "That's Alan's job"—whether they're talking about a decision, a product, a process, or simply who makes the coffee; they're talking about a division of labor. When they regularly pass a certain information resource to Alan for processing, and get a different resource back, that's a division of labor too. How do you capture these?

Observations. Observe how people handle information and artifacts at the site. Does an individual or group always give a certain resource to others? Does an individual or group characterize others, such as, "They always do things that way"?

Interviews. Confirm those observations. Start with what you find about communities. Do the divisions you observed break down along community lines? Why do these divisions form?

Artifacts. As with communities, start with the organizational chart, if there is one. But also examine the artifacts, particularly resources that get passed between divisions. How are they processed, annotated, changed, or fed into other resources?

Characterizing the Activity

Now that you have developed the activity system, you can step back and characterize it more fully. To do that, start again with the objective: the thing that the activity is meant to cyclically transform. Understanding that objective can help you to understand why the activity is configured the way it is. To better understand the objective, examine two aspects:

Is it known or emergent? Some activities are set up to transform the same objective in the same way, over and over, with very little variation. The objective is *known*. For instance, a factory churns out hundreds of machines that are as identical as possible. A school educates children so that they all reach the same competencies. A utility delivers water that meets EPA requirements for water quality. In all of these cases, the endpoint is known and the activity isn't successful unless it achieves that endpoint over and over.

But other activities are set up to reach emergent objectives; each objective is unique and the participants in the activity don't know the endpoint until they get there. These objectives are usually creative. For instance, artwork, graphic design work, and open-ended problem solving work this way. Sometimes business pitches work this way too. An emergent objective involves an interplay among the actors and community stakeholders: they must collectively decide when the objective has been reached.

Is it internal or shared? Some objectives are internal to the activity. For instance, if an organization assigns a task force to develop an employee training manual, that objective is probably internal: It will be used to help new employees as they begin working inside the organization. The employee manual probably won't be posted on the website or given to stockholders—and those other audiences wouldn't likely be interested in it anyway.

On the other hand, some objectives are shared across activities. For instance, a software company might develop a new mobile app specifically for sharing documents in enterprises. They don't want to keep that app to themselves; they want it to be bought by users and integrated in those users' activities. And they will price it so that it can compete against other solutions.

When you characterize the objective in these two ways, you may notice a pattern. As Figure 20.2 shows, the kind of objective implies the way the activity is organized.

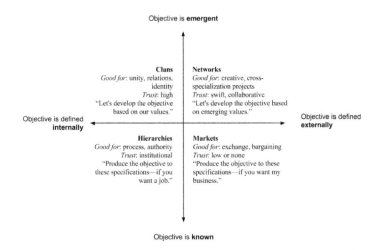

Figure 20.2. Organization types and the objectives they tend to produce. (Based on Spinuzzi 2015.)

For instance, a factory will tend to be run as a *hierarchy*, with definite lines of authority and tight tolerances, because that's the easiest way to transform an objective and get the same result each time. On the other hand, if the object is a creative solution that taps the expertise of different groups, you'll tend to find that the activity is organized as a *network*.

Of course, the larger the scope of your activity, the more likely it is to use several different forms of organization. For instance, in the SEO case, specialists worked on creative problems in a network configuration—but performance reviews, hiring, and firing happened via a hierarchical configuration.

Sometimes these different configurations mesh well. But sometimes they don't. And in that case, we can describe that failure to mesh as a *contradiction*.

Detecting Contradictions in the Activity System

Contradictions are points at which an activity system encounters basic frictions at or across the elements. Like activities, contradictions take a bit of time to form, and can take a long time to work themselves out, if they are tractable at all.

In this section, we'll refer to the Activity System Contradictions Worksheet (figure 20.3). We'll look at two kinds of contradictions:

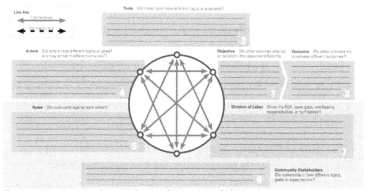

Figure 20.3. Activity System Contradictions Worksheet.

Within a point. For instance, suppose that the activity system involves two tools that are incompatible, usually originating in two different activities. Or suppose that the system has two contradictory rules. For instance, salespeople might be told to focus on corporate rather than residential accounts, but they might also be told that they must fill a sales quota, which sometimes requires them to pick up residential accounts.

Across points. For instance, perhaps someone must fill out a form that assumes they have certain information, but because of the local division of labor, someone else has it.

As we'll see in the next chapter, there's a third kind of contradiction. So we'll return to this worksheet in that chapter, once we look for that kind of contradiction, and add it to the others.

Contradictions are strategic disturbances. They're tensions that form and often increase as activities develop. But they're also a source of innovations. When you see innovations, workarounds, or clever practices in the activity; they are usually symptoms of contradictions.

One more thing: although we can *detect* contradictions, that doesn't mean we will be able to *solve* them, nor that we *should*!

Sometimes contradictions are so embedded and intractable that they have to work themselves out over time. Maybe an organization faces a contradiction in which it gives lip service to equality and fairness, but actually operates unequally (e.g., a "good old boy network"). Although you might point out the issue, you probably won't be able to resolve it with a recommendation report.

Sometimes contradictions, as sites of innovation and change, are actually productive for the organization. For instance, you might find that an organization faces a "culture clash" in its cross-functional teams; team members from different parts of the organization see things very differently, and thus they disagree on how to understand and address tasks. On the surface, this contradiction may lead to arguments. But if those arguments are productive—if the teams can avoid the mistakes that they might make, if they all came from the same perspective—then the contradiction is actually a useful site of innovation.

Exercises

- Now that you have a good idea how to examine your site as an activity, fill out Figure 20.1. Base your descriptions on the data you collected, and make sure you can point to a piece of data for every assertion you make about the activity.

- Use Figure 20.2 to help you characterize the activity. Is it focused on an internal objective or a shared one? Is the endpoint of the objective known or emergent?

- Use Figure 20.3 to identify possible contradictions. Not every activity has a blatant contradiction, and certainly activities usually don't have every single type of contradiction. What contradictions can you detect? Base your descriptions on the data you collected, and make sure you can point to a piece of data for every assertion you make about each contradiction.

- **Within a point.** Do two sets of tools have different logics? Do different actors come from very different backgrounds? Look for critical differences at each point.

- **Across points.** Do different communities of stakeholders expect different rules to be in play? Do the tools assume a division of labor that's not in place at the site? Look for critical differences across points.

Example

Figure 20.4 and 20.5 show activity system components and contradictions for the SEO case.

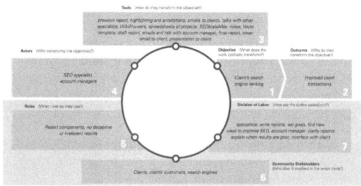

Figure 20.4. Activity system components for the SEO case.

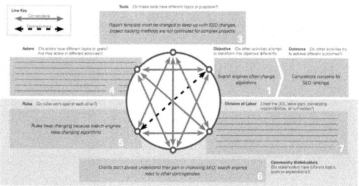

Figure 20.5. Activity system contradictions for the SEO case.

CHAPTER 21

Activity Networks

In Chapter 20, we saw how to model macro-level activities and the contradictions that build up within them. But these activities also connect to other activities, and these can develop contradictions *between* them.

Think about it this way. Activities don't exist in isolation; they're interlinked and thus impacted by each other. If your organization is a restaurant, for instance, it gets a lot of *rules* from the health department; *tools* come from suppliers (e.g., someone prints the menus and provides software for managing seating arrangements); actors come from all over (e.g., cooking schools, high schools, and universities); and so forth. Your restaurant is impacted by all of these linked activities.

Sometimes those impacts include contradictions. For instance, perhaps your restaurant has special seating, but the seating software doesn't provide a way to handle it. Perhaps the local cooking school doesn't specialize in the kind of food your restaurant serves. Perhaps the health department mandates signs that don't make sense. For instance, in Texas, I often see signs informing us that pregnant women shouldn't drink alcohol. These signs are posted in *men's restrooms*, where pregnant women presumably will not see them.

We won't be able to map out every single link to other activities. But sometimes we can detect specific, deep ways that other activities impact the one we're examining; that's when we put together an *activity network*: a network model that lets you map out how activity systems interact.

Developing the Activity Network

Figure 21.1 shows an activity network, which we'll discuss throughout the chapter.

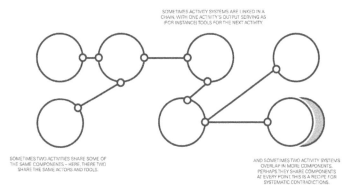

Figure 21.1. An Activity Network.

To help you develop your own activity network, we'll begin with the Activity System Links Worksheet (figure 21.1), starting from our original activity system to find links from the research site's activity to adjoining activities. This worksheet helps us to look for impacts like the ones we saw in the restaurant example at the beginning of the chapter. Once we've filled it out, we'll map out how this activity interacts with other activities. And doing so helps us to understand some of the quirks we may be seeing at our sites, quirks that can't be explained by looking at the site itself.

Activities can network with each other in two ways: chained and overlapping.

Chained activities

As the Activity System Links Worksheet suggests, each corner of an activity system comes from somewhere. Sometimes it is developed within the activity, but often it is developed somewhere else and imported. But from where?

Tools. We pick up tools from other activities. Sometimes they come to us as part of a chain. For instance, in the restaurant example, someone designed the seating software, which was their *objective*. Then they sell it to us, and it becomes our *tool*.

Actors. People in an activity don't just appear there; they are trained or educated somewhere then hired, drafted, or otherwise persuaded to join in an activity. Their past experiences, training, and norms are sometimes carried into the new activity. For instance, if someone is trained to manage their tasks with to-do lists in school, they will likely carry that strategy into the job they get after graduation.

Community. The actors interact in communities, including trades, fields, and disciplines. Graphic designers, for instance, have professional organizations and contacts beyond their own workplace. So do cooks and chefs. Those communities have their own values and expectations, which are carried into the new activity and sometimes don't match with that activity's values and expectations. For instance, although graphic designers want to solve their clients' problems, they also want to create pieces that could win AIGA awards—and the two audiences may have different sets of criteria.

Rules. Professional standards, legal standards, and rules of politeness often come from outside the activity. For instance, a restaurant has to follow health regulations that it did not invent; a graphic designer may want to follow professional standards of originality that are not significant to the client.

Division of Labor. Similarly, the division of labor might come from somewhere else. For instance, someone who forms her own company might take the organization of other companies as a model; a student organization may need to fill officer positions that are required by the university.

Objective. Finally, the activity's objective may be the input for some other activity. For instance, web developers might spend time developing and updating a website for a company. That website can serve as a *tool* for customers wanting to buy the company's products and services.

The first step in mapping out these interconnections is to start with your activity system. In the last chapter, you described the components of your site's activity system. Now you'll build on that work: use Figure 21.2 to find out where each of those components comes from.

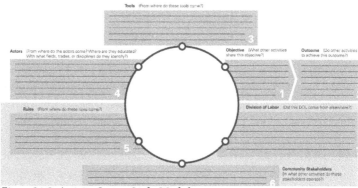

Figure 21.2. Activity System Links Worksheet.

To understand the links to other activities, follow these steps.

- **Fill out the Activity System Links worksheet**. As you do,

- base your descriptions on the data you collected, and make sure you can point to a piece of data for every link you assert about the activity.

- If you aren't sure about a component, put a question mark in the box, then investigate further. You might look over your data again or collect additional data.

- **Consider mapping out some of the linked activities**. If your data indicate strong intersections between your site's activity and these other chained activities—for instance, if some of the tools are clearly designed for different actors—strongly consider mapping out these activity systems as well. You can develop the Activity System Components Worksheet and the Activity System Links Worksheet for each of these contributing activities.

Once you have followed these steps, you'll have a good idea of how the components of your activity flow *from* other activities or *into* other activities. But activities can also relate in a second way: they can overlap.

Overlapping Activities

Activity systems aren't just chained together. Sometimes they intersect in other ways. For instance, two activities can share the same objective. In fact, as we saw in the last chapter, objectives are frequently shared in *network* and *market* configurations. In these configurations, the objective is by definition the focus of at least two different activities, each of which is trying to transform it in a different way.

Let's consider an example: a web design team. In this case, the team's objective is the website, but that website is also the objective of other teams: the web design team wants to make it *effective and attractive*, while the company's legal team want to make it *accurate and compliant with legal restrictions*. These two aims (that is, these ways of transforming the objective) aren't necessarily incompatible, but they are different. They share the same objective—the website—but they need to transform it in entirely different ways.

This overlapping usually requires the two activity systems to develop ways to coordinate their efforts. If handled improperly, it can lead to frictions and mistakes: more on that in a moment.

But other components might also be shared. Suppose that someone at your research site has other relationships with her customer. Maybe they go to the same church; maybe they belong to the same club: maybe they're married—or divorced. The same actors interact in two different activities, using two sets of rules, communities, etc.

To detect these instances, take a second look at the Activity System Links Worksheet.

- Does the activity overlap other activities you can identify?

- Rather than originating somewhere else, are the components active in different activities in ways that identifiably overlap?

- Are other activities attempting to transform the same objective?

- Are other activities attempting to achieve the same outcome?

- Do other activities share components of the activity system in identifiable ways?

As you ask these questions, look for evidence for each point. You may have to do some follow-up investigation. For instance, if you're studying the web design team, you may see some evidence that they are fighting with the legal team about the content of the site; you can confirm this disagreement by talking to someone in Legal or looking at the legal team's mission statement.

Detecting Contradictions in the Activity Network

In the last chapter, we saw that activity systems tend to develop internal contradictions. But contradictions build up *between* activities as well. In fact, in the examples above, you can see how these contradictions can easily develop.

In this section, we'll systematically examine such contradictions. To do so, we will return to the Activity System Contradictions Worksheet that we began in the last chapter. This time, we'll look at another kind of contradiction.

Across activities. For instance, suppose that the web developers have created an elegant site that provides clear information to customers, but the legal department insists that they include a long disclaimer on each page, wrecking the design.

As I said in the last chapter, contradictions are strategic disturbances—tensions that form and often increase as activities develop. But because they create tensions, they also tend to produce innovations. When you see participants creating and using innovations and workarounds, they are usually trying to address contradictions in the work. When those contradictions happen across activities, you may find considerable opportunities for improving how those activities interact.

To explore these contradictions, use the Activity System Contradictions Worksheet. Identify possible contradictions in *chained* and *overlapping* components.

Not every activity has a blatant contradiction. Certainly, activities usually don't have every single type of contradiction, but they will usually have some. What contradictions can you detect across activities?

- Start with chained relationships, going through the Activity System Links worksheet to identify where components come from. For instance,

- Do rules originate from another activity that's at cross-purposes with the one at your site?

- Are people trained in different areas, with different norms and values, before entering your site?

- Next, consider points at which the activity system overlaps with others:

- Is another activity also attempting to transform the objective your site is trying to transform?

- Does the activity system involve actors who also interact in other activity systems? Might these other activities interfere with how they relate in this one?

As you identify potential contradictions, write them down on the Activity System Contradictions Worksheet. Although you can *speculate* about contradictions here, you will want to go back to your data (and perhaps collect more data) to *confirm* whether these contradictions are actually there.

For instance, if you're studying a family business, you might *speculate* that some of the frictions you see in this activity system are due to the family's personal dynamics (an overlapping activity system). That seems reasonable, but *confirm* it with data.

Developing a Consolidated Activity System

Although we are interested in how your site functions in the context of its activity network, the real focus is the site itself. So, once you have mapped out the activity system and its contradictions, you'll bring those insights back to the activity system of your site.

In concrete terms, that means that once you explore these links across activity systems, you should create a final activity system that includes

- Its components

- Its contradictions, both internal and external

You'll get a consolidated picture similar to figure 21.5.

Examples

Below are examples from the SEO case: activity system links, an activity network, and a consolidated activity system.

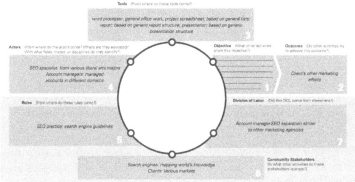

Figure 21.3. Activity system links, SEO case.

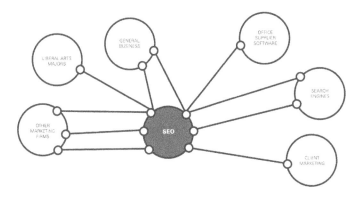

Figure 21.4. Activity network for SEO case, showing connections between the SEO firm and other activities.

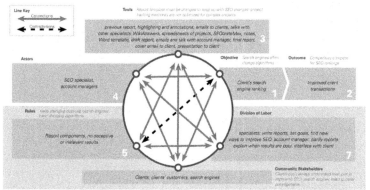

Figure 21.5. A consolidated activity system, based on the work in chapters 20-21.

CHAPTER 22

Creating New Models

Before we get to the final Topsight model, recall that in Chapter 15 I said that you might consider creating your own models for special purposes. Models are meant to help you identify and isolate relationships in the data. The models in chapters 16-21 cover basic types of relationships that we often see in repeated, text-heavy work.

But in your unique study, you may find that you need different models to help you pull out those unique aspects. If that's the case, you can consider trying out other *variants of models*, *supplemental models*, or *combinations of models*

Variants of Models

Chapter 15 suggests three basic models: matrix, flow, and network models. All of the Topsight models are based on these three types. But you can develop other variants of these models as well.

For instance, a while back one of my students was interested in how startups go through growth phases. She interviewed three different entrepreneurs and examined their website and other artifacts. But then she got stuck: it was hard for her to apply the topsight models effectively because her project wasn't focused on repeated work.

I suggested she back up and start with *comparisons*.

For instance, the three entrepreneurs all addressed various aspects of company growth, and some talked about certain aspects more than others: Person A discussed leadership more, while Person B talked more about the startup phase. I suggested that my student confirm by systematically comparing the number of times each subcode came up during the interview, using a **matrix**.

This made me wonder whether Person B, who had much more experience, had specific phases of company growth in mind, while Person A, who was new to entrepreneurship, might have a less defined idea. So I suggested comparing quotes from their interviews to see if that was the case. A **network diagram** allowed her to check how the participants connected different experiences to different aspects of company growth.

Finally, in their interviews, the participants described a sequence for company growth. I suggested that she use a **flow diagram** to show that sequence and to map out decision points. She could then compare the three participants' flow diagrams to see whether they were describing different sequences—and how those sequences differed.

"As you do these things," I told her, "you may see other points of comparison, connection, or sequence. For instance, you might track metaphors that they use for company growth. You might identify how they connect growth phases with other events or trigger points: do they seek funding 'when I reach $250k in sales' or 'when I feel it in my gut' or 'when I can't eat ramen anymore'?"

Supplemental Models

Although matrix, flow, and network models cover three major types of relationships, you may sometimes see other relationships that you want to explore as well. In that case, you could adopt or invent models based on different principles. These models will likely play a supplemental role in your field research.

Here are two examples of supplemental models that you might consider:

Traffic maps. You may find that your site has an unusual layout that causes people to move through it in unusual ways. For instance, perhaps the shared printer is in a hallway, causing traffic jams when people need to print things. That spatial relationship will not show up in the standard Topsight models, but you can model it by creating a map of the space and tracing the routes that people take through that space.

Word clouds. As you look through a set of documents at a particular site, you may get the impression that two sets of training materials emphasize two different sets of concerns. Perhaps this disjuncture is related to the contradictory answers about values that you are getting in your interviews, you think. But how can you systematically confirm your impression? One simple way could be to run each set of documents through a word cloud generator—a free application that analyzes the frequency of words, sizing the words to show how frequently they are used. Word clouds are not sophisticated tools, but they can give you a quick, easy way to compare frequency: if one word cloud's biggest words are "customer" and "fun," while the second word cloud's biggest words are "rules" and "compliance," you may have found a thematic difference between these two sets of training documents.

As you consider supplemental models, try to articulate why you need this model, what relationship you'll explore with it, and how systematically it will let you explore that relationship. Once you have articulated these three things, you can consider whether the supplemental model is the best fit—and you might iterate the model to make it a better fit.

Combinations of Models

Finally, in specific cases, you might find that a combination of existing models will work better for you than one model type alone might.

For instance, a while back my colleagues and I were trying to examine how entrepreneurs learn and use information resources to develop their pitches:

> Spinuzzi, C., Nelson, S., Thomson, K. S., Lorenzini, F., French, R. A., Pogue, G., & London, N. (2016). How Magnets Attract and Repel: Interessement in a Technology Commercialization Competition. *Written Communication*, 33(1), 3–41.

We started out by putting these in a resource map (a network model). But we realized that the *sequence* was important as well—they learned these information resources in a specific sequence and they often copied text from one resource to another. That implied a flow model. Furthermore, the entrepreneurs learned these information resources in specific phases—so the phases had to make their way into the model too. The resulting model consolidated the different data, allowing us to see the relationships among information resources over time (Figure 22.1).

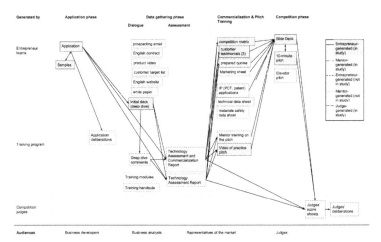

Figure 22.1. A combination model based on Spinuzzi et al. 2016.

As you work through your unique data, you may find similar points at which you have to combine different models to get at the relationships you need to explore.

CHAPTER 23

Topsight Tables

So far, our analytical models have allowed us to examine our research sites at three different levels: macro, meso, and micro (see table 23.1).

Table 23.1. Analytical models, time scale, and disruptions.

Levels	Models	Time scale	Disruptions	Essential Questions
Macro (Organization)	Activity systems Activity networks	Days, weeks, months, years	Contradictions	Why?
Meso (Human)	Resource maps Handoff chains Triangulation tables	Minutes, hours	Discoordination	What?
Micro (Habit)	Breakdown tables	Seconds	Breakdowns	How?

As I mentioned, each model lets us pull out and systematically examine a particular relationship. And these relationships as the table shows, operate at different levels of activity.

But the relationships and levels are *analytical constructs*. That is, we separate them out temporarily to examine them, but in real life, they work together.

Think about it this way. When you learn a sun salutation in yoga, a power clean in weightlifting, or a swing in golf, your instructor breaks down the moves for you. You practice the pieces, then put them together. In the end, these pieces shouldn't stay as pieces—they should turn into a single smooth movement.

Similarly, the models let us look at different relationships at play in the activity. But in the end, it's all the same activity. All those second-by-second operations at the micro scale make up the minutes and hours at the meso level and the longer cycles of work at the macro level. The levels are connected—and, more importantly for us, the *disruptions* at each level are connected.

How do we make the case for those connections? How do we get from the symptoms to the disease? That is, how do we link the disruptions (e.g., the contradictions, discoordinations, and breakdowns) so we can understand the systemic issues at work?

We'll do this work with our final matrix model, the *topsight table* (table 23.2). This table allows you to

- detect possible affinities among the disruptions at each level;

- drill down into your models and evidence at each level to confirm or disconfirm whether these disruptions are related; and

- organize your reasons and evidence for characterizing this systemic issue.

Table 23.2. A topsight table.

Disruptions	
Macro (Contradictions)	Activity network: Activity system:
Meso (Discoordinations)	Resource map: Handoff chain: Triangulation table:
Micro (Breakdowns)	Breakdown table:

This table integrates all of the analytical work you have done so far. In this chapter, we will

- examine the relationships among the models;

- examine how the topsight table can unify the models into a "big picture" view of the systemic issue;

- use the K-J Method to develop a topsight table;

- title the topsight table, naming the systemic issue it describes.

1. Understanding Topsight Tables

Looking at the individual levels, we might find it hard to make connections. But pulling the different disturbances into a single table helps us to make these connections more easily, letting us name the different issues that our participants face. Topsight tables represent findings in our research— findings pointing to recommendations.

Those findings might represent systemic issues or, even more remarkably, the lack of systemic issues.

Systemic issues

In most organizations, you'll notice several disruptions at each level: macro-level contradictions, meso-level discoordinations, and micro-level breakdowns. You will sometimes be able to spot relationships across the different levels—that is, you can trace several different symptoms to a common underlying issue. At that point, you'll be able to suggest ways to address that underlying issue.

The lack of systemic issues

But what if you can't detect contradictions, discoordinations, and breakdowns in an aspect of the organization? Frankly, that's headline news in itself. In organizations, we *usually* find systemic issues.

The lack of a systemic issue is unusual and remarkable, in the sense that you should remark on it in your findings.

To demonstrate that the organization works well across levels, you might rework the topsight table to demonstrate how the different levels are in alignment with *harmonies* rather than contradictions, *coordinations* rather than discoordinations, and *fluencies* rather than breakdowns (see table 23.3).

Table 23.3. A topsight table lacking disruptions. How does the organization work so well?

Disruptions	
Macro (Harmonies)	Activity network: Activity system:
Meso (Coordinations)	Resource map: Handoff chain: Triangulation table:
Micro (Fluencies)	Breakdown table:

As I said, this situation is remarkable and worth examining more carefully. You can use this table to explore why things are working so well.

In either case, if you were to write a Findings section based on these tables, each table would represent a different finding. Let's use these tables as examples for developing our own.

2. Developing Topsight Tables

To develop topsight tables, you first need to list disruptions (i.e., contradictions, discoordinations, and breakdowns) or the lack of disruptions (i.e., harmonies, coordinations, fluencies) from each model. Once you do that, you'll start to see congruencies among them.

For instance, in the SEO case, we can see discoordinations and breakdowns clustering around certain resources across all the models. The activity system showed that some of these problems came from the interactions among different activities. To nail down the issue, I developed a topsight table that pulled in disruptions from each model, making sure that I could point to evidence for each disruption.

You'll do the same thing. If one finding is that two different resources are incompatible, you might

- show with an activity system and activity network that the resources come from two separate activities;

- show with your resource map that people are using other, unofficial resources to help them work between the two incompatible resources;

- show with your handoff chain that people regularly have to relate the two incompatible resources to get work done;

- show with your triangulation table that although people use a lot of different unofficial resources as workarounds, they all do basically the same thing—they fit the same niche; or

- show with your breakdown table that people frequently encounter breakdowns, across all participants, when they try to relate the incompatible resources, and that they find different ways to recover.

You might come up with something like table 23.4.

Table 23.4. A topsight table for the SEO case.

Disruptions	
Macro (Contradictions)	*Activity system:*
	Activity network: Rules keep changing because search engines keep changing algorithms.
Meso (Discoordinations)	*Resource map*: Sonia must ask Elizair for clarification when search rankings drop due to algorithm changes.
	Handoff chain: Clarification results in additional rounds of email between Sonia and Elizair.
	Triangulation table: Elizair doesn't proactively address algorithm changes, but Craig always includes a note about them when presenting his draft report to Sonia.
Micro (Breakdowns)	*Breakdown table*: When reading the draft report, Sonia initially doesn't understand the rankings drop. She asks the other account representatives if they understand it, then emails Elizair.

As you go through your topsight table, you may find disruptions that don't quite fit. That's fine: They may belong in a different topsight table, representing another cluster of issues.

How do you make this happen? You'll use a method called the K-J Method: a procedure that helps you to inductively develop categories from "flat" input. I suggest that you do this exercise in a group—that means that you'll have to explain your reasoning out loud, making it explicit.

Follow these steps:

Step 1: Write disruptions on sticky notes

1. Get out all of the models you have developed. Each model depicts a specific relationship, but it also depicts disruptions that you have identified through that model.

2. Copy each disruption from each model onto a separate sticky note. Note which model each disruption came from.

3. Put all of the sticky notes on a big flat surface (such as a table, wall, or big sheet of paper).

Now you have an inventory of all disruptions—your "symptoms."

Step 2: Cluster the sticky notes

1. If you see a relationship between two notes, put them together (cluster them). *You don't even have to name the relationship at this point.*

2. If you see a cluster forming and you have a note that may fit into that cluster, put it there.

3. If you disagree with where someone has placed a note, grab it and put it where you think it should go.

4. If you see someone else taking your note, decide whether you agree with their new clustering.

Now you have clusters of related notes—clusters of related symptoms that point to underlying systemic issues.

Step 3: Label the clusters

1. As a group, discuss each cluster. What do all the notes have in common? Especially consider the macro-level disruptions.

2. As a group, formulate a sentence that summarizes the cluster. Write it on a sticky note (and make it a different color from the other ones).

3. Use the summary sentence as a label. Put it next to the applicable cluster.

4. Repeat for all clusters.

Now you have named the underlying issues for each cluster. You have a good idea of how the individual disruptions relate.

Step 4: Turn the clusters into Topsight tables

1. Create a blank Topsight table in your favorite medium (paper, spreadsheet, etc.).

2. Write (or type) the summary sentence above the Topsight table.

3. Copy the symptoms from the sticky notes into the Topsight table at the appropriate place. For instance, if the sticky note describes a macro-level contradiction from the activity system, write it in the table on the macro row, next to "Activity system."

4. Repeat step 3 for all sticky notes.

5. Repeat steps 1-4 for all clusters.

Now you have Topsight tables that succinctly describe the underlying issues, similar to Table 23.4.

3. Generating Findings from Topsight Tables

At this point, you have developed a topsight table and captioned it with a summary phrase. *This summary phrase is your finding.*

For instance, the summary phrase for table 23.4 could be something like:

Since search engines keep changing their search algorithms, the organization has limited control over search rankings, but their internal and external communication patterns haven't addressed this problem consistently.

It's a simple claim, but one that you can back up with several pieces of related evidence working at different levels.

This last step seems simple, but it's crucial to get it right. Use a phrase that can describe your topsight at all levels. This phrase is the main takeaway that readers will absorb for this point, and it's also the basis for a corresponding recommendation. So don't oversimplify.

Example

Table 23.5 shows a topsight table for the SEO case. In this table, based on the entire case, not just the pieces we've seen here, we can see that changing algorithms create related disruptions at all levels.

Table 23.5. A topsight table for the SEO case.

Disruptions	
Macro (Contra-dictions)	*Activity network*: Rules keep changing because search engines keep changing algorithms.
Meso (Discoordi-nations)	*Resource map*: Sonia must ask Elizair for clarification when search rankings drop due to algorithm changes. *Handoff chain*: Clarification results in additional rounds of email between Sonia and Elizair. *Triangulation table*: Elizair doesn't proactively address algorithm changes, but Craig always includes a note about them when presenting his draft report to Sonia.
Micro (Break-downs)	*Breakdown table*: When reading the draft report, Sonia initially doesn't understand the rankings drop. She asks the other account representatives if they understand it, then emails Elizair.

REPORTING THE RESULTS

You've finished your analysis and achieved topsight. But how do you turn topsight into something that can improve the organization? In this section, we'll address two questions:

- How do you communicate your analysis?

- How do you develop a solid set of recommendations?

CHAPTER 24

Describing
Systemic Issues

In the last section, you developed several models to help you better understand your participants' work. And with the last model, the topsight table, you used the "symptoms" (i.e., disruptions) to diagnose the underlying "illness" (i.e., systemic issue). As we saw in the last chapter, you might have also been able to describe things that go surprisingly right with the organization—the harmonies, coordinations, and fluencies that make it work against all odds. And since all of your models are based directly on the data you collected, you can easily point to strong evidence for the issues you have identified.

That's great. But how do we turn this into something that other people can understand? In this chapter, we'll take the first step; we'll walk through the process of turning the models into a set of claims—that is, findings—supported by reasons and evidence.

In this chapter, we will

- examine the relationship among claims, reasons, and evidence;

- translate models and data into claims, reasons, and evidence; and

- develop a claim with supporting reasons and supporting evidence.

This work prepares us for developing recommendations in Chapter 25.

Claims, Reasons, and Evidence

First, let's get our terms straight. What are claims, reasons, and evidence?

A *claim* is a statement that you believe to be true and that you can justify. We make claims all the time, often with little evidence:

- "This restaurant is the best Thai restaurant in town."

- "My party's economic policies make sense; your party only cares about constituency X."

- "Men should not wear shorts."

But in this book, the claim is a statement of a systemic issue—a finding. And it turns out that you've already developed at least one claim. It's what you titled your topsight table.

A *reason* is a statement of why you believe your claim is true. Claims are backed with reasons. If they're not, they are not claims, they're *opinions*. For instance, for the claims above, you might provide the following reasons:

- "The true test of a Thai restaurant is its Masaman curry, and that's their specialty."

- "My party's proposed budget was scored by the Congressional Budget Office and the results clearly show that its budget will help people of all constituencies, at all economic levels."

- "When men wear shorts, they look like overgrown boys."

In this book, you've already developed reasons too. The reasons are the models you developed, showing the patterns of activity and the disruptions that occur at each level.

Evidence consists of specific facts (i.e., data) supporting a reason. Just as claims are backed with reasons, reasons are backed with evidence. For instance, for the reasons above, you might provide the following evidence:

- "This restaurant's Masaman curry got five stars on Yelp."

- "Specifically, look at the table of figures on page 62 of this Congressional report."

- "Look at that guy wearing those shorts. Doesn't he look like Sluggo?"

In this book, your models are developed on evidence—your data. You can pull out examples of those data, such as quotes from interviews, stories from your field notes, and examples from the artifacts you collected.

As I mentioned, each claim is backed by one or more reasons, which in turn are backed by one or more pieces of evidence. The relationship among claims, reasons, and evidence looks like figure 24.1.

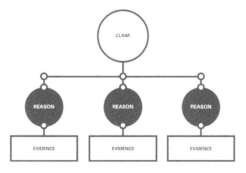

Figure 24.1. The relationship among claims, reasons, and evidence.

So how do you translate this structure into something you can use in a recommendation?

Turning Your Models into Claims, Reasons, and Evidence

Your models and data can translate directly into claims, reasons, and evidence (see figure 22.2).

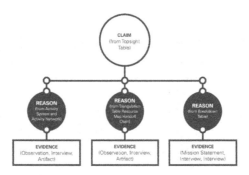

Figure 24.2. Translating models and data into claims, reasons, and evidence.

As you can see, all of your hard work is about to pay off; you should have everything you need in order to put together one or more strong claims backed by reasons and evidence.

Developing the Claim

A claim expresses a systemic issue you've found through the topsight table. And that means that you'll have as many claims (i.e., findings) as you have topsight tables.

To develop that claim, do the following:

- State the claim as a claim: an interpretation that you can justify.

- Make sure the claim summarizes what you know across all levels of the topsight table.

State the claim as a claim: an interpretation that you can justify.

Let's take the SEO case as an example. As you remember, we found that the organization was having trouble addressing the rapid changes in search-engine algorithms. I described these in a single topsight table (see table 23.5). Based on that table, I can develop this claim:

> Since search engines keep changing their search algorithms, the organization has limited control over search rankings, but their internal and external communication patterns haven't addressed this problem consistently.

This is a definite claim, justified via the models at each level.

Make sure the claim summarizes what you know across all levels of the topsight table.

This claim isn't only justifiable. It also summarizes what I know across all levels of the topsight table. I can view the models at each level and confirm that their discoordinations are addressed by the claim.

Notice that the claim isn't too broad or too narrow. A claim that is too broad might be difficult to justify. Take this one:

> Constant search engine changes result in total confusion and wasted time.

This claim is too broad. The organization isn't in complete disarray, and in fact, we can see that Craig has developed an innovation to help address the problem. Just as bad is this one:

> Elizair's way of presenting the reports to Sonia results in confusion and wasted time.

This claim is too narrow. It's not just Elizair that is having this problem. Even when Craig presents the report with his innovation, Sonia still has to translate the issue for the customer.

Finally, the more broadly you can justify the claim, the stronger it is. You justify the claim through reasons. So let's talk about them next.

Developing the Reasons

As we've seen, each claim is a summary of a topsight table. The reasons that back that claim are the things that your models tell you at each level of the topsight table.

State each reason as an insight from a model supporting the claim.

We've seen how I summarized the topsight table with a definite claim. But now I have to make sure that he can clearly express my reasons. Preferably, I can summarize each model in a sentence or two.

For instance, here's my summary of the resource map for this case:

> Account managers must contact SEO specialists repeatedly, both by email and in person, to clarify why search rankings drop in specific instances.

I can then point to the resource map, which shows exactly how many information resources I observed account managers using for this purpose. I can also show any discoordinations that I detected in the resource map.

Remember; the more broadly you can base each reason on evidence, the stronger it is. You justify the reasons through evidence. So let's talk about evidence next.

Developing the Evidence

Think of evidence as the specific instances from your data: quotes from interviews, stories from your field notes, or copies of resources.

Of course, you don't want to present all the data you have. No one wants to read all of your field notes, for instance. But if you can provide representative data to back each model, you can clearly and convincingly demonstrate what that model is based on.

For instance, to support the statement above, I could give this piece of evidence from my field notes:

> Sonia read Elizair's draft report silently, then stopped at the rankings. "This doesn't look right," she said to another account manager. "Have you ever seen anything like this?" After discussing it, they agreed that she needed to ask Elizair for an explanation. She emailed him, but his response only confused her further. "I'll need to iron this out in person," she said as she got up to visit his office.

By giving us this observation—and by contrasting it with what another staff member does—I can show what my resource map was based on.

Furthermore, you can use specific examples then demonstrate that these examples are representative.

In the next chapter, we'll turn these validated claims into general recommendations.

Exercises

- In groups, examine a caption from one of your topsight tables.

- Is it stated as a claim?

- Does it summarize all of the related models?

- How broadly can you justify it? That is, how many models can you use as reasons for this claim?

- In groups, examine how you summarized models in one of your topsight tables.

- Is each one stated as an insight from the model that supports the claim? If not, either modify the claim or restate the reason.

- Is each one supported with evidence? How broadly? Do you need to qualify it?

- In groups, examine the evidence supporting your reasons.

- Can you provide one or more specific instances from your data to support each part of the model?

- Can you identify specific instances that can serve to illustrate the data (e.g., quotes, instances, or artifacts)?

- Can you demonstrate that your specific instances are representative?

- Can you triangulate the data?

CHAPTER 25

Developing Recommendations

In Chapter 24, you constructed a basic argument for your findings: a claim, supported by reasons, which in turn are supported by evidence. Now you can confidently describe at least one finding—at least one systemic issue faced by the organization you studied.

Up to this point, your work has been *descriptive and analytical*. That is, you have described what you saw and analyzed what it means. Based on that work, you have argued for one or more findings. You're essentially saying, "Here's what's going wrong."

But if you want to help improve things at the organization, you have to turn from description to *prescription*—that is, you have to develop specific recommendations for dealing with the systemic issues you've found. You're saying, "Here's how to solve the problem."

In some cases, these recommendations may seem obvious—at first. But since you're looking at systemic findings, which tend to be complex problems, you'll often have to put a lot of thought into developing the right recommendations. After all, every problem can have multiple solutions. What are the right recommendations? They should meet the following criteria:

They should flow from the findings. That is, they should respond directly to the systemic issues you have identified.

They should be general at this stage. That is, you should outline a direction, not an implementation.

They should address the systemic issues without doing harm. Since work is so interconnected, as we've seen, when you develop recommendations you need to make sure not to create *other* issues or interfere with *other* parts of the work.

Meeting these criteria turns out to be tricky. But I'll walk you through how to meet them. In this chapter, we will discuss

- how to move from descriptive findings to prescriptive recommendations;

- how to generate recommendations at an appropriate level of abstraction; and

- how to test whether a recommendation is aligned with the systemic issue, with other parts of the work, and with the client's goals.

This work prepares us for writing the recommendation report.

From Descriptive Findings to Prescriptive Recommendations

Let's turn to the SEO case. As we saw, one finding was:

Since search engines keep changing their search algorithms, the organization has limited control over search rankings, but their internal and external communication patterns haven't addressed this problem consistently.

We were able to establish this claim by drawing on reasons and evidence from our different models. Now, we have a good thick description of the systemic issue. So what's the solution? Dozens come to mind. Here are a few:

- Mandatory all-hands meetings whenever search algorithms change

- A daily email bulletin describing algorithm changes

- A new section in the monthly report describing algorithm changes

- An internal blog describing algorithm changes

- New training so that account managers will be able to recognize algorithm changes

- A new role: a separate individual whose job is to collect and communicate news on algorithm changes

- New organization (e.g., outsource the detection of algorithm changes to another organization)

- New direction (e.g., don't discuss algorithm changes at all)

Some of these are terrible ideas. Some might work pretty well. But all are possible solutions that would address the finding. In fact, they all address our first two criteria for findings:

- Flow from the findings (i.e., systemic issues)

- Are general at this stage (e.g., Not, "Start a Wordpress blog in which specialists A, B, and C would post daily bulletins in which they classify search algorithm changes along these eight categories", but "Adopt an internal blog describing algorithm changes").

But do they accomplish the third goal?

- Address the systemic issue without creating other issues or interfering with other parts of the work.

To find out, ask these key questions:

- Will the recommendation solve the systemic issue?

- How will it solve the systemic issue at each level of scope (i.e., macro, meso, and micro)?

- Will it create other problems in adjacent parts of the work?

- Will it be acceptable to the organization?

For example, outsourcing the detection of algorithm changes to another organization might be a great way to lift the burden from the organization's workers, but it also puts the organization at the mercy of another, more specialized firm, instead of developing that expertise in-house. Will that be acceptable to the organization?

Will the Recommendation Solve the Systemic Issue?

To answer this question, examine the possible impact of the recommendation at each level:

Macro. Align the recommendation to the activity's objective in the activity system and activity network. Does it maintain the objective while easing contradictions?

Meso. Align the recommendation to the resource map, handoff chain, and triangulation table. Does it maintain the information resource relationships and the handoff chains while eliminating discoordinations?

Micro. Align the recommendation to the breakdowns table. Does it leverage the workers' current working habits while addressing breakdowns?

How Will It Solve the Systemic Issue at Each Level of Scope?

To answer this question, examine how the recommendation will impact each individual level. This involves *revising* each model to represent how you expect it to work once the new recommendation is implemented.

Macro. Revise the activity system and activity network to demonstrate how the change will maintain the objective while easing contradictions.

Meso. Revise the resource map, handoff chain, and triangulation table to demonstrate how the change will maintain the information resource relationships and the handoff chains while eliminating discoordinations.

Micro. Revise the breakdowns table to demonstrate how the change will leverage the current working habits while addressing breakdowns.

Will It Create Other Problems in Adjacent Parts of the Work?

Does the recommendation eliminate, change, or make redundant other important aspects of the work? Be careful here, since changing one part of the work might very well solve local problems, while creating problems elsewhere. Carefully examine these aspects:

Roles/divisions of labor. Examine the activity system and triangulation table. How will your changes impact these?

Tools and information resources. Examine the activity system and resource map. Will your changes eliminate or change tools or information resources that are being used elsewhere? Will you need to add tools or resources to integrate your changes with the current activity?

Rules and regulations. Examine the activity system and resource map. Will your changes eliminate or change rules or regulations? Will you need to add rules or regulations to integrate your changes with the current activity?

Routines and procedures. Examine the handoff chain and break-downs table. Your participants likely have elaborate routines and procedures to help them get through their work. Do your changes impact these? How will participants handle these changes?

Rationales, goals, and outcomes. Examine the activity system. Do your changes impact the objective or outcome of the activity?

Connections to other organizations. Finally, examine the activity network. The organization is already connected to many other activities. How will your changes impact those other activities? For instance, will the organization break off a relationship with a supplier, become too specialized to deal with a specific type of client, or require a new kind of service or software?

If the change will create problems with adjacent parts of the work, evaluate whether you want to recommend that change. Keep the scope manageable.

Will It Be Acceptable to the Organization?

Finally, compare the recommendation to the organization's stated goals.

During your data collection, you've examined how the organization represents itself at the macro level (i.e., via mission statements, annual reports, etc.) and the organization's objective and outcome. But you may have also talked with representatives of the organization about other factors that will influence whether a given solution is acceptable. Those factors may include:

Budget. If the organization doesn't have a large budget or has higher priorities, it may not accept a solution that is too expensive to develop, test, or implement. For instance, the Internet marketing firm was relatively small and new; I knew they wouldn't be able to afford to hire large numbers of people or invest in lots of new equipment.

Platform. If the organization has already committed to a certain platform, it may prefer to build on that platform rather than adopt a new one. For instance, the Internet marketing firm had developed their SEObrateMax system in-house, and were actively developing it; they were unlikely to switch to a new system.

Organization. The organizational structure itself might bear on whether a solution is acceptable. For instance, you may find that a strongly hierarchical organization will not consider a solution that gives a lot of discretion to workers; whereas, a flatter organization, such as the Internet marketing firm, might resist creating new levels or consolidating functions under a specific manager.

Strategic considerations. Finally, the organization may be committed to a specific strategic direction that will work against your recommendations. For instance, if the Internet marketing firm is planning to push into international markets, it may be less willing to consider services or software that aren't oriented toward those markets.

Consider all of these factors as you refine your recommendations.

Make Sure Recommendations Match Findings

Now that you've done this work, you'll want to make sure your recommendations are still well aligned with the findings. The principle is to *address each finding (i.e., systemic issue) with a recommendation.* That is, always make sure to offer a solution to each problem you raise, and don't offer solutions unless they clearly address a problem.

You might use one of these configurations:

Provide matched findings and recommendations. That is, if you raise findings A, B, and C, you'll match them with recommendations A, B, and C. For each finding you offer a matching recommendation.

Address a single finding with multiple recommendations.
That is, you may raise a single, complex finding that requires more than one recommendation to solve.

Address multiple findings with a single recommendation.
That is, you may raise several findings, but offer a single, complex recommendation that solves all of them.

I suggest matching these findings and recommendations with a simple table, like Table 25.1.

Table 25.1. Matching findings and recommendations.

Findings	Recommendations

In the SEO example at the end of the chapter, the first finding is addressed with two recommendations, while the second finding is addressed with just one.

Once you've developed recommendations for your findings, you're ready to write the recommendation report.

Exercises

In groups, try brainstorming possible solutions.

- Select one finding.

- Brainstorm **terrible** recommendations—ones that you know won't work.

- Brainstorm **fantasy** recommendations—ones that could work with magic. What makes these so attractive?

- Brainstorm **doable** recommendations—ones that could do the same job as the fantasy recommendations, but that could work under the existing constraints of the site.

- Test your doable solutions against criteria. Will each solution address the systemic issue? In groups:

Align the recommendation to the different models.

Explain your reasoning to the other group.

How will each solution solve the systemic issue at each level? In groups:

- Sketch revised models at each level to visualize whether the recommendation will solve the systemic issue.

- Look for potential disruptions and discuss whether to modify the recommendation to avoid them.

Will each solution create other problems in adjacent parts of the work? In groups:

- Compare the old and new models. Identify changes in roles; tools; rules and regulations; routines and procedures; rationales, goals, and outcomes; and connections to other activities.

- Discuss whether these changes will impact other parts of the work (e.g., eliminating a tool that is key to someone's work).

Will each solution be acceptable to the client? In groups, compare the recommendation to the client's stated goals.

- Budget

- Platform

- Organization

- Strategic considerations

Example

Table 25.2 lists findings from the SEO case along with corresponding recommendations.

Table 25.2. Findings and recommendations for the SEO case.

Findings	Recommendations
Since search engines keep changing their search algorithms, the organization has limited control over search rankings, but its internal and external communication patterns haven't addressed this problem consistently.	Develop a note in SEObrateMax to indicate search algorithm changes. Develop a SEObrateMax routine to automatically detect algorithm changes.
No standardized project tracking, resulting in confusion when specialists have to communicate projet status to each other or account managers.	Establish standardized project tracking.

Recommendation Report

In Chapter 24, you identified systemic issues (i.e., findings). In Chapter 25, you developed specific recommendations for dealing with the systemic issues you've found. Now, in Chapter 26, you'll pull these together into a recommendation report for your client.

Frankly, this step won't be too hard if you've kept up with the other steps. The findings and recommendations are the heart of the report.

In this chapter, we will

- examine the recommendation report outline as an argument;

- develop the report's introduction and methods sections; and

- turn the models, findings, and recommendations into report sections.

As we discuss each of these, we will look at the recommendation report example at the end of the chapter. (This example is of a written recommendation report, but you can use the same principles to develop a slide deck instead.)

The Recommendation Report Outline as an Argument

Recommendation reports are specific types of arguments. Each major "slot" is part of the basic logic that makes up the argument of the recommendation report:

- **Introduction.** "Here's what you asked us to do."

- **Methods.** "Here's how we did it."

- **Findings.** "Here's what we discovered."

- **Recommendations.** "Here's what we recommend you do about it."

Let's make this outline more specific for the field studies covered in this book:

- **Introduction:** Describe the goals of the engagement and forecast the rest of the report.

- **Methods:** Describe your investigation in brief.

- **Findings:** Describe your findings as claims, backed by your analysis (i.e., reasons) and evidence (i.e., data).

- **Recommendations:** Describe your general recommendations, based on the findings.

Introduction and Methods provide the context for your recommendations. Findings provides the description of the systemic issues you found. And Recommendations provides clear, general guidance for addressing those issues.

Developing the Report's Introduction and Methods Sections

As I said, the Introduction and Methods are the context of the report. So let's set up that context.

Writing the Introduction

The report's Introduction has basically three jobs:

- Remind the client that you conducted this particular study. (They might forget—they have a lot going on.)

- Specify that you will describe findings and recommendations.

- Forecast the rest of the report.

In a short recommendation report, such as the one at the end of the chapter, you can usually accomplish this context-setting in just a paragraph or two.

Writing the Methods

The Methods section describes how you investigated the organization. You can handle this section in one of two ways.

- If your organization is interested in how you collected data, you can list the data collection methods from your matrix as well as the models you used for data analysis.

- If your organization is not particularly interested in how you collected data, just list the models.

Writing the Findings

Whereas the Introduction and Methods provided context, Findings provides a description of each systemic issue you found, as well as a justification of the findings. As you write the Findings section, make sure to include:

- An opening paragraph that briefly mentions each finding

- A subsection for *each* finding (i.e., claim), including

- A subheading for the finding (i.e., claim), based on the topsight table's caption (i.e., systemic issue)

- The topsight table and an explanation of how it represents the systemic issue

- A discussion of each model (i.e., reason) supporting the finding, along with representative data (i.e., evidence) backing each model

Here's where your hard work really starts to pay off. Make sure to keep all of your work handy as you write this section, including your models from Phase IV and the findings/recommendations table you developed in Chapter 25.

In Chapter 1, I told you to approach your field study as if you were a doctor examining symptoms so you could diagnose an illness, or a detective examining clues to solve a mystery. Well, the Findings section is where you deliver the diagnosis or tell everyone how you solved the mystery. But they might not believe you unless you make a strong, solid case for your conclusions. So make your claims, present your reasons and evidence, and make sure you've presented a compelling case.

Writing the Recommendations

In the Findings, you build a case for the systemic issues you've found. But the organization is also going to wonder, what do we do about it? Here, you'll build a separate case—a case for each recommendation you generated in Chapter 25.

In this section, you should include

- an opening paragraph that briefly mentions each recommendation; and

- a subsection for each recommendation, including

- a description of the recommendation, specifying which finding(s) it addresses;

- a discussion of how each recommendation will translate into changes at the different levels; and

- a discussion of how the recommendation will address the client's stated goals (e.g., budget, platform, organization, and strategic objectives).

Again, you'll base this work on the findings/recommendations table from Chapter 25.

Above, I reminded you that you can think of Findings as diagnosing the organization's "illnesses". But if a doctor stopped with diagnosing your illness, you probably wouldn't be very happy with him. You want him to tell you what to do about it. What's the cure? How much will it cost? Will it be effective? Will it impact your quality of life, and if so, how?

Your organization will wonder the same thing. Do your best to describe the recommendation, how it will solve the systemic issue, and how it will impact the organization in other ways.

Example

On the next page is a recommendation report based on the SEO case.

Recommendation Report

Tim—

I'm writing to follow up on the Interim Report that I sent you a few weeks ago. Having had more time to study the data, I am now able to provide a more detailed analysis, including identifying systemic issues at SEObrate and recommending ways to address these issues.

In this report, I first discuss the analytical models I used to pinpoint these issues then describe my findings and recommendations. Since you've indicated that you can implement changes in your in-house software, SEObrateMax, I've recommended changes to that software.

Methods

Four team members were involved in the study: three SEO specialists and one account manager. During the study, I observed each team member twice, two hours per observation. After each observation, I interviewed the team member for up to 15 minutes. Finally, with their permission, I collected texts and other artifacts that they used, and I took photos of their work areas.

I applied the following analytical models to the data:

Activity systems and activity networks. These models allowed me to examine the context of the work at SEObrate. They depict how the organization cyclically works, the components of that work, and how those components connect to other organizations. They also depict the systemic contradictions that have developed at SEObrate.

Resource maps. These models map out the information resources (such as documents, emails, and presentations) that workers used and how they used those resources together to get things done. Resource maps show the widely recognized information resources, but also the innovations that workers developed. In addition, they show the disruptions workers encounter as they try to use information resources in concert.

Handoff chains. These models allowed me to examine the routines people followed as they regularly handed off information resources (such as documents, emails, and presentations) to each other. Handoff chains also helped me to map out common disruptions that occur during these handoffs and to see how workers recovered from these disruptions.

Triangulation tables. These tables allowed me to compare how different individuals and groups use information resources to perform sequences of work. This model synthesizes insights from resource maps and handoff chains to cross-reference how people are using information resources similarly or differently—and where they encounter disruptions.

Breakdown tables. These tables allowed me to catalogue and examine micro-level disruptions, when they happened, and how workers recovered from them.

Topsight tables. Finally, these tables synthesized the disruptions across all of the other models, helping me to identify the systemic issues that underlie them.

The topsight tables are presented inline; the rest of the models are in the appendix.

FINDINGS

Through these analytical models, I identified two systemic issues:

Issue 1: Since search engines keep changing their search algorithms, SEObrate has limited control over search rankings, but internal and external communication patterns haven't addressed this problem consistently.

Disruptions	
Macro (Contra-dictions)	Activity system: Activity network: Rules keep changing because search engines keep changing algorithms.
Meso (Discoor-dinations)	Resource map: Sonia must ask Elizair for clarification when search rankings drop due to algorithm changes. Handoff chain: Clarification results in additional rounds of email between Sonia and Elizair. Triangulation table: Elizair doesn't proactively address algorithm changes, but Craig always includes a note about them when presenting his draft report to Sonia.
Micro (Break-downs)	Breakdown table: When reading the draft report, Sonia initially doesn't understand the rankings drop. She asks the other account representatives if they understand it, then emails Elizair.

As represented in this topsight table, SEObrate faces the challenge of optimizing sites to address continually changing search algorithms. This is perhaps the central challenge of

SEO, and as the activity network demonstrates (figure 1), the changing algorithms are beyond SEObrate's control.

But beyond that, SEObrate has not standardized its internal or external communication to deal with these changes. As the resource map (figure 3) and handoff chain (figure 4) both demonstrate, most SEO specialists and account managers don't share a succinct way to communicate these changes and their repercussions. In many instances, account managers must contact SEO specialists repeatedly, both by email and in person, to clarify why search rankings drop in specific instances. In one observation, Sonia had to contact Elizair twice—first over email, followed by a 10-minute meeting at his desk—to figure out why her client's rankings had dropped 22 places in a week.

Because SEO specialists don't share a common way to communicate these issues, account managers frequently run into problems when interpreting monthly report drafts. For instance, the breakdown table (see table 2) shows that Sonia encountered multiple breakdowns when trying to figure out why the client's rankings fell so dramatically. For instance, at one point Sonia read Elizair's draft report silently, then stopped at the rankings. "This doesn't look right," she said to another account manager. "Have you ever seen anything like this?" After discussing it, they agreed that she needed to ask Elizair for an explanation. She emailed him, but his response only confused her further. "I'll need to iron this out in person," she said as she got up to visit his office.

Although the SEO specialists don't share a common way to communicate these issues, some have developed innovations to address them. For instance, the triangulation table (see table 1) shows that when Craig emails his monthly reports to Sonia, he always includes a section in his email describing any algorithm changes.

Issue 2: No standardized project tracking exists, resulting in confusion when specialists have to communicate project status to each other or account managers.

Disruptions	
Macro (Contradictions)	Activity system: SEO specialists use tools that are not meant to manage complex projects.
	Activity network:

Example

Meso (Disco-ordinations)	Resource map: Elizair manages his projects with a custom spreadsheet, while Craig uses a list and Dani uses a notebook; all have trouble tracking their progress on a given project.
	Handoff chain: Craig and Dani sometimes drop tasks on projects when conveying reports to the account manager.
	Triangulation table: Elizair doesn't drop tasks on projects, but Craig and Dani do.
Micro (Break-downs)	Breakdown table: Craig and Dani both encounter several breakdowns when managing project tasks; Elizair encounters a few.

This topsight table suggests that SEObrate currently doesn't provide support for managing complex projects, and consequently, the SEO specialists have all developed their own systems—with varying degrees of success. The result, for some, is wasted effort and repetition.

The activity system (figure 2) shows that although specialists have identified information resources to help them track project management, these tools have come from other domains; Elizair uses a spreadsheet he improvised himself, while Craig models his text list on other lists he's used, and Dani models her notebook on the class notes she took during college (see figure 3). These resources have different sorts of capabilities. As the triangulation table (see table 1) suggests, Elizair's resource seems more successful than the other specialists'.

Similarly, the breakdown table (see table 2) suggests that Elizair encounters fewer breakdowns during project management tasks than Craig and Dani do.

RECOMMENDATIONS

Based on the findings, I recommend three changes to address these issues—develop a note in SEObrateMax to indicate search algorithm changes; develop a SEObrateMax routine to automatically detect algorithm changes; and establish standardized project tracking.

Develop a note in SEObrateMax to indicate search algorithm changes

Although Craig currently makes life easier for account managers by describing search algorithm changes in his emails, this information doesn't seem to circulate any further than this one communication. Furthermore, other specialists have not integrated this sort of communication into their routines at all.

Rather than asking these other specialists to add something else to their to-do lists, I recommend integrating this information directly into your internal SEO system, SEObrateMax. Doing so will standardize the information, make it part of their workflow, integrate it directly into the auto-generated reports, and track it permanently. In addition, it should be easy to implement; it should involve just one additional field in the SEObrateMax interface and just one additional routine to automatically drop it into the report draft—approximately 6 hours of scripting.

Develop a SEObrateMax routine to automatically detect algorithm changes

Along these lines, SEObrateMax should be able to automatically detect probable algorithm changes as it collects rankings. Building this capability into SEObrateMax would not only save time for the SEO specialists, it will also provide more historical context for algorithm changes. Currently, SEObrate is aware of these changes, but doesn't systematically track them.

In the medium term, then, I recommend building this routine to save time and to auto-detect such issues, which can then be examined more thoroughly by specialists. SEObrateMax has the basic capacity already. Although this recommendation involves a larger scope of work than the first recommendation, it should provide additional dividends that could keep SEObrate at the forefront of SEO.

Establish standardized project tracking

Finally, I recommend adopting a shared project tracking or project management system and training SEO specialists and account managers how to use it collaboratively. As we've seen, SEO specialists don't share a common way to track projects, and the results have been hit-and-miss.

Establishing a common system should help them to improve their own project management as well as communicating project status to each other. Fortunately, several inexpensive off-the-shelf solutions exist that could meet this need.

Tim, I am confident that these three recommendations will address the systemic issues I've detected at SEObrate. I hope that these recommendations serve SEObrate well as you begin addressing these issues. Let's discuss how to move forward on these recommendations.

Example

APPENDIX: MODELS

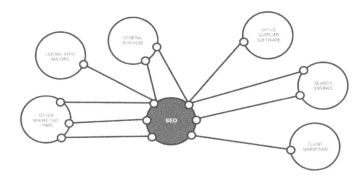

Figure 1. Activity network.

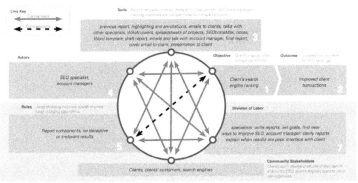

Figure 2. Activity system.

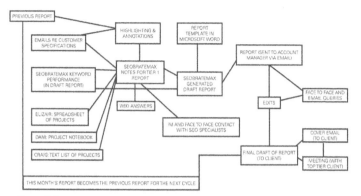

Figure 3. Resource map.

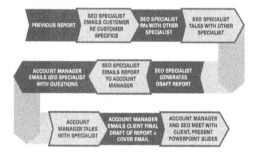

Figure 4. Handoff chain.

Example

Table 1. Triangulation table, showing how different team members used different resources.

	Prepare for report	Write report	Deliver report
Elizair	Previous month's report, highlighting and annotations on previous month's report, emails with client, spreadsheet of projects, IMs and talks with Craig, WikiAnswers	Emails from customers, SEObrateMAX, report template, notes, email to Sonia	Final draft of report, client presentation, PowerPoint slides
Craig	Previous month's report, highlighting and annotations on previous month's report, emails with client, keyword logs, text file listing projects, IMs and talks with Dani	Emails from customers, SEObrateMAX, report template, notes, email to Sonia	Final draft of report, client presentation, PowerPoint slides
Dani	Previous month's report, highlighting and annotations on previous month's report, emails with client, notebook listing projects, IMs and talks with Craig	Emails from customers, SEObrateMAX, report template, notes, email to Sonia	Final draft of report, client presentation, PowerPoint slides
Sonia		Email from Elizair, emails with customers, talk with Elizair	Final draft of report, cover email to client, client presentation, PowerPoint slides

Table 2. Breakdown table.

Partici-pant	Breakdown	Recovery
Dani	Excel: Accidentally enters date range in graph, resulting in straight line.	Copies proper range and pastes in Excel.
Dani	Excel: Graph only shows one line.	Deletes graph, selects entire data range, pastes into Excel.
Dani	SEObrateMAX: Fills out info for client. SEObrateMAX hangs.	Cancels, hits Try Again.

Example

312

Topsight 2.0

Redesigning an Implementation

Now that you have a recommendation, you need to figure out how to implement it. That's easier said than done! In this section, we'll answer two questions:

- How do you redesign parts of the work to address the organization's systemic issues?

- How do you communicate your changes?

CHAPTER 27

Designing Solutions

At this point, you've developed a *recommendation*. It's based on your deep analysis of the organization, and it provides that organization with a *general* solution. But a general recommendation isn't specific enough for you to implement. The next step is to design a concrete solution based on that recommendation, one that *can* be implemented.

Recommendations are General; Design is Specific

For instance, in the example at the end of the last chapter, the report recommends three solutions:

- "Develop a note in SEObrateMax to indicate search algorithm changes"

- "Develop a SEObrateMax routine to automatically detect algorithm changes"

- "Establish standardized project tracking"

These three recommendations tell the readers *what* they need to do, but not *how* to do it. For example, they might consider many different systems for tracking projects. Which specific implementation would be best for them? Which one would be most likely to meet their needs without conflicting with other parts of their ongoing activity or causing further contradictions? That is, *how* should they address that need by implementing the recommendation?

Recommendations are:

- **General**. "Develop an electronic filing system with character-istics A, B, and C."

- **Abstract**. The recommendation has many different potential implementations.

- **Testable against abstract characteristics**. You can test whether it fits, based on the models you've developed to describe your data.

But *design* is:

- **Specific**. "Here's a working electronic filing system with char-acteristics A, B, and C."

- **Concrete**. The recommendation has a single realized imple-mentation.

- **Testable in actual use**. You can test whether it works in real situations—and you can learn things from how it is used.

Design implementation can be tricky because you have to make specific decisions and (often) compromises. More than that, the implementation has to harmonize with the people who will use it. After all, when people don't like an implementation, they will often route around it, bringing in tools and practices from elsewhere instead of using the ones that are given to them by the organiza-tion. In fact, that's why the resource maps of most organizations look so eclectic: people route around the official solutions, bringing in unofficial ones.

Design is Hard to Get Right the First Time

As you can imagine, designing a solution can be a high-stakes gamble: you don't (yet) know whether a specific design will be ac-

ceptable to your participants. If you make a big change and participants reject it, you've put a lot of time and effort into the project
for nothing—and you've disrupted people's lives in the process.

Worse, designing a solution is hard to get right because of several
constraints:

- **Limited data**. You haven't been able to see every scenario.

- **Tacit knowledge**. People don't know what they know; they
  may not be able to put into words what they do. They might
  not be able to provide good feedback until they actually use
  the design in their activity.

- **Design language**. You and the users may not have a shared
  vocabulary or set of concepts.

These mean that even if your recommendation is solid, the design
implementation might not be on target. *It might fail.*

The solution is not to try really hard to make the design perfect.
You probably can't make it perfect—you don't have enough data to
do that. Instead, *fail faster*.

Solution: Fail Faster

In other words, as you design an implementation, make lots of
low-stakes gambles that allow you to test your changes piece by
piece.

To do that, you'll use an approach called *participatory design*. In
this approach, you don't design an implementation for users—you
design it *with* users. You will:

- Create ways for people to experience a designed solution
  within their activity (or a simulation of it).

- Design solutions cheaply.

- Design solutions to generate feedback.

- Iterate designs based on feedback so you can evolve a better solution.

Failure is good—if it provides useful feedback. And that is what participatory design should do for us.

Participatory Design

To understand participatory design, let's briefly discuss its origin and its principles. (If you would like to learn more about this fascinating history, see Spinuzzi 2002, 2005a, 2005b.)

Participatory design originated in the Scandinavian countries in the 1970s and 1980s. At that point, industries such as typesetting relied on the deep craft expertise of workers with lifelong employment. But changes were happening. Computer technologies held the promise of automating parts of this work—but they also threatened to make the workers' deep craft knowledge, which had been built up over decades, suddenly obsolete. After all, these workers had never seen computers (except in science fiction movies), and they were worried that bringing in computers would mean relearning their jobs from the ground up. And if that had to happen, they reasoned, how long would it be before management just gave up on the experienced workers and hired new (and cheaper) workers right out of school?

Beyond representing a sharp break from workers' traditional ways of working, computer systems also threatened to exert greater and greater control over the fine details of the work. The workers worried that they would have less and less discretion over their own work.

But what could the workers do? Since they did not know how to design computer technologies themselves, they were put into the position of either accepting or rejecting computer systems. And they could only reject these systems for so long before their work became obsolete.

But in the UTOPIA Project, some Scandinavian researchers set out to develop a third way. This approach provided a set of "language games" (Ehn and Kyng 1991, pp. 176-177) that would help software developers and workers to collaborative on developing new technologies. As a result, the computer systems could be developed *based on* the workers' expertise, as a clear extension of what the workers already knew, rather than as a completely new paradigm.

To do this, the researchers and union representatives developed an approach called participatory design. Participatory design has three stages; people can *iterate* these stages, looping through them until they are satisfied with the solutions they have developed. Each stage helps researchers and participants to cocreate solutions.

The stages are:

Stage 1: Initial Exploration of Work

In this stage, researchers and participants meet and the researchers become familiar with the ways in which the participants work together. They examine the technologies, workflow and work procedures, routines, teamwork, and other aspects of the participants' work.

Stage 1 usually involves observations, interviews, and artifact analysis. In fact, it looks a lot like the field studies we discussed earlier in *Topsight*.

Stage 2: Discovery Processes

In the second stage, researchers and participants use different techniques to help them discover, talk about, understand, and prioritize aspects of their work, as well as envisioning what they would like from a future workplace. During this stage, researchers and participants work together to clarify the participants' goals and values and to agree on what they want out of the project.

Stage 3: Prototyping

In this stage, researchers and participants iteratively shape tools to fit into the workplace they envisioned in Stage 2. They can conduct prototyping on site or in a lab. It involves one or more participants. And it can be conducted on-the-job if the prototype is a working prototype.

Through these three stages, the researchers used several participatory design techniques to codesign with participants. These techniques included:

- **Mockups**: Common objects (such as cardboard boxes) used to represent technologies with which workers are unfamiliar (such as laser printers).

- **Paper prototypes**: Paper versions of interfaces with which workers could eventually interact. Workers could directly change these.

- **Cooperative prototypes**: Computer-based prototypes that researchers could quickly change based on workers' feedback.

- **Organizational games**: Games based on familiar ones (such as Monopoly), representing aspects of workers' decisions or routines.

- **Future workshops**: Workshops to discuss the concerns workers have about the future. What are their (activity-level) expectations, hopes, and fears for this activity?

- **Role playing**: Having workers imagine using a new tool as they pretend to complete a task.

- **Organizational toolkits**: A set of icons or stickers that people can use to represent a process and common problems with it.

- **Storyboarding**: Representing a current problem in a storyboard or comic strip, then representing how the same scenario could play out with the proposed innovation.

- **Card sorting**: Writing different procedures, information resources, etc. on index cards, then asking users to group and sort them.

As I mentioned, the three stages of participatory design can be used as a *feedback loop*. And that's important. As we discussed earlier in this book, participants often have *tacit* (unspoken, un-articulated) knowledge, and they have to make it *explicit* in order for researchers to take that knowledge into account. To make that happen, they have to be put in a position in which they can recognize and articulate that knowledge. You've started them on this road in Stage 1, through your observations and interviews—but you'll need techniques from Stages 2 and 3 to try out possible interventions, see if they work, and (more importantly) see why they *don't* work. You'll be able to elicit feedback such as:

- The workers' interactions

- The workers' feedback during the process

- Confusion and disagreements

- The resulting conversations

Because participatory design is a design research approach, the point of these interventions is not to "pass the test." It's to learn progressively more about participants' tacit knowledge in order to better synchronize your interventions with their work. And that means that your feedback loop should involve intervening in small controlled ways, examining the results of the intervention, and iterating in response to those results.

Implementing Participatory Design with Topsight

So how do we handle a participatory design project within the Topsight approach? That's what this final section is about.

Iterating and feedback. In Chapter 28, we will discuss the basics of iterating and feedback. We'll talk about how to "fail faster" without failing disastrously or losing the confidence of your participants. This is the heart of any design research approach, and it should help you to develop a right-fit implementation for your participants.

Chapters 29-32 will discuss specific participatory design techniques.

Mockups and prototypes. If your recommendation is to develop or modify an *information resource*, mockups and prototypes are a good way to develop an implementation. Chapter 29 explains the difference between the two, discusses how to iterate them, and provides examples.

Organizational games. On the other hand, if you're recommending a new *process* that affects organizational or group-level routines, you might consider developing an organizational game to probe how well a high-level process change might work. Chapter 30 discusses organizational games, describing what they do and providing examples.

Future workshops. Finally, you might recommend changes in the broader *activity*, such as rethinking its objective. This sort of change requires real discussion among the people in the activity, and that's where future workshops come in. Chapter 31 discusses future workshops and provides guidance on how to conduct them.

Looping through feedback. Finally, Chapter 32 gives you parting advice on how to take the feedback from these techniques and drive it into the next round of design work.

Exercise: Select the Recommendation to Address

- **Review your recommendations**. Which one would be either most important (the biggest win) or easiest to design (the easiest win)?

- **Think about design options**. Does one seem most appropriate for this recommendation?

CHAPTER 28

Iterating and Feedback

As we've seen, a field study tells you what the problem *is* and helps you to guess what changes will result from an intervention.

But an organization is a complex system. Don't bet that you know everything about it. In fact, expect that you don't! Your brief field study helped you to detect systemic issues, but now you must figure out how to design a solution that won't cause unintended effects in the rest of the organization—a solution that won't create further problems.

Here, we will treat design as a way to further probe the organization and how it might react to interventions—*before* we implement them organization-wide. We will *fail faster*.

Fail Faster

I mentioned in the last chapter that "design solutions should help you to fail faster." The phrase *fail faster* is widely used in entrepreneurship (see Ries 2011), but it's also widely misunderstood.

The idea behind "fail faster" is to allow our efforts to fail in *small, controlled ways that provide more actionable data*. "Failing faster" in low-stakes situations (such as small-scale tests) helps us to learn and adjust so that we can succeed in high-stakes situations (such as rolling out a new information system or a fundamental change in work organization).

"Fail faster" is an acknowledgement that we aren't perfect, we don't have a perfect understanding of the organization in which we want to intervene, and we won't be able to generate a perfect intervention right off the bat. We may know the recommendation, but we need the users' tacit knowledge to develop the right solution. So, using participatory design techniques, we will

- Put them into the situation we want to improve.

- Provide a solution that they could see themselves using.

- Watch them as they try to use it; identify observable problems as they do.

- Provide easy ways for them to give their own feedback; identify otherwise invisible problems *and* get the participants' own ideas on how to solve them.

So, rather than going away, designing a solution, and presenting it as a complete solution to users, we will create probes—probes that encourage users to provide feedback at each step, cocreating solutions with us and participating in their design.

A Feedback Loop in Pseudocode

So what would such a feedback loop look like? Here's a pseudocode (or stepwise process) representation of it:

1. Provide a recommendation

2. Design an implementable solution to the recommendation

3. Gather feedback from participants through the appropriate participatory design techniques

4. IF feedback is fatal GOTO 1

5. IF feedback is substantial GOTO 2

6. ELSE END

If your feedback is *fatal*, you may have misconstrued the problem; you might have to rethink your recommendation entirely (*punt*). If your feedback is *substantial*, you may have to redesign your solution (*persevere*) or even design an entirely new solution to test (*pivot*). We will discuss these moves in Chapter 33.

But at some point your feedback won't be substantial. Participants may make suggestions about minor wording or format changes, but they respond well to the design in general. At that point, you know you have a winner—and you can end the participatory design process.

As discussed in the previous chapter, we will discuss these types of probes:

- Mockups and prototypes (for tools)

- Organizational games (for processes)

- Future workshops (for activities)

We'll begin this discussion in the next chapter.

Example Reading

Evia and Patriarca used participatory design in a study described in this article:

> Evia, C., & Patriarca, A. (2012). Beyond Compliance: Participatory Translation of Safety Communication for Latino Construction Workers. *Journal of Business and Technical Communication*, 26(3), 340–367.

In this study, the authors addressed an important problem: the problem of developing effective workplace safety and risk communication materials for Latino construction workers. These workers faced a set of problems: culture and language differences on many job sites, as well as low levels of literacy and lack of proper training. To address these issues, the authors used direct creative input from Latino construction workers to create safety and risk communication products. These products were evaluated as effective and culturally relevant for these workers and their peers.

To develop these products, the authors followed these stages:

1. **Initial stage**: Observed, attended talks, conducted interviews.

2. **Discovery stage**: Future workshop, organizational game.

3. **Prototyping stage**: Comic strip or storyboard narrative; TV sitcom made with stop-motion animation.

By following the participatory design approach, the authors were able to codesign with workers, creating products that had a high chance of being useful and productive.

Exercise: Plan your Intervention

In groups or alone:

1. **Identify** an intervention.

2. Develop a plan to **instantiate** the intervention (e.g., make a prototype).

3. Develop a plan to **test** the intervention (e.g., how you'll present the prototype).

4. Identify the **kinds of data** you'll collect (e.g., remarks and their modifications).

5. Think through how your data will provide **feedback** for further design.

CHAPTER 29

Mockups and Prototypes

Let's go back to the SEObrate case. As you recall, one of the recommendations was:

"Develop a note in SEObrateMax to indicate search algorithm changes"

This recommendation is for a new feature within the software—a new tool they can use to explain their work. But this recommendation just tells them *what* they need. You haven't yet solved *how* the note will be implemented. It could be implemented in many ways, including

- A regular field in an existing window

- A hidden field in an existing window, which becomes visible if they click a checkbox

- An optional separate window in a sequence

- A pop-up window

Beyond its form, it could have many different features. Here's just a few:

- It could be optional or mandatory

- It could alert others

- It could list recent comments so the user can see what others have noted about it

- It could restrict input by having users select keywords

And the design choices go on and on. Once you begin to consider implementation, you find that you must make many choices, each of which could impact your users in ways you may not anticipate.

Furthermore, your participants may not have the explicit knowledge necessary to tell you what choices are good ones. Features that sound good to them in a meeting might turn out to conflict with their tacit knowledge about their work.

How do you probe this tacit knowledge—and how do you do it without spending lots of time and money on developing an implementation for them to test?

When you're faced with a situation like this, in which you need to design and test a *tool*, you can turn to two related design probes: mockups and prototypes.

Mockups and Prototypes as "Language Games"

As mentioned, mockups and prototypes are meant to probe how a new tool might affect the organization. In the participatory design tradition, they have been developed to provide a common "language game" for designers and users to "play."

Mockups

Mockups are great for representing large, vaguely defined equipment at the beginning of a process, especially if the participants haven't used that equipment before.

In the UTOPIA project (see Chapter 28), researchers had begun by using traditional design description methods such as scenarios and data flow. But workers had difficulty understanding these unfamiliar notations, so the enrolled parties turned to mock-ups to give workers a frame of reference (Bødker et al. 1987, p.263). "The principle behind the mock-up was simple. Using sheets of paper, matchboxes, some plywood, etc., one 'builds' a workstation with a 'high-resolution display,' a 'mouse,' etc." (Ehn 1993, p.335). Then, under the researcher's guidance, workers used the mock-ups to simulate work (Ehn and Kyng 1991).

These mockups—low-fidelity prototypes of computers, laser printers, and other hardware and software—provided a way for workers to play with, interact with, and imagine possibilities for new computer technologies before actual development was begun. Rather than having to work with fully developed technologies that conflicted with their practices, experiences, and goals, workers could interact directly with designers to help design the technologies they would use and how those technologies would impact their work.

Thus mockups provided a language game that made sense to all participants, a way for researchers and workers to pool their expertise and share design responsibility for the project (Ehn and Kyng 1991, p.176–77). This language game meant that workers could even modify the prototypes to better suit their tacit knowledge of their craft (183). That meant that the resulting design was actually *codesigned* with the workers. Mockups provided a way to establish a common ground; using mockups pulled workers into the design process rather than excluding them.

Prototypes

Prototypes are similar to mockups, but are more detailed.

In the UTOPIA project, researchers would mock up a laser printer with a box labeled "laser printer." That's fine for understanding broad impacts: how big the laser printer is, where a worker might prefer to put it, and how workers might adjust their workflow to use it. But it's not great for understanding finer details and impacts—say, how a specific note field in SEObrate should be designed. For that level of detail, prototypes are better.

Prototypes are detailed representations of the tools the researcher might develop for the participants. For instance, in the UTOPIA project, software developers created paper "screens" that gave the workers an idea of what an actual interface might look like. In participatory design, prototypes typically start out as low-fidelity *paper prototypes*: typically hand-drawn and hand-lettered, with features such as pop-up windows represented by sticky notes. If a paper prototype represents a sequence, that sequence can be simulated with several pieces of paper.

Why should paper prototypes start out with such low fidelity? Wouldn't it be simpler, faster, and more legible to design these in a layout program and print them for use? Maybe—but the hand drawing and lettering signals to the participants that *this prototype is not serious*. They're not dealing with a finished piece of work and they won't hurt your feelings by grabbing a marker and making their own changes to it—which is exactly what you want them to do.

The Feedback Loop for Mockups and Prototypes

When you use mockups and prototypes, remember that these function as probes. These probes should encourage the participants to make their tacit knowledge explicit and to capture that feedback. In other words, mockups and prototypes *should* fail—that is, participants should be able to tell you what's wrong with these probes and how you can fix them. You can expect to go through this feedback loop at least a few times.

The feedback loop looks like this:

- Rough out the tool

- Put participants in a scenario

- Ask participants to "use" the tool

- Ask participants to modify the tool

1. Rough out a Tool

As mentioned above, it's fine—probably preferable—for the mockup or prototype to be obviously rough. This roughness signals to the participants that this tool is not the product of a lot of work, so it can be criticized. *It's just a probe.*

Signal that probe status.

- If you are using a prototype, strongly consider making it out of paper. Hand-draw and hand-letter the prototype, using pens, pencils, markers, and sticky notes.

- Similarly, if you use a mockup, consider using cardboard boxes, construction paper, Styrofoam, or other inexpensive materials that signal how rough the mockup is.

The initial objective of this tool isn't to give them a complete solution, it's to give them a starting place for discussion.

2. Put Participants in a Scenario

The participants will need to envision using the tool to do things within their work context. But what?

- Go back to your models, then your field notes and interviews, to get a good idea of the context in which they might need to use these tools. Look at your models and your raw data to understand what.

- Next, develop a scenario based on the models and raw data.

- When you're ready to try out the tool, describe the work scenario to them. Make sure they have the information needed to pretend they are in this situation. (For instance, if we were testing a prototype for SEObrate notes, we might describe a scenario in which they have found an algorithm change.)

3. Ask Participants to "Use" the Tool

Sometimes when you present a scenario and tool to a participant, she or he will want to critique it rather than using it. But when this happens, they are activating their *explicit* knowledge, the knowledge that they have been able to verbalize. You need to activate their *tacit* knowledge instead: the things they know without being able to verbalize. To make sure that you activate their tacit knowledge, ask them to "use" the tool in the fictional scenario.

As they do, they will be able to identify different critiques, situated within their normal workflow and other information resources. This is the feedback you need. Make sure to record it in notes or on video.

4. Ask Participants to Modify the Tool

Beyond your recording, though, encourage them to record their own feedback directly on the prototype or mockup. Tell them they can change it to better suit what they want to do. And give them plenty of ways to do that—markers, pens, sticky notes.

As they modify the tool, encourage them to explain why. Doing this will help you to understand the reasoning behind their changes. That's critical, since—let's be honest—some of their designs will be ugly and unworkable. They're not trained designers. But this step should allow them to explain why the current design is so unsatisfactory and what they need from a new design.

Refining the Tool

At the end of the process, you'll have notes and recordings from each session, plus the actual mockups and prototypes that the participants changed.

Now, look across the feedback you received. Are there consistent themes? Do people identify some of the same issues, even though their solutions are all over the place?

Based on this feedback, refine the mockup or prototype.

- If your participants suggested lots of deep modifications, keep the mockup or prototype rough. Use the same materials as before; get more feedback before proceeding.

- But if your participants suggested only a few superficial modifications, consider producing the mockup or prototype in more permanent, realistic materials.

Example: Using a Prototype to Design a New Tool

Suppose that you have identified a problem at the workplace you studied. They're trying to track inventory via pen and paper, but this system doesn't work well for a number of reasons. So you have recommended that they move to an iPad-based database.

But what should this database look like—how should it be implemented? You know that if the workers don't understand the interface, they might just go back to the old system. So you have to hook into the workers' tacit knowledge about how they track inventory so he can make sure the solution works.

Since the design problem involves designing a tool, you decide to try paper prototyping. You come up with the following plan:

- You create an interface on paper with sticky notes and put the paper on a clipboard to simulate a tablet. You bring some markers and extra sticky notes as well.

- For each participant, you do the following:

    a. Meet, preferably in the context where they do this work.

    b. Have them pretend to take inventory using the prototype. This should let you see them deal with actual situations, and they should be able to feel like this exercise is realistic, triggering their tacit knowledge.

    c. Since the prototype interface has different screens (represented by different pieces of paper), you ask them to touch the interface drawing, flipping to different drawings to show the changes in the interface.

    d. Ask them to use the markers and extra sticky notes to change the interface, showing you what they would prefer.

You can do this for 3-4 people and see what sorts of problems they encounter.

If workers provide you with a lot of feedback, you can keep iterating paper prototypes until the workers seem pretty happy with one. At that point, you can begin developing an actual iPad app (testing further as you go).

CHAPTER 30

Organizational Games

Let's go back to the SEObrate case again. As you recall, one of the recommendations was:

"Establish standardized project tracking"

This recommendation is for a new process that, if implemented well, will allow them to work more effectively. But, again, this recommendation just tells them *what* they need. You haven't yet solved *how* project tracking will be implemented. It could be implemented in many ways, including

- A centralized process in which one person tracks the projects and handles coordination; everyone else reports to her

- A distributed process in which every worker shares the same tracking system and updates their own work

- A hybrid system in which certain kinds of tasks are centralized or overseen by domain experts, while others are distributed across team members

- A regular morning meeting in which everyone identifies what they plan to accomplish that day and that week

Not only might the processes look different, each could cycle at a different level of frequency: daily, weekly, or monthly.

Which implementation would be the best for SEObrate? You may have an idea based on your fieldwork, but again, you won't be able to mine the tacit knowledge of your participants unless you have them try out these processes. In fact, you might have to have them try these processes out in different ways, with different combinations of participants—a process might work just fine for participants in one role, but conflict with those in adjacent roles.

One way to test an implementation is with an *organizational game*.

Organizational Games as "Language Games"

Like mockups and prototypes, organizational games were developed during the UTOPIA project to give researchers and workers a common "language game" for understanding the work and how the researchers could intervene in it.

The idea is this: When a worker is *describing* what she does, she might not be able to make her tacit knowledge explicit. When a worker *does* her work (and is being observed), it's hard to separate specific contingencies from the general workflow. The worker needs a little structure for representing her work processes, and at the same time, a little distance so she can see these work processes in a different way. Furthermore, if the researcher wants to describe a new process, that process has to be represented in a way that the worker can understand and evaluate. They need a common language game in which they can represent, try out, and reflect on this intervention.

In the UTOPIA project, the researchers and workers didn't have much in common in terms of work. The researchers really didn't understand what the workers did and the workers didn't really understand the capabilities of the computer systems the researchers were proposing to design. But both sets of people had played games—board games, card games. So they decided to use common, well-known games to represent organizational processes.

After all, many games already do something like this:

- A certain **board game** represents real estate speculation. The players go around the board, encountering buying opportunities, deciding whether to buy real estate, and encountering random contingencies. At the end of each trip around the board, they receive a "week's" pay.

- A certain **trading card** game represents single combat. Each round, each player can choose a combatant and has the option to also choose cards representing defensive or offensive capabilities that boost the chances of the combatant.

Games often represent situations we already understand, but with simplified rules and rapid gameplay. Actual real estate speculation is much more complicated than a board game and takes a lot longer—and actual combat is more complex and dangerous than a card game.

An organizational game can similarly represent a process at work, one with simplified rules, a compressed timeframe, and a chance to examine the process from a distance. For instance,

- A **board game** might represent a work project, with each trip around the board representing a new day. What strategy does a worker use to track and manage the project? How does he handle random contingencies and get back on track? What resources does he choose to "buy" to make the project work?

- A **card game** might represent decision-making with resources. If the researcher "plays" a contingency from her deck, what resource cards does the worker choose from his deck?

And unlike store-bought games, these games can be modified:

- Workers can change the **board game** by rearranging the squares on the board or writing new ones to better represent their day; by adding new contingency cards and/or getting rid of ones that they think don't match their real work; and by adding new types of resources they use.

- Workers can change the **card game** by making their own resource and contingency cards and adding these to the deck.

As workers change the games, they can explain why—an important piece of feedback as you consider how to modify the game further.

The Feedback Loop for Organizational Games

When you use organizational games, remember that these function as probes. These probes should encourage the participants to make their tacit knowledge explicit and to capture that feedback. In other words, organizational games *should* fail—that is, participants should be able to tell you what's wrong with these probes and how you can fix them. You can expect to go through this feedback loop at least a few times.

The feedback loop looks like this:

- Develop an organizational game to address the aspect you need to probe

- Play the game with one or more participants

- Discuss the game with the participant(s)

- Refine the game

1. Develop an Organizational Game

We can't possibly categorize all of the games with which people are familiar, and each type of game might tell you something different. But here are three common types of organizational games:

- **Board games**: These work well for representing routines and time structuring. They also work well for multiple participants, allowing them to demonstrate different strategies and use those to talk about their reasons for selecting each strategy.

- **Card games**: These work well for representing contingencies and resources. They typically work best in pairs.

- **Card sorting**: Card sorting involves creating a deck of cards with different things or concepts. Each participant then puts the cards in groups and then discusses why they are grouped in this way. Card sorting is typically done with one participant and works well for understanding how people define categories.

Remember, organizational games are grounded in what your people know, but they are abstracted into a rapid environment with simplified rules. To get the most out of them, either

- model your game after one that your participants know, or

- create a game with clear, simple rules

Recall that the point of the organizational game is to represent a process in the organization: either a process as it currently exists or a proposed process that could improve the organization. When you design your organizational game, select a type of game that allows you to represent that process and explore what you need to know about it.

2. Play the Game

Once you've designed the game, you'll need to do the following:

- **Select participants**. Choose people who are engaged in the process you're exploring. If the process involves people in different roles—such as project tracking—make sure to get participants who represent these different roles.

- **Explain the rules**. Tell the participants what the rules of the game are, and make sure they know that the game represents a process from work. (If they argue about your rules, that's data too!)

- **Facilitate gameplay**. You will need to enforce the rules and encourage the participants to play. As you do this, make sure to record the gameplay and their conversations about it. You could videorecord the game, write down notes, or have a second person keep notes for you.

- **Allow them to change the rules and game**. Once they have played a few rounds, ask them to suggest new rules, write new cards, or rearrange the board. What could improve the process?

Make sure there's a defined endpoint—either a set number of rounds or a time constraint. Otherwise participants might get bored and want to end the game early—or play even longer.

3. Discuss the Game

The game is an opportunity for your participants to reflect on work at a level they may not always be able to access. So take advantage of that—spend some time at the end discussing the results. What would they suggest to improve the process further? What do they think will and won't work in real life, and why? Where do different participants agree and where do they disagree?

4. Refine the Game—Or Try a New One

If the game gave you a lot of feedback, consider refining it and bringing it back to the same participants.

On the other hand, playing one game may suggest that you need a different game to probe aspects that you weren't able to probe adequately with this one. Drive your insights into selecting and designing that new game.

Below, I offer three sample organizational games: a board game, a trading card game, and a card sorting exercise.

Example: Using a Board Game to Examine Workflow in an Office

The Scenario

Suppose that you're interested in examining workflow in an office. Your recommendation was to clarify this workflow so that people don't spend so much time switching between tasks. But to implement this recommendation, you'll need to know which tasks are necessary, which are routine, and which are urgent.

Summary of the Game

This board game is designed to help investigate overall workflow in a chronological sequence, represented by a track running around the board, and random disruptive events, represented by two stacks of cards in the middle of the board. Workers can reconfigure the game by adding and modifying cards and by changing the squares on the track.

Gameplay

The events on the board include standard parts of the participant's day, including office hours, regular meetings, client meetings, checking email, checking the inbox, and talking with other office workers in the hallway.

Random disruptive events are delivered in two ways:

- **Email cards**. If the worker lands on a Check Email square, he draws an Email card. Email events might include administrative requests, attempts to schedule client meetings, and correspondence from clients and coworkers.

- **Inbox cards**. If the worker lands on a Check Inbox square, he draws an Inbox card. Inbox events might include paperwork, junk mail, and package deliveries.

Whenever the worker draws a card or lands on a square, she should explain how she might handle the situation. She can also critique, modify, and add to the cards and squares.

Concluding the game

At the end of the game, researchers and participants can engage in the following activities:

- Go through the Inbox and Email cards, ranking them by priority.

- Critique the squares and add/remove/change them.

Example: Using a Card Game to Explore Contingency Handling in an Office

The Scenario

Now suppose that you want to explore contingency handling in an office.

Summary of the Game

You develop a duelling card game modeled after trading card games. It's designed to allow you to mix and match contingencies and see how the participant draws upon resources to address them. It's not designed to explicate an *overall picture* of the workflow, just *particular pieces* of it. In addition to the supplied cards, the deck contains blank cards that participants can use to add resources and contingencies.

If the participant cannot address the event with the cards in her hand, she can discard up to five cards and draw new ones, or she can elect to fill out a blank card.

The game consists of two decks and four types of cards.

The Researcher's Deck

The researcher has a deck that she uses to create events to which the worker must react. This deck includes Challenge and Contingency cards. The designer always has five cards total in play or in her hand.

- **Challenge cards** represent basic challenges the participant might face related to sharing information, such as scheduling a meeting, circulating information, or responding to clients. In addition to the defined cards, this deck includes six blank cards that the participant can define.

- **Contingency cards** represent contingencies that might close off certain possibilities for dealing with the challenges, such as email being down, the website being down, staff being out sick, or the participant getting sick. In addition to the defined cards, this deck includes four blank cards that the worker can define.

The worker's deck

The worker's deck represents resources she may draw on to address the events represented in the cards played by the researcher. Resources include Tools and People.

- **Tools** include physical and electronic artifacts used in the course of work. Tools include email, the website, the phone, paperwork, and new documents that the participant writes (such as letters or meeting minutes). In addition to the defined cards, this deck includes four blank cards that the worker can define.

- **People** include key personnel in the office, such as individual staff members, team members, and managers. In addition to the defined cards, this deck includes four blank cards that the worker can define.

Concluding the game

At the end of the game, the researcher and participant can do one or more of the following:

- Sort the different types of cards in terms of priority/severity (challenge and contingency cards) and usefulness/importance (tools and people cards).

- Go through the filled-out cards and discuss what other cards might be filled out.

- Go through challenge cards and discuss how a new process might address each.

Example: Using Card Sorting to Help Workers Deal with Stray Tasks

Suppose you have discovered that people in the organization aren't clear on their roles, so lots of tasks keep getting dropped—each person thinks it's someone else's problem. In your recommendation report, you have recommended providing clearer, better defined roles for workers.

But how can you implement this recommendation? You have some ideas, but you want to test out how well those ideas work. So you come up with a low-stakes way to test the solution: *card sorting*. To develop this solution, you:

1. take a lot of index cards, write a name of a dropped task on each, and bring along some blank cards as well;

2. meet with each participant;

3. hand the participant the set of cards;

4. ask the participant to group the tasks by role—that is, to say which tasks should be tackled by which role;

5. ask the participant to write down other stray tasks they have noticed being dropped, and assign these to roles as well; and

6. discuss why the participant assigns each task to each role, so you can understand their thinking.

You do this for 3-4 people, then see how closely the answers are grouped.

With this plan, you'll be one step closer to assigning tasks. And you'll be able to see if they think the tasks can be handled by an existing role or whether they think a new role should be created to handle it.

CHAPTER 31

Future Workshops

Up to this point, we have been looking at the SEObrate case, considering how to implement the recommendations in the recommendation report. For those recommendations, techniques such as prototyping and organizational games help us to envision new tools and processes.

But, as discussed in Chapter 20, sometimes deeper *contradictions* form within or between activities, and these contradictions can sometimes threaten the entire organization. How do we address this kind of issue? One way is through a *future workshop*. To understand what this technique is and when you might use it, let's turn away from SEObrate and try a completely different case.

Case: The Photography Club

Suppose that you have investigated a student photography club at the local university. (We briefly discussed this scenario in Chapter 2.)

The photography club has been around since the late 1980s. It was started by a student who wanted to become a professional photographer: she wanted to learn professional skills from other photographers, organize trips so she could practice photography in different conditions, and network with other students who also aspired to become professional photographers. In the early days, the club arranged for its members to have access to a darkroom so they could develop their own film. It also had a speaker series in which professional photographers discussed their own techniques.

The club's charter and mission still reflect that orientation.

However, over time, photography has changed considerably. Now photography is primarily digital, which means that it's cheaper and doesn't require a darkroom. Increasingly, people are interested in photography as a hobby rather than a profession, and many of the new club members share their photos on Instagram or other low-fidelity photo-sharing outlets. Some of them actually take pictures on their phones, using special lenses, rather than using expensive SLRs. And some are branching out from still photography to limited video, using new capabilities of the latest generation of digital cameras.

That is, although the club's charter and mission have not changed, many of the current club members don't really subscribe to the old charter and mission. But others do. And this tension is showing up in a lot of places:

- The club members are forming cliques (or factions).

- Different cliques are showing up to different events. For instance, the professional photography clique will attend one speaker event but not the next; the phone photography clique will attend an urban field trip but not a nature trip.

- Members are disagreeing about how membership fees should be spent.

- Every year, members elect their officers. For the last few years, these elections have devolved into fights between cliques.

As you investigated the organization, you found that its objective had developed a contradiction: is the objective to *prepare members to be professional photographers*, or is it to *facilitate photography as a leisure pursuit*? That contradiction cannot be addressed by introducing new tools or processes because it's at the heart of what it means to be part of this organization.

So how do you address a problem like this one, a fundamental disagreement about the objective of the organization? Since the organization is made up of members, each of whom have a say in the organization, how do you get those members to talk openly about their goals, listen to each other, and compromise?

Future Workshops: Collaborative Visioning

A similar problem was faced in the UTOPIA project. The software developers needed to understand the users' needs, but they also needed to understand the broader context of the work and how the changes they made would affect the future of their users' work. To address this question, they turned to an approach called *future workshops*.

Future workshops were originally developed by Robert Jungk, a German citizen who had fled Nazi Germany in 1933 and had attempted to alert the European media to the menace. Jungk wanted to encourage workers to take control of their own lives, especially in the face of totalitarian regimes:

"What is a future workshop all about? Well, the man in the street has practically no say when it comes to jobs, the environment or the way the future is shaped. All of these aspects of our lives are in the hands of the politicians, the industrialists and the experts. To remedy this non-democratic state of affairs and to show that things can be done better, Robert Jungk and his co-workers, over a decade ago, developed the future workshop method. The idea behind it is that the silent majority actually has plenty to say about what our towns and neighbourhoods should be like, about jobs and industry [and] energy and all their other needs" (Jungk and Mullert 1988, pp.51-52).

The idea behind the future workshop was that rank-and-file workers, who were normally not brought into the decision-making processes of their organizations, could get together to methodically discuss their interests and propose changes.

In adopting the future workshop approach, the Scandianvian software developers organized weekend workshops with union representatives. In those workshops, workers collaboratively critiqued the current work arrangement; envisioned an ideal future in which those critiques would be satisfactorily be answered, and identified changes that they could implement in order to get to that future (see Muller 2008). The future workshop, in other words, helped the workers to get an activity-level view of their work so they could talk through what they wanted from changes.

The Topsight approach already involves sketching out the activity-level view in our investigation (via activity systems and activity networks). This means that if you were to run a future workshop, you can use these two models as a starting place for discussing the current state of the organization with participants.

The Feedback Loop for Future Workshops

Future workshops, like the other techniques, function as probes. In this case, the probes should help the participants to have an honest conversation about what objectives they see as being important in the organization—and how they might reimagine the organization to better address the needs of multiple participants.

Like the other probes, future workshops can result in failures. In fact, one real possibility is that the *organization itself* will "fail": members may decide that the best way to reach different objectives is to split the organization rather than expanding to address everyone's concerns. That's not necessarily a bad thing, and only the members can decide and justify it.

The feedback loop for a future workshop looks like this:

- Define the issue

- Invite the representatives

- Convene the future workshop

- Summarize the results

Define the Issue

Using the activity system and activity network models, articulate what you believe is the essential contradiction. Think in terms of the organization's *objective and outcome*. What are its mission and vision, and do you have indications that these are contradicted by other parts of the system?

In the case of the photography club, you have already noted a contradiction in the objective, one that you can substantiate with your data.

Invite the Representatives

When Jungk developed the future workshop approach, he wanted to involve people who didn't usually make decisions—he wanted them to take control of their own work. When the UTOPIA project picked up this technique, they involved union leaders, who functioned as political representatives for the workers.

In your case, you will need to decide who the best representatives will be for your organization. Consider selecting a variety of people with different roles, job descriptions, and (if applicable) factions. Do *not* just invite leadership—unless the problem is genuinely affecting only leaders.

In the case of the photography club, you should consider inviting people from each of the factions you were able to identify. You might also get a sample of long-time club members and new members. Since the future workshop is a way for them to have a conversation about what the club should accomplish, it's a good idea to have many different perspectives at the table.

For a larger organization, consider working through existing channels rather than inviting individuals (something that may make you look like you're playing favorites). Or consider selecting a random sample of people from different levels and departments, making a "diagonal slice" through the organization chart (Waterman 1993).

When you invite people to the future workshop, give them clear expectations:

- Where they will meet

- When to meet and how long it will take

- Why they're meeting

- Who they're meeting with

- What they'll be doing

- What the meeting will accomplish

Convene the Future Workshop

Make sure to block out several hours for this workshop, and put the relevant activity system and activity network on a wall so everyone can reference them.

During the future workshop, your role is as a facilitator. You will help participants as they do the following:

1. Collaboratively Critique the Current Activity

Structure this part of the session so that everyone gets a chance to discuss what they think is and isn't working with the current situation. Make sure to refocus the discussion on the activity system and activity network—participants might gravitate toward specific gripes and pet peeves, but they need to discuss the basic contradiction. Take notes on a large sheet of paper with a marker so that everyone can see the main issues you are capturing.

Once they have critiqued the current activity, tape your notes on the wall next to your models.

2. Envision an Ideal Future

Now, lead the participants to describe an ideal future in which those critiques would be satisfactorily be answered. At this point, they should not be trying to figure out how to *get to* the solution. Instead, they should discuss what the *results* of the solution would be.

For instance, the participants in the photography club might envision a future in which there are no cliques; everyone feels that they have a voice; they have clear guidelines about what speakers to book; and they know which field trips will unite members.

Participants will sometimes envision aspects of the future that conflict with each other. For instance, one member of the club might envision a future in which "we don't have boring speakers talking about F-stops," and another might immediately object. In those cases, guide the participants to backtrack to a future with which they can both agree (such as "clear guidelines about what speakers to book").

Again, write notes on a large sheet of paper. When you're done, tape it to the wall next to the previous one.

3. Identify Changes

Now comes the tough part. How can they get from the current situation to the future they envisioned?

Participants should be able to identify steps to get them from the current situation to the future one. For instance, they may agree that currently there are no agreed-upon guidelines to select speakers, and in an ideal future they would have those guidelines. So how do they develop these guidelines? This discussion should lead to a more extensive one about how to determine the organization's priorities. The result might be:

- **A resolution**: Participants might develop an action on the spot that can achieve the change.

- **A proposition**: Participants might develop a proposed action that they can then bring to the organization for consideration, e.g, through a formal vote.

- **A direction**: Participants might develop a possible action, then ask a task force—or you—to flesh it out for consideration.

Again, write down each of these changes as you go.

Summarize the Results

Finally, summarize the results of the future workshop. You're the facilitator, so you're in the best position to provide this summary in a form that other members of the organization can absorb it.

As I mentioned earlier, future workshops—like the other techniques we have discussed in this last section—should be treated as a feedback loop. Although you might conduct just one future workshop, depending on the problem, you might conduct a series of them. The more deeply embedded the disagreements are in the organization, the more future workshops you might need in order to unearth these disagreements and come up with constructive solutions.

Example Reading

Evia and Patriarca used future workshops in a study described in this article:

> Evia, C., & Patriarca, A. (2012). Beyond Compliance: Participatory Translation of Safety Communication for Latino Construction Workers. *Journal of Business and Technical Communication*, 26(3), 340–367.

In this study, the authors were interested in how participants envisioned a safer workplace. Through future workshops, they found that "The participants were interested in developing and using materials that would lead to a safer job site. But their 'envisioned future' indicated that maintaining good communication with their supervisors was, in many cases, even more important than safety measures" (p.15). This insight helped them to better understand the complexity of these work sites and design better tools through later prototyping.

CHAPTER 32

Looping through Feedback

In Chapter 28, I said that each of the techniques in this section is a *probe*, providing a feedback loop to help you make better design choices. I also advised you that in the design phase, these feedback loops should set up opportunities for small-scale, low-stakes failures from which you could learn and improve.

Failure can be good—if it is experienced in low-stakes situations and if it provides high-value insights. And that's what these probes are designed to do. If the probe fails and it still gives you information, *that's a good thing* (see Ries 2011).

But it doesn't always *feel* good. Inevitably, some of your feedback will represent failure. Maybe a participant tries out your prototype and declares "this sucks!" Or two participants try to play your organizational game, then tell you that it has absolutely nothing to do with their actual processes. Or a future workshop ends with the participants saying that you've wasted their time because they couldn't come to agreement. When these things happen, it's easy to get discouraged.

That's fine. Take five minutes to feel discouraged.

Are you back? Great. Now let's make this feedback useful.

What's your Next Action?

When you receive feedback from your probes, you'll get a new set of information to supplement the data you already have. But more than that, you'll get new ideas on how to proceed. Your next step could fall under one of three major headings: *persevere*, *pivot*, or *punt*. (See Ries 2011, where he talks about persevering vs. pivoting.)

Persevere

If your feedback is largely positive, but has some negative aspects, you should *persevere*.

For instance, suppose you addressed this recommendation by developing a paper prototype:

"Develop a note in SEObrateMax to indicate search algorithm changes"

When you tested the prototype, participants liked the basic idea, but wanted to change a lot of things. One of them grabbed a marker and wrote all over the prototype. Another just crossed out the entire prototype, then grabbed a blank piece of paper and drew their own ideas. A third didn't write anything, but talked for 20 minutes about how it should work differently.

Notice what they *didn't* do:

- **They didn't ignore the prototype**—they really engaged with it, giving you a lot of feedback.

- **They didn't argue with you about the problem**—they agree that the problem you diagnosed is a real problem that needs a solution.

- **They didn't tell you that the prototype itself was useless**—they agreed that the basic approach (a tool) was the right way to go.

This first probe has been *successful*! You have confirmed that you have identified the problem correctly, addressed it with a reasonable approach (a tool), and developed that tool enough to get detailed feedback.

Keep iterating. You are on the right track, but you need to refine the prototype. And now that you have all of this feedback, you have a lot of guidance on how to refine it.

Pivot

On the other hand, suppose that you tried to probe this recommendation with an organizational game:

"Establish standardized project tracking"

When you asked people to play the organizational game (a board game), they understood the rules of the game quickly. But they disagreed with the process just as quickly. One said that they understood the point of standardized project tracking, but the work environment was too variable and depended on too many outside events to make it work—there really was no "standard" project. Another pointed out that this process cut across the domains of three different managers, so implementing it as one process would be really difficult. Both thought a process simply wouldn't work.

In this case, the news is more discouraging—but again, notice what they didn't do.

- *They didn't ignore the organizational game*—they really engaged with it, giving you a lot of feedback.

- *They didn't argue with you about the problem*—they agree that the problem you diagnosed is a real problem that needs a solution. They just don't think this solution is on the right track.

In other words, this probe was successful too. It tells you that although you have identified the problem, your solution is probably not going to work. And notice that it told you these things early in the process, before you made the mistake of spending time and effort putting together a finished solution!

The feedback from this probe suggests that you should *pivot*: you've confirmed the problem, but you need to try another direction for this recommendation. You might consider a different process, or you might even rethink the problem in terms of tools.

Punt

But sometimes you receive very discouraging news. Suppose you ran a future workshop for the photography organization discussed in Chapter 31. And no matter how you facilitated the workshop, the participants just couldn't seem to come to agreement about the problem.

Some people denied that there even was a problem: "The organization is fine. It does everything it's supposed to do. I don't know why we're even discussing this." Others agreed that there was a problem, but it wasn't theirs: "The mission clearly states that this club is for people who want to be professional photographers. We just have to get back to that mission." And still others agreed that there was a problem, but the solution wasn't a future workshop: "We just need a democratic process for deciding how to select events. Let's put these to a vote."

This probe brings back what could be the most discouraging news: Not only do people disagree on your solution, they disagree on whether a problem actually exists. And it's hard to get an organization to change when it doesn't even acknowledge that there is a problem.

In the terms I used in Chapter 28, this feedback is "fatal": you can't proceed because the stakeholders don't even agree on whether the recommendation is valid.

In this (comparatively rare) scenario, sometimes your best option is to *punt*: to decide that this recommendation is intractable. You might still believe that the recommendation is a good one, but unless the stakeholders can be persuaded, your time (and theirs) may be better spent on addressing other issues.

Getting Ready for Round Two

Now that you have decided how to handle your feedback, it's time to loop. You have three basic options for the next round, depending on your feedback from this one:

- **Persevere**: In this case, your best course of action may be to refine the probe based on feedback, then use it to gather more feedback. For instance, you can fold the participants' feedback into the next prototype.

- **Pivot**: In this case, consider trying a completely different probe. If people didn't see any potential for the process you described, try a different process in a different organizational game. Or rethink the problem in tool terms, generating a prototype.

- **Punt**: In this case, keep your feedback, but turn to a different recommendation.

CHAPTER 33

Conclusion

Here we are at the end of the book—and the end of your first engagement with the Topsight approach. Congratulations!

You've covered a lot of ground in the process. You started with an organization and a vague question of concern about it then moved through the process to develop a solid, evidence-backed, multi-leveled argument for change—and concrete probes to turn that argument into real solutions. Along the way, you've learned how to approach organizations and people; collect and manage data; use and integrate models; turn findings into recommendations; and use a design research approach to gain new insights. Not bad.

More than that, you've learned the basics of field research, including some tips and tricks that most research guides don't cover. And you've learned basic participatory design techniques that you can use in a number of other contexts.

Of course, there's still more you can do.

The approach I've described here is one that I've used for many studies. But that doesn't mean it's appropriate for everything, nor has this book done more than scratch the surface of field research.

For instance, I mentioned in Chapter 1 that this approach only touches on organizational culture; if you want to understand culture further, you might consider reading about ethnography, which focuses more squarely on culture. Similarly, in Chapters 20-21, I discussed how certain contradictions will prove to be intractable using this approach; if you face these sorts of contradictions, you might consider approaches such as participatory action research. In Chapter 19, I discussed how to approach operations and breakdowns from a field methods perspective; you might also take a look at more fine-grained approaches, such as usability testing. The last section provides tools based on participatory design; you might also look at the similar tools provided by Design Thinking (see Di Russo 2016).

If you have become really interested in methods and methodology, there are many, many other books out there. Appendix A lists a few of them, including some landmark books on qualitative research methods.

Finally, if you want to learn more about the theory and methodology behind *Topsight*, take a look at the publications that I authored and coauthored in Appendix A. A good place to start might be my first book, *Tracing Genres through Organizations,* where I first described some of these models. Another might be the 2006 article I wrote with William Hart-Davidson and Mark Zachry, where we first discussed the relationships among the meso-level models (there, called genre ecology models, communication event models, and sociotechnical graphs).

For further resources, see the book's website:

http://clayspinuzzi.com/book/topsight/

Good luck!

Resources

If you're interested in learning more about field studies or some of the other topics discussed in this book, consider some of these resources.

Research Methods, Methodologies, and Techniques

Becker, H. S. (2008). *Tricks of the trade: How to think about your research while you're doing it*. University of Chicago Press.

Bernard, H. R. (2002). *Research methods in anthropology: Qualitative and quantitative approaches* (Third edition). New York: AltaMira Press.

Corbin, J., & Strauss, A. C. (2008). *Basics of Qualitative Research: Techniques and Procedures for Developing Grounded Theory* (Third edit., p. 400). Thousand Oaks, CA: Sage Publications, Inc.

Creswell, J. W. (2006). *Qualitative inquiry and research design: Choosing among five traditions*. Thousand Oaks, CA: SAGE Publications.

Ladner, S. (2014). *Practical Ethnography: A Guide to Doing Ethnography in the Private Sector*. Walnut Creek, CA: Left Coast Press.

Maanen, J. Van. (2011). *Tales of the Field: On Writing Ethnography* (Second Edi.). Chicago: University of Chicago Press.

Whyte, W. F. (1984). *Learning from the Field: A Guide from Experience*. Newbury Park, CA: Sage.

Zuboff, S. (1988). *In the age of the smart machine: The future of work and power.* New York: Basic Books.

Research Design

Shuttleworth, M. (2009). Hawthorne Effect. Retrieved 23 Aug. 2012 from Experiment Resources: http://www.experiment-resources.com/hawthorne-effect.html

Smagorinsky, P. (2008). The Method Section as Conceptual Epicenter in Constructing Social Science Research Reports. *Written Communication*, 25(3), 389–411.

Yin, R. K. (2003). *Case study research: Design and methods* (Third Edit.). Thousand Oaks, CA: SAGE Publications.

Research Ethics

Anderson, P. V. (1998). Simple gifts: Ethical issues in the conduct of person-based composition research. *College Composition and Communication*, 49(1), 63-89.

Belmont Report. (1979). The Belmont Report: Ethical principles and guidelines for the protection of human subjects of research. Retrieved August 23, 2011 from http://www.hhs.gov/ohrp/humansubjects/guidance/belmont.html

Cross, G. A. (2004). Protecting the Voices of Our Research: Appropriately Verifying Qualitative Data. *Journal of Business and Technical Communication*, 18(4), 491–504.

McKee, H. A. (2008). Ethical and legal issues for writing researchers in an age of media convergence. *Computers and Composition*, 25(1), 104–122.

McNely, B. J. (2009). Backchannel Persistence and Collaborative Meaning-Making. In B. Mehlenbacher, A. Protopsaltis, A. Williams, & S. Slattery (Eds.), *SIGDOC '09: Proceedings of the 27th ACM international conference on Design of communication* (pp. 297–303). New York: ACM.

Research Analysis

Hart-Davidson, W. (2003). Seeing the project: Mapping patterns of intra-team communication events. *ACM SIGDOC 2003 Conference Proceedings* (pp. 28–34). New York: ACM.

Miles, M. B., Huberman, A. M., & Saldaña, J. (2014). *Qualitative Data Analysis: A Methods Sourcebook* (Third Edit.). Thousand Oaks, CA: Sage.

Saldaña, J. (2013). *The coding manual for qualitative researchers*. Thousand Oaks, CA: Sage Publications.

Slattery, S. (2007). Undistributing work through writing: How technical writers manage texts in complex information environments. *Technical Communication Quarterly*, 16(3), 311–326.

Spinuzzi, C. (2002). Modeling genre ecologies. *Proceedings of the 20th annual international conference on computer documentation* (pp. 200–207). ACM Press.

Spinuzzi, C., Hart-Davidson, W., & Zachry, M. (2006). Chains and ecologies: Methodological notes toward a communicative-mediational model of technologically mediated writing. *SIGDOC '06: Proceedings of the 24th annual international conference on Design of communication* (pp. 43–50). New York, NY, USA: ACM Press.

Zachry, M., Spinuzzi, C., & Hart-Davidson, W. (2007). Visual documentation of knowledge work: an examination of competing approaches. *SIGDOC '07: Proceedings of the 25th annual ACM international conference on Design of communication* (pp. 120–126). New York: ACM.

Zachry, M., Hart-Davidson, W., & Spinuzzi, C. (2009). Visualizing patterns of knowledge work in organizations: a workshop. *SIGDOC '09: Proceedings of the 27th annual ACM international conference on Design of communication* (pp. 305–306).

Field Studies Using Models Related to Topsight

Gygi, K., & Zachry, M. (2010). Productive tensions and the regulatory work of genres in the development of an engineering communication workshop in a transnational corporation. *Journal of Business and Technical Communication*, 24(3), 358–381.

Hart-Davidson, W. (2003). Seeing the project: Mapping patterns of intra-team communication events. *ACM SIGDOC 2003 Conference Proceedings* (pp. 28–34). New York: ACM, Inc.

Hart-Davidson, W., Spinuzzi, C., & Zachry, M. (2007). Capturing & visualizing knowledge work: results & implications of a pilot study of proposal writing activity. In D. G. Novick & C. Spinuzzi (Eds.), *SIGDOC '07: Proceedings of the 25th annual ACM international conference on Design of communication* (pp. 113–119). New York, NY, USA: ACM.

McCarthy, J. E., Grabill, J. T., Hart-Davidson, W., & McLeod, M. (2011). Content Management in the Workplace: Community, Context, and a New Way to Organize Writing. *Journal of Business and Technical Communication*, 25(4), 367–395.

Spinuzzi, C. (2010). Secret sauce and snake oil: Writing monthly reports in a highly contingent environment. *Written Communication*, 27(4), 363–409.

Spinuzzi, C. (2012). Working Alone, Together: Coworking as Emergent Collaborative Activity. *Journal of Business And Technical Communication*, 26(4), 399–441.

Spinuzzi, C. (2014). How Nonemployer Firms Stage-Manage Ad-Hoc Collaboration: An Activity Theory Analysis. *Technical Communication Quarterly*, 23(2), 88–114.

Spinuzzi, C., Nelson, S., Thomson, K. S., Lorenzini, F., French, R. A., Pogue, G., & London, N. (2016). How Magnets Attract and Repel: Interessement in a Technology Commercialization Competition. *Written Communication*, 33(1), 3–41. doi:10.1177/0741088315614566

Design Research

Bannon, L. J., & Bodker, S. (1991). Beyond the interface: Encountering artifacts in use. Cambridge University Press.

Beyer, H., & Holtzblatt, K. (1998). *Contextual design: Defining customer-centered systems*. San Francisco: Morgan Kaufmann Publishers, Inc.

Bodker, K., Kensing, F., & Simonsen, J. (2004). *Participatory IT Design: Designing for Business and Workplace Realities*. Boston: MIT Press.

Bødker, S. (1991). *Through the interface: A human activity approach to user interface design*. Hillsdale, NJ: L. Erlbaum.

Bodker, S. (2009). Past experiences and recent challenges in participatory design research. In A. Sannino, H. Daniels, & K. D. Gutierrez (Eds.), *Learning and expanding with activity theory* (pp. 274–285). New York: Cambridge University Press.

Bødker, S., Ehn, P., Kammersgaard, J., Kyng, M., & Sundblad, Y. (1987). A UTOPIAN experience: On design of powerful computer-based tools for skilled graphical workers. In G. Bjerknes, P. Ehn, & M. Kyng (Eds.), *Computers and democracy -- A Scandinavian challenge* (pp. 251–278). Aldershot, England: Avebury.

Bødker, S., & Grønbaek, K. (1991). Design in action: From prototyping by demonstration to cooperative prototyping. In J. Greenbaum & M. Kyng (Eds.), *Design at work: Cooperative design of computer systems* (pp. 197–218). Hillsdale, NJ: Lawrence Erlbaum Associates.

Di Russo, S. (2016). *Understanding the behaviour of design thinking in complex environments*. Swinburne University of Technology. Retrieved from http://researchbank.swinburne.edu.au/vital/access/manager/Repository/swin:48637

Ehn, P. (1989). *Work-oriented design of computer artifacts*. Hillsdale, NJ: Lawrence Erlbaum Associates.

Ehn, P. (1993). Scandinavian design: On participation and skill. In D. Schuler & A. Namioka (Eds.), *Participatory Design, Principles and Practices*. Mahwah, NJ: Lawrence Erlbaum Associates.

Ehn, P., & Kyng, M. (1991). Cardboard computers: Mocking-it-up or hands-on the future. In *Design at work: Cooperative design of computer systems* (pp. 169–196). Hillsdale, NJ: Lawrence Erlbaum Associates.

Evia, C., & Patriarca, A. (2012). Beyond Compliance: Participatory Translation of Safety Communication for Latino Construction Workers. *Journal of Business and Technical Communication*.

Holtzblatt, K., Wendell, J. B., & Wood, S. (2005). *Rapid contextual design: A how-to guide to key techniques for user-centered design*. San Francisco: Morgan Kaufmann Publishers, Inc.

Jungk, R., & Mullert, N. (1988). *Future workshops: How to create desirable futures*. London: Institute for Social Inventions.

Muller, M. J. (2003). Participatory design: the third space in HCI. In *The human-computer interaction handbook: Fundamentals, evolving technologies and emerging applications* (pp. 1051–1068). Lawrence Erlbaum Associates, Inc.

Muller, M. J., Wildman, D. M., & White, E. A. (1993). Taxonomy of PD practices: A brief practicioner's guide. *Communications of the ACM*, 36(4), 26–27.

Spinuzzi, C. (2002). A Scandinavian challenge, a US response: Methodological assumptions in Scandinavian and US prototyping approaches. *Proceedings of the 20th annual international conference on Computer documentation* (pp. 208–215). New York: ACM Press.

Spinuzzi, C. (2005a). Lost in the translation: Shifting claims in the migration of a research technique. *Technical Communication Quarterly*, 14(4), 411–446.

Spinuzzi, C. (2005b). The methodology of participatory design. *Technical Communication, 52*(2), 163–174.

Organizations

Adler, P. S., & Heckscher, C. (2007). Towards Collaborative Community. In C. Heckscher & P. S. Adler (Eds.), *The Firm as a Collaborative Community: Reconstructing Trust in the Knowledge Economy* (pp. 11–105). New York: Oxford University Press.

Mintzberg, H. (1979). *The Structuring of Organizations*. New York: Prentice Hall.

Ries, E. (2011). *The lean startup: How today's entrepreneurs use continuous innovation to create radically successful businesses*. New York: Crown Books.

Waterman, R. H. (1993). *Adhocracy*. New York: Norton.

Developing Arguments

Booth, W., Colomb, G.C., & Williams, J.M. (2008). *The Craft of Research, Third Edition*. Chicago: University of Chicago Press.

Freed, R. C., Freed, S., & Romano, J. (2010). *Writing winning business proposals: Your guide to landing the client, making the sale and persuading the boss*, third edition. Chicago: McGraw-Hill.

Sociocultural Theory

Bazerman, C. (1988). *Shaping written knowledge: The genre and activity of the experimental article in science*. Madison, WI: University of Wisconsin Press.

Bazerman, C. (1994). Systems of genre and the enactment of social intentions. In P. Freedman, Aviva And Medway (Ed.), *Genre and the new rhetoric* (pp. 79–99). Bristol, PA: Taylor & Francis.

Bazerman, C. (2013a). *A rhetoric of literate action: Literate action, Volume 1*. Fort Collins, CO: WAC Clearinghouse.

Bazerman, C. (2013b). *A theory of literate action: Literate action, Volume 2*. Fort Collins, CO: The WAC Clearinghouse.

Engeström, Y. (2014). *Learning by Expanding*. New York: Cambridge University Press.

Engeström, Y. (1990). *Learning, working, and imagining: Twelve studies in activity theory*. Helsinki: Orienta-Konsultit Oy.

Engeström, Y. (1992). *Interactive expertise: Studies in distributed working intelligence*. Helsinki: University of Helsinki.

Engeström, Y. (2008). *From Teams to Knots: Studies of Collaboration and Learning at Work*. New York: Cambridge University Press.

Latour, B., Mauguin, P., & Teil, G. E. (1992). A note on socio-technical graphs. *Social Studies of Science*, 22, 33–57.

Miller, C. R. (1984). Genre as social action. *Quarterly Journal of Speech*, 70(2), 151–167.

Russell, D. R. (1997a). Rethinking genre in school and society: An activity theory analysis. *Written Communication*, 14(4), 504–554.

Russell, D. R. (1997b). Writing and genre in higher education and workplaces: A review of studies that use cultural-historical activity theory. *Mind, Culture, and Activity*, 4(4), 224–237.

Russell, D. R. (2009). Uses of Activity Theory in Written Communication Research. In A. Sannino, H. Daniels, & K. D. Gutierrez (Eds.), *Learning and Expanding with Activity Theory* (pp. 40–52). New York: Cambridge University Press.

Russell, D. R. (2010). Writing in multiple contexts: Vygotskian CHAT meets the phenomenology of genre. In C. Bazerman, R. Krut, K. Lunsford, S. McLeod, S. Null, P. Rogers, & A. Stansell (Eds.), *Traditions of Writing Research* (pp. 353–364). New York: Routledge.

Russell, D. R., & Yañez, A. (2003). "Big picture people rarely become historians": Genre systems and the contradictions of general education. (C. Bazerman & D. R. Russell, Eds.) *Writing Selves/writing Societies: Research from Activity Perspectives*. Ft. Collins, CO: WAC Clearinghouse and Mind, Culture, and Activity. Retrieved from http://wac.colostate.edu/books/selves_societies/

Spinuzzi, C., & Zachry, M. (2000). Genre ecologies: An open-system approach to understanding and constructing documentation. *ACM J. Comput. Doc*, 24, 169–181.

Spinuzzi, C. (2003). *Tracing genres through organizations: A sociocultural approach to information design*. Cambridge, MA: MIT Press.

Spinuzzi, C. (2004). Four ways to investigate assemblages of texts: Genre sets, systems, repertoires, and ecologies. *SIGDOC '04: Proceedings of the 22nd annual international conference on Design of communication* (pp. 110–116). New York: ACM.

Spinuzzi, C. (2007). Who killed Rex? Tracing a message through three kinds of networks. In M. Zachry & C. Thralls (Eds.), *Communicative practices in workplaces and the professions: Cultural perspectives on the regulation of discourse and organizations* (pp. 45–66). Farmingdale, NY: Baywood Pub. Co.

Spinuzzi, C. (2008). *Network: Theorizing knowledge work in telecommunications.* New York: Cambridge University Press.

Spinuzzi, C. (2015). *All edge: Inside the new workplace networks.* Chicago: University of Chicago Press.

Rolling Your Own QDA

This appendix is based on my 2008 blog post:

http://spinuzzi.blogspot.com/2008/10/rolling-your-own-free-customized-free.html

Qualitative data analysis (QDA) tools are expensive. When I came to the University of Texas at Austin in 2001, I had the university spend $500 on one popular QDA tool, NVivo. It was going to change the way I did research. I installed it, played around with it, and was not impressed, so I abandoned it.

Much more recently, I decided to try HyperResearch on the advice of a graduate student. Again, UT sprang for the $400 needed to buy it. I used it for two studies and again, I was not impressed; in some ways it was very limiting, particularly in terms of relating various types of data and coding. The interface was clunky.

And look: $900 spent for nothing.

But between those two times, I managed to analyze 89 sets of observations, 84 interviews, and assorted artifacts. This work followed me across three platforms (i.e., Linux, MacOSX, and OpenZaurus). It didn't involve an off-the-shelf qualitative research tool. I'm coming back to this solution for managing the data in the SEObrate study—a study of collaboration and project management at a high tech organization. It offers better print formatting, more flexible data analysis, and multiple interfaces that can be chosen for the specific type of analysis or data entry. It's multiplatform. Fast. And it didn't cost me a dime.

So how do you save $400, $500, or even $900 on your next qualitative research project? It takes a little setup, but you can do it.

Needs

When you're analyzing qualitative data, you might have several different kinds of data. Here are the data types I regularly use:

- *Interviews* (e.g., audio recordings and transcriptions)

- *Observations* (e.g., transcribed field notes)

- *Artifacts* (e.g., usually digital photos or paper that can be scanned; I have also recorded ambient noise at sites)

You might also use other data, such as system logging.

In addition, you typically have administrative data, such as information on participants (I include first and last name, pseudonym, and title at minimum).

For each of these data, qualitative analysis includes coding. You can code in several different ways, but let's keep it simple and think of *coding* as free-form tagging.

So how do you make sense of all this? Let's start with some don'ts:

Don'ts

Don't use Excel or other spreadsheets. Spreadsheets only offer two dimensions, and that means you're very limited in how you analyze the data. You'll end up doing one of the following:

- Creating a spreadsheet for each datatype. So you'll have spreadsheets for observations, for interviews, etc. Since spreadsheets don't provide an intuitive or robust way to link data between spreadsheets, you'd have to do that connective work by hand.

- Creating a single spreadsheet into which all data go. This will involve tremendous redundancy, with several fields going empty in every entry and lots of redundant data, since you'll have to tag name and date for every entry.

Don't try to manage all this outside of a table. Sure, you could dump your data in a big Word file and use comments for tagging, and sure, you could search text and comments. But you lose a lot of granularity that way, as well as the ability to gain a top-level view (e.g., how many times did I use this code vs. that code?).

Don't store your data online. Several free web-based services offer great solutions. But your data may not be secure. In many cases, you simply won't be allowed to store your data on an unencrypted server that isn't administered by the university.

So that's what you don't do. Now here's what I do.

Overview of My System

I use a MySQL database to store the data, with a different database table for each kind of data. The first table to set up is the Participant table, with each participant receiving a key index number. Other tables are all indexed by that participant number, so I can join tables based on participant.

Each table has a CODES field where I can insert codes from a list. I keep the list of codes in a text editor and surround each one with asterisks like this:

COMPANY_HISTORY

The asterisks allow me to search across a table and pick up just the codes—searching for "**COMPANY" picks up codes that start with that string, while searching for "COMPANY" might pick up uses of the actual word in interview or observational notes.

To analyze the data, I have used several MySQL front ends, including YourSQL, CocoaMySQL, and phpMySQL. These front ends are all free; they afford different views of the data; but they all work on the same underlying data. The result is far more flexibility than I would get from an off-the-shelf QDA tool.

Limitations

Obviously, this solution isn't for everyone:

- You don't have to learn SQL, but learning just a little bit will make your life a lot easier.

- You may have a hard time storing files in your SQL database, depending on your front end. I typically store them on the hard drive and store filenames and metadata in the database.

- This method allows you to code by line, not by line portions or longer blocks.

How to Set it Up

The setup is not hard, but you'll need to be comfortable with uncertainty. Or get your system administrator to do it.

1. Download and install MySQL.

Go to mysql.com (or mysql.org) and download the free software. It has versions for several operating systems. The site also has a ton of documentation; keep a window open for installation.

2. Download one or more MySQL front ends.

Cruise on over to sourceforge.net and search for SQL. You should get a large list of SQL utilities and clients, some of which will be applicable, many of which won't be. I am using OS X, so I downloaded the following front ends:

- YourSQL

- CocoaMySQL

- phpMySQL (This one runs on your internal web server, so it works across platforms, just like MySQL. It will take some additional setup.)

3. Create a database.

Follow your MySQL installation instructions to set a root user and password. (You can set different user and permission levels; if you're the only one using the database, why bother?)

Once you do this, run your front end—or one of them, if you downloaded several—and follow instructions to connect to MySQL. Then create a database. I suggest naming it something descriptive, not "research". For instance, I named the database for my current project "research-pm", the same name I used for my tags in GMail and Google Drive for the same project.

4. Create a table for participants

Now you create tables within the database. MySQL is a relational database, which means that you can relate the tables in different ways once you have them set up. I typically make the participants table the "handle" for most of the rest of the database, since most of my analysis focuses on what individuals do and say. So we create that one first.

So what do you need to know about your participants? I usually put in the following information:

- *pkey*: A participants key. It's a unique integer that identifies the participant. When you refer to participants in other tables—such as observational notes—you can use that same number to designate the same participant in these other tables.

- *lname*: Participant's last name.

- *fname*: Participant's first name.

- *fname_p*: Pseudonym.

- *position*: Text field for their job title or similar information that might be relevant, such as profession.

- *site*: If the study includes multiple sites, use either a text string or a number to indicate each.

- Observation and interview dates: Depending on the data collected, you might or might not include these dates. Usually you can get these from querying the appropriate data tables.

Once you have roughed out the participant table, fill it out with information about each participant.

5. Create tables and rows for each kind of data you collect.

Each will be indexed to the participant table. For a recent study, I created:

- observations;

- interviews;

- interviewfiles;

- artifacts; and

- site notes.

For each of these, create at least the following:

- *key*: The unique key for this piece of data. If it's from an observation, you might call this "okey".

- *pkey*: This field links the individual to their data. If a given observation was of participant 1, you'd put a 1 here.

- *date*: The date you collected the data. If it's an observation, you might call it "obsdate".

- *text*: The data itself. For instance, if you're filling in observational notes, "obstext" would contain perhaps a paragraph from your notes. If it's an interview, "inttext" would contain an answer or paragraph from the transcribed interview.

- *codes*: The codes you assign to this piece of data.

- *notes*: Any additional information you might want to insert that doesn't fit into the fields above. Sometimes I use this to make notes about further investigation, artifacts I should collect, or methodological issues.

6. For each table, fill out rows.

You can do this manually via one of the front ends. You'll find that each front end has advantages and disadvantages in terms of data entry.

If you don't mind learning a little SQL, you can take your raw data (e.g., observational notes or transcribed interview notes) and insert the appropriate SQL around them with some search and replace commands. Once you do that, you can plug the whole mess in as a single query and it'll update the table with that data. That's what I do. It's much faster as long as you're willing to spend half an hour learning the appropriate SQL command (INSERT).

7. Code the table.

Now that the data are in the tables, code each table. In this scheme, that means filling the "codes" field for each row of each table. Codes can come from your starter codes, open coding, axial coding, or all three. I typically put them all in the same field; you could differentiate them or place them in different fields if you think you need that level of complexity.

Note: If you code thousands of lines of data with a code (say, **WORKPLACE**) and then decide you really need to rename this code (say, to **WORK**), you can do a search-and-replace with the "update" command. See documentation for details.

Similarly, you can do auto-coding with an "update" command. For instance, suppose you want to make sure that each mention of "msword" in the field notes is coded with **SOFTWARE_OFFICE**. You can use "update" to search for those incidents and code them appropriately. Brute-force coding can be tricky; you risk false positives and broad-brush characterization of the data. Depending on your data, it can also be very useful and gain a lot of traction quickly.

How to Search

Now that you've entered and coded the data, you can do simple and complex searches.

1. Simple searches within tables

These are searches within one table. For instance, suppose you want to find a mention of msword in your observational notes just so you can look up the context. Or you want to see how many interview notes are coded with **SOFTWARE_OFFICE**. I usually use these two tools:

Search-as-you-type (YourSQL)

I love search-as-you-type. The idea is that as you start typing the string, the results reduce. Eventually you have zeroed in on the data you want, even before you're done typing.

The advantage is that you get the results quickly. The disadvantage is that this method searches across all fields, so you might get false positives. Suppose you're looking for "software" in the observational notes, but you catch all instances of **SOFTWARE_OFFICE** in the codes.

Search by string (CocoaMySQL)

This method allows you to specify the field and the relationship before you search. So you might set "obskey=1" to catch all observations of participant 1, or codes like "%**SOFTWARE_%" to catch all observations where the codes field includes a code starting with "**SOFTWARE_".

The advantage is that the search is fine-grained and focuses on just one field. The disadvantages are that (a) it's not as fast as search-as-you-type and (b) you can't set up searches that look in more than one field.

But if you want to set up more complex searches that go across tables, you'll have to learn a little more SQL.

2. Complex searches joining tables

Since MySQL is relational, you can link these tables you've set up, and the result is a much more powerful set of queries.

Here's an example from the Telecorp study that became my second book. I had the following tables:

- "workers"

- "interviews"

Now suppose I want to grab all interview notes for Customer Service workers that are coded ***JOB_DESCRIPTION*** then append the workers' first names and pseudonyms to them so I can remember who they are. I ran this query so that I could see how the many different CS workers understood their jobs, especially so that I could zero in on differences in those understandings.

That's too complex for the simple queries earlier. So I ran the simple SQL query. The names after dots (e.g., workers.fname) are field names in the given table.

select workers.wkey, workers.fname, workers.fname_p, interviews. notes, interviews.codes from workers, interviews where ((workers. area='Customer Service') and (workers.wkey=interviews.wkey) and (interviews.codes like '%**JOB_DESCRIPTION**%'))

So we can get really specific searches that join the different tables and allow us to slice the data in different ways. I could have added further codes beyond job description, searched across additional areas, specified a date, etc. In fact, I did do all of these, and I occasionally joined three tables to yield really interesting connections among the different types of data.

Formulating these can be a pain, so I formulate them once, make sure they work, and then save them. If I want to run it again with a different code, I copy and paste.

How to Print

One big problem with HyperResearch is that it does an appalling job printing data. In the system I've described, you could print in a number of ways. The best two are:

- Use phpMySQL to generate the table you want then print from the browser.

- Use MySQL from the command line to dump the query into an HTML file.

As always, see the documentation.

About The Author

Clay Spinuzzi is a professor of rhetoric and writing at The University of Texas at Austin. Spinuzzi's interests include research methods and methodology, workplace research, and computer-mediated activity. He has written four books: *Tracing Genres through Organizations* (MIT Press, 2003); *Network* (Cambridge University Press, 2008); *Topsight* (via Amazon CreateSpace, 2013; second edition Urso Press, 2017); and *All Edge* (University of Chicago Press).

Find out more at http://www.amazon.com/Clay-Spinuzzi/e/B001JSE7II/ref=sr_ntt_srch_lnk_1?qid=1465231091&sr=8-1

Or visit clayspinuzzi.com.

CPSIA information can be obtained
at www.ICGtesting.com
Printed in the USA
LVHW031639201122
733652LV00007B/443

9 781981 360741